Learning Ruby

Other resources from O'Reilly

Related titles
Ruby Cookbook™
Ruby in a Nutshell
Ruby on Rails: Up and
  Running

Ajax on Rails
Rails Cookbook™

oreilly.com
oreilly.com is more than a complete catalog of O'Reilly books. You'll also find links to news, events, articles, weblogs, sample chapters, and code examples.

oreillynet.com is the essential portal for developers interested in open and emerging technologies, including new platforms, programming languages, and operating systems.

Conferences
O'Reilly brings diverse innovators together to nurture the ideas that spark revolutionary industries. We specialize in documenting the latest tools and systems, translating the innovator's knowledge into useful skills for those in the trenches. Visit *conferences.oreilly.com* for our upcoming events.

Safari Bookshelf (*safari.oreilly.com*) is the premier online reference library for programmers and IT professionals. Conduct searches across more than 1,000 books. Subscribers can zero in on answers to time-critical questions in a matter of seconds. Read the books on your Bookshelf from cover to cover or simply flip to the page you need. Try it today for free.

Learning Ruby

Michael Fitzgerald

O'REILLY®

Beijing · Cambridge · Farnham · Köln · Paris · Sebastopol · Taipei · Tokyo

Learning Ruby
by Michael Fitzgerald

Published by O'Reilly Media, Inc., 1005 Gravenstein Highway North, Sebastopol, CA 95472.

O'Reilly books may be purchased for educational, business, or sales promotional use. Online editions are also available for most titles (*safari.oreilly.com*). For more information, contact our corporate/institutional sales department: (800) 998-9938 or *corporate@oreilly.com*.

Editor: Simon St.Laurent
Production Editor: Lydia Onofrei
Proofreader: Lydia Onofrei
Indexer: John Bickelhaupt

Cover Designer: Karen Montgomery
Interior Designer: David Futato
Illustrators: Robert Romano and Jessamyn Read

Printing History:

May 2007:   First Edition.

RepKover. This book uses RepKover™, a durable and flexible lay-flat binding.

ISBN-10: 0-596-52986-4
ISBN-13: 978-0-596-52986-4
[M]   [8/07]

Robert Wayne Darrah
1950–2006
Till we meet again

Table of Contents

Preface

Ruby has gotten a lot of attention since the appearance of Ruby on Rails, the web application framework written in Ruby. The attention is way past due. Ruby has been around as long as Java but enjoyed only limited attention outside of Japan until around 2000. In the last few years, Ruby's popularity has steadily grown, and with good reason.

Who Should Read This Book?

Generally, I figure two kinds of readers will buy this book: experienced programmers who want to learn Ruby, and new programmers who want to learn to program. I have the interesting job of catering to both while trying not to tick off either. It's a balancing act, and this is how I'll handle it: I am going to address you as if you are already a competent programmer, but I'll also provide plenty of help for beginners, mostly in the form of notes or sidebars. I'll let you know when you can skip a section if you are already a heavy hitter.

If you're a fairly experienced programmer, you might just want to read the code examples first, from the beginning of the book to the end, skimming the explanations surrounding the examples as needed. You should be able to see what's going on fairly quickly just by keeping your eyes on the code. The code is laid out in a more or less logical fashion (to me at least), so you should be able to figure out Ruby in fairly short order. If you are new to programming, I have attempted to make your job a little easier by explaining things as I go along.

How This Book Works

Do you have to know everything about a car before you start driving? Did you have to know anything about fuel injection, combustion, or timing belts to drive? Of course not.

It's the same with programming in a new language. I am going to show you lots of Ruby programs, many of them just one-liners, and then tell you how and why they work—just enough to get you rolling down the road. I take this approach because I believe we do most of our learning by observing, imitating, and playing. I plan to do a lot of that in this book.

You should know up front that this is a just-get-in-and-drive book. In other words, you can drive a car even if you don't know whether its got six or eight cylinders.

David Heinemeier Hansson, inventor of Ruby on Rails, said something I like: "People learn by changing a little thing, reloading, and seeing the change." He's right on. That's my experience: over the years I have learned more by hacking code than by reading about it.

I also move as quickly as possible, not getting bogged down in the quicksand of details. The details will come in time, as they are needed; the main thing I want to give you now is forward movement and momentum.

If you just follow along with what I'm doing, running the programs and altering them to your taste, you'll learn quickly. The more you run these programs, the more fluency you'll develop, and before long, you'll start thinking and even dreaming in Ruby. Then you'll just take off on your own.

The latest stable version at the time I am writing this is 1.8.6. That's the version I'll be using. You can probably get along using an older version, but unless you have 1.8.6 or later installed, I can't guarantee that all the programs in this book will work as advertised, though they most likely will.

About the Examples

I think we learn best by observing what others do, then imitating what we observe. That's how we learn as children, anyway. And that's why you'll find code examples—to observe and imitate—on nearly every page of this book.

Many of the examples are available for download from *http://www.oreilly.com/ catalog/9780596529864*. The idea is that you will have enough examples in your hands to start most of the basic programming tasks.

How This Book Is Organized

Learning Ruby is organized into 11 chapters. A brief synopsis of each follows:

Chapter 1, *Ruby Basics*
> Introduces many Ruby basics, such as where to get Ruby, how to install it, and how to run a large cross-section of programs to enable you to start using Ruby immediately.

Chapter 2, *A Quick Tour of Ruby*
Gallops over the Ruby terrain at a brisk pace, covering briefly the most important features of Ruby.

Chapter 3, *Conditional Love*
Explains and demonstrates how to use conditionals (like if and while) in Ruby, including looping mechanisms.

Chapter 4, *Strings*
Introduces how to manipulate strings in Ruby (includes a section on regular expressions).

Chapter 5, *Math*
Shows you how to use operators, basic math functions, functions from the Math module, rational numbers, etc.

Chapter 6, *Arrays*
Talks you through Ruby arrays.

Chapter 7, *Hashes*
Demonstrates hashes in detail.

Chapter 8, *Working with Files*
Reveals how to process files with Ruby, including reading and writing files, and so on.

Chapter 9, *Classes*
Discusses Ruby classes in detail, including a tiny introduction to object-oriented programming (OOP), instance variables, instance methods, class variables, class methods, modules, and mixins.

Chapter 10, *More Fun with Ruby*
Introduces a variety of topics of interest, including RubyGems, reflection, metaprogramming, exception handling, and more.

Chapter 11, *A Short Guide to Ruby on Rails*
Gets you acquainted with some of the essentials of Rails and includes a short tutorial. (You have to give credit to Ruby on Rails for improving the visibility of Ruby.)

Appendix A, *Ruby Reference*
Presents all the reference material from the book in one location.

Appendix B, *Answers to Review Questions*
Provides answers to the review questions found at the end of the chapters (more than 100 questions and answers).

Glossary
Provides a list of terms related to Ruby programming and their definitions.

Conventions Used in This Book

The following font conventions are used in this book:

Italic is used for:

- Pathnames and filenames (such as program names)
- Internet addresses, such as domain names and URLs
- New terms where they are defined, or for emphasis

Constant width is used for:

- Command lines and options that should be typed verbatim in a file or in *irb*
- Names and keywords in Ruby programs, including method names, variable names, and class names

Constant width italic is used for:

- User-supplied values

Constant width bold is used to:

- Draw attention to parts of programs

 This icon indicates a tip, suggestion, or general note.

 This icon indicates a warning or caution.

Comments and Questions

Please address comments and questions concerning this book to the publisher:

O'Reilly Media, Inc.
1005 Gravenstein Highway North
Sebastopol, CA 95472
800-998-9938 (in the United States or Canada)
707-829-0515 (international or local)
707-829-0104 (Fax)

There is a web page for this book, which lists errata, examples, or any additional information. You can access this page at:

http://www.oreilly.com/catalog/9780596529864

To comment or ask technical questions about this book send email to:

bookquestions@oreilly.com

For more information about books, conferences, Resource Centers, and the O'Reilly Network, see the O'Reilly web site at:

http://www.oreilly.com

Safari® Enabled

 When you see a Safari® Enabled icon on the cover of your favorite technology book, that means the book is available online through the O'Reilly Network Safari Bookshelf.

Safari offers a solution that's better than e-books. It's a virtual library that lets you easily search thousands of top tech books, cut and paste code samples, download chapters, and find quick answers when you need the most accurate, current information. Try it for free at *http://safari.oreilly.com*.

Acknowledgments

Once again, I want to thank my editor Simon St.Laurent for giving me the chance to write this book. Simon's encouragement has kept me afloat through four book projects!

I also appreciate the comments from the technical reviewers Ryan Waldron and Joey Franklin. They hauled me back on deck when I was floundering in heavy seas. Thanks, guys.

Finally, and most importantly, I want to thank my wife, Cristi, and daughters, Melissa, Amy, and Aubrey, for supporting me and believing in me. You make it all worthwhile.

## CHAPTER 1

Ruby Basics

Perhaps like you, I've learned to program in a number of languages over the years—BASIC, FORTRAN, C, C++, C#, Java, and JavaScript among others—but so far Ruby is my favorite. It has been the most fun to learn and use. Why? Because of its syntax. If you have a background in a variety of other languages, Ruby is easy to figure out. And it's flexible: Ruby lets you do things in a variety of ways, not just one way, so you can decide how to do things *your* way.

Ruby is an interpreted rather than a compiled language. You can call it a scripting language, an object-oriented language, a refreshing language. It's not a perfect language. It doesn't have to be. It's still my favorite. It has that certain *je ne sais quoi*. If it didn't, why would I spend hundreds of hours writing a book about it? Certainly not for money and fame.

To me, one of the best aspects of Ruby is its composability. *Composability* is the degree to which you can express logic by combining and recombining parts of a language (see James Clark's "The Design of RELAX NG" at *http://www.thaiopensource.com/relaxng/ design.html#section:5*). Ruby's got that, big time.

Also, Ruby isn't under committee or corporate control. It's open source. It was written by Matz, with some help from his friends. (It was written in C, by the way, and can take C extensions.)

"Matz" is short for Yukihiro Matsumoto (from Japan). He started working on Ruby in 1993, and first released it to the world in 1995, the same year Java came out. It took a while for Ruby to emerge in the West, but once it did, around the year 2000, it started to take off. With the help of people like Dave Thomas, Andy Hunt, Hal Fulton, and others, Ruby got a foothold. Now it has a fan base.

And Ruby has a killer app. It's called Ruby on Rails (*http://www.rubyonrails.org*). Heard of it? It's a web application framework for producing web sites with databases quickly and easily. A lot of people really like Rails. Not everyone, but a lot of people. And those people are discovering that one of the main reasons they like Rails is because it was written in Ruby.

Hello, Matz

I know many readers are expecting a "Hello, World" example right about now. In spite of a moral and ethical obligation to provide a "Hello, World" example, I have decided to change the first example to "Hello, Matz." Given all that Matz has done for the programming world, don't you think he deserves some acknowledgment?

Before you go any further, find out if you already have Ruby installed on your computer. If you are on Mac OS X or a Linux distribution of some sort, it might already be there, though it's probably an older version; Tiger (Mac OS X 10.4 or later) ships with version 1.8.2, for example.

To discover if Ruby is lurking inside your box, just go to a shell prompt on a Unix/Linux system (this won't work on a standard Windows system) and type:

```
$ which ruby
```

See if you get a reply like this one (good news if you do):

```
/usr/local/bin/ruby
```

Or just type a command to check the version of Ruby (this works on Unix/Linux and Windows):

```
$ ruby -v
```

or:

```
$ ruby --version
```

If Ruby is installed, you should get an answer that looks like this:

```
ruby 1.8.6 (2007-03-13 patchlevel 0) [powerpc-darwin8.9.0]
```

 If Ruby is not installed on your box, and you're a little nervous about figuring out how to install it on your own, go to the section "Installing Ruby," later in this chapter. Follow the instructions there to install Ruby on your platform. Then come right back!

A Very Short Ruby Program

Now that you have Ruby up and running, type the following line in a plain-text editor such as TextPad or vim:

```
puts "Hello, Matz!"
```

This line of code is a programming *statement*, an instruction that you want the program to carry out. The instruction will print the string Hello, Matz! on your screen, followed by a newline character.

You can end a statement with a semicolon (;) if you want, just like in C or Java, but you sure don't have to: a newline will do fine. (Most Ruby programmers don't use ; except when writing multiple statements on one line.)

Save the little program in a file as plain text and name it *matz.rb*. (The *.rb* file extension is the conventional extension for Ruby programs.)

 It's a good idea to save the file in a directory or folder where you plan to do your Ruby work so that all your Ruby files will be readily accessible in one location.

You run the program by running the Ruby interpreter. To do this, type the following at a shell or command prompt:

```
$ ruby matz.rb
```

The output from the program is displayed by default on the screen:

```
Hello, Matz!
```

Placing a # at the beginning of a line tells the interpreter to ignore that line:

```
# a nice greeting for Matz
puts "Hello, Matz!"
```

Add the # and some text following it to your program *matz.rb*. This is called a *comment*. Whatever follows the # is hidden from the Ruby interpreter. You'll learn more about comments in Chapter 2.

Shebang!

If you run a Ruby program on Windows, you generally have to use the ruby command before the Ruby filename (unless you associate the file extension *.rb* with a file type; to learn how to do this, see "Associating File Types on Windows," later in this chapter). You can avoid typing ruby each time on Unix/Linux systems by adding something called a shebang line (#!) at the top of your Ruby file. Add a shebang line to the top of *matz.rb*:

```
#!/usr/local/bin/ruby
# a nice greeting for Matz
puts "Hello, Matz!"
```

The shebang lets the system know where to find the Ruby interpreter, that is, in */usr/local/bin*, which is a conventional place to install Ruby executables (see "Installing Ruby on Mac OS X Tiger," later in this chapter). A more general alternative is *#!/usr/bin/env ruby*. Choose what works for you. I use the latter.

 As mentioned earlier, Tiger comes installed with an older version of Ruby, version 1.8.2, which is stored in */usr/bin*. We won't bother using that version.

Go to a prompt on your Mac or Unix/Linux system and enter the filename by itself:

```
$ matz.rb
```

You'll get the same answer as before:

```
Hello, Matz!
```

 If you get a permission denied message when running *matz.rb*, and you aren't sure what to do about it, I'd like to offer you a hand. Go to the section "Permission Denied" near the end of this chapter to find out what to do.

I'll now show you more ways you can output the text Hello, Matz!, which will give you a glimpse of the power of Ruby. At this point, I won't get very deep into detail about what's going on. Just follow along, typing in and testing as much code as you want. To test the code, follow these steps.

1. Delete the previous code in *matz.rb*.

2. Enter the new code.

3. Run the program with the Ruby interpreter from the prompt to see the output.

You'll be deleting the old code in *matz.rb* and inserting new code, unless another Ruby file with a different name is presented in the text. You can either recreate these other files with the given names, or you can download all the files that come with this book from *http://www.oreilly.com/catalog/9780596529864*. After downloading the ZIP archive, extract the files into the directory or folder of your choice. That's where you'll do your work. Navigate to the directory in a shell or command window using the cd command.

Issue a System Command

You can run an operating system command with system:

```
system "echo 'Hello, Matz!'"
```

Try this with and without single quotes ('), where shown.

You can also submit each part of a command separately, as an argument to system:

```
system "echo", "Hello,", "Matz!"
```

The exec command is similar to system, but it replaces the current process and, after the command is finished, exits—not always what you want to do.

Appending a String

Append one string to another with the + method:

```
puts "Hello, " + "Matz!"
```

You can also append a string with the << method:

```
puts "Hello, " << "Matz!"
```

Multiply

What if you want to print out a line of text three times? How about:

```
puts "Hello, Matz! " * 3
```

This would give you:

```
Hello, Matz! Hello, Matz! Hello, Matz!
```

Or you could use the `times` method:

```
5.times { print "Hello, Matz! " }
```

It will show your enthusiasm:

```
Hello, Matz! Hello, Matz! Hello, Matz! Hello, Matz! Hello, Matz!
```

You could just print one word three times, then add or append more text with +:

```
puts "Hello, " * 3 + "Matz!"
```

Then you'd get:

```
Hello, Hello, Hello, Matz!
```

Inserting a Shell Command

Let's insert some output from a shell command:

```
puts "Hey Matz, I'm running " + `ruby --version`
```

When you run this, the output from the shell command inside the grave accents or backticks (`ruby --version`) is inserted into the output:

```
Hey Matz, I'm running ruby 1.8.6 (2006-08-25) [powerpc-darwin8.8.0]
```

Using a Variable

You can give a value a name by assigning it to a variable:

```
hi = "Hello, Matz!"
puts hi # => Hello, Matz!
```

hi is an example of a *local variable*. You can tell because its name starts with a lower-case letter. You'll learn more about local and other kinds of variables in Chapter 2 in the section "Variables."

 In code examples, => will always follow a comment character (#). Whatever follows => is the output you can expect from the line or block of code, or from the whole program.

Put two or more variables together with the + method:

```
hi = "Hello, "
person = "Matz!"
puts hi + person # => Hello, Matz!
```

Expression Substitution

Another way of inserting the value of a variable in a string is with *expression substitution*—a very handy feature of Ruby:

```
person = "Matz!"
puts "Hello, #{person}" # => Hello, Matz!
```

The #{...} is replaced with the result of the expression inside it. For example, #{2+2} would yield the result 4.

Using expression substitution, you can grab an argument off the command line and add it to the output.

```
#!/usr/bin/env ruby

puts "Hello, #{ARGV[0]}!"
```

Ruby stores command-line arguments in a predefined Ruby variable called ARGV. ARGV[0] refers to the first item on the command line, the 0th element in ARGV. Run the *matz.rb* program you just edited with an argument to see the results:

```
$ matz.rb Matz
Hello, Matz!
```

Formatting a String

You can change the output on the fly with the %s format flag and %:

```
hi = "Hello, %s"

puts hi % "Matz!" # => "Hello, Matz!"

puts hi % "people!" # => "Hello, people!"

puts hi % "universe!" # => "Hello, universe!"
```

You can also use % like this:

```
"%s, %s!" % [ "Hello", "Matz" ]
```

% is a method from the String class that formats a string. It is like using sprintf:

```
sprintf( "Hello, %s", "Matz!" ) # => "Hello, Matz!"
```

Use printf to print the output to your display (the default standard output device).

```
printf( "Hello, %s", "Matz!" ) # => Hello, Matz!
```

You will learn about formatting strings with sprintf in Chapter 10 in the section "Formatting Output with sprintf."

The eval Method and -e Option

The eval method evaluates a string enclosed in quotes as a Ruby statement or expression and returns the result. It's handy for testing.

```
eval "puts 'Hello, Matz!'" # => Hello, Matz!
```

Similarly, there is a way you can print Hello, Matz! without using a separate file at all—with the -e (execute/evaluate) option:

```
ruby -e "puts 'Hello, Matz!'"
```

Notice that you use single quotes inside of double quotes when using the -e option. You can also use multiple -e options:

```
ruby -e "print 'Hello, '" -e "puts 'Matz!'"
```

Using both of these will give you the same output as before (or what looks like the same output):

```
Hello, Matz!
```

I used print in the first -e option because it doesn't add an end-of-line or newline character at the end of the line like puts does. If I used puts with both -e options, the result would be:

```
Hello,
Matz!
```

You can use multiple statements, separated by semicolons, inside a single -e if you want:

```
ruby -e "three = 3; puts 'Matz! ' * three"
```

This will give you:

```
Matz! Matz! Matz!
```

Getting Input from the Keyboard

You can use the gets method to read from standard input (text from your keyboard, by default).

```
#!/usr/bin/env ruby

print "Who do you want to say hello to? "
hello = gets
puts "Hello, " + hello
```

The program prints the message Who do you want to say hello to? The gets method reads what you type and assigns it to the hello variable. puts prints Hello, plus whatever is held in hello, to the standard output (your computer display, by default). Run the program, then type your answer to the question.

```
$ matz.rb
Who do you want to say hello to? Matz!
Hello, Matz!
```

Methods

You've had a chance to use a few methods like system and eval; now you'll define your own method with def/end:

```
def hello
  puts "Hello, Matz!"
end

hello # => Hello, Matz!
```

The method called hello contains a single statement that prints Hello, Matz!. To see it in action, call the method by invoking its name, hello.

The block

Redefine hello so that it contains only a yield statement, then call the new version of hello with a *block* (the code in braces).

```
def hello
  yield
end

hello { puts "Hello, Matz!" } # => Hello, Matz!
```

The yield statement executes the block of code in braces (that is, { puts "Hello, Matz!" }) associated with the method call to hello. You'll learn more about blocks in the section "Blocks" in Chapter 2.

The each Method

Let's go a step further. Let's print all the elements in an array using the each method followed by a block:

```
[ "Hello, ", "Matz!"].each { |e| print e }
```

An array is an ordered list of elements. The method each uses a block—again, the code enclosed in braces—to iterate over, or repeatedly process, all the elements in the array. The |e| represents the elements fed from the array; the print e statement prints each element in the array. You'll learn much more about arrays in Chapter 6.

The proc

You can convert a block into an object. This object is called a *proc* (procedure). The nice thing about procs is that they preserve their execution environment and pack it along with them. The lambda method is one way to create a proc object. I'll use it here to create a now familiar greeting.

```ruby
prc = lambda { |name| puts "Hello, " + name }
```

The proc is stored in prc as the result of a call to lambda, which stores the block as an object. You can now call the proc with an argument; call executes the proc with an argument, yielding a string.

```ruby
prc.call "Matz!" # => Hello, Matz!
```

You'll learn more about procs in the section "Procs" in Chapter 2.

XML

For XML processing, REXML is built into Ruby. Use it to greet the revered founder of our feast, as shown in Examples 1-1 and 1-2.

Example 1-1. matz.xml

```xml
<hello>Matz!</hello>
```

Example 1-2. matz_xml.rb

```ruby
#!/usr/bin/env ruby

require "rexml/document"

file = File.new( "matz.xml" )
doc = REXML::Document.new file
puts doc.to_s
```

When you run it, the program grabs the XML file *matz.xml* and displays it.

The Class

Use the class Hello to greet Matz, as shown in Example 1-3.

Example 1-3. hello.rb

```ruby
class Hello

  def initialize( name )
    @name = name
  end

  def hello_matz
```

Example 1-3. hello.rb (continued)

```
    puts "Hello, " + @name + "!"
  end

end

hi = Hello.new( "Matz" )
hi.hello_matz # => Hello, Matz!
```

You'll learn a bit about classes in Chapter 2. Chapter 9 is dedicated to bringing you fully up to speed on Ruby classes.

The Tk Toolkit

Create a graphical version of "Hello, Matz!" with the Tk toolkit (see *http://www.tcl.tk*), as shown in Example 1-4.

Example 1-4. matz_tk.rb

```
#!/usr/bin/env ruby

require 'tk'
hello = TkRoot.new
TkLabel.new( hello ) do
    text "\n  Hello, Matz!  \n"
    pack
end
Tk.mainloop
```

The require method loads the Tk library. The next line creates a new TkRoot object called hello. TkLabel.new adds a label to that object with the text Hello, Matz!. Tk.mainloop makes the graphical event happen, displaying the graphic shown in Figure 1-1. You can run the program by typing the following at a shell prompt:

```
    matz_tk.rb &
```

The & puts the process in the background on a Unix/Linux system. You'll learn more about the Tk library and other graphical user interfaces in the section "Using Tk" in Chapter 10.

Figure 1-1. Tk version of Hello, Matz! on Mac OS X

Editing and Running Ruby in TextMate

If you own a Mac, you will get more joy out of life if you get yourself a copy of Text-Mate. (Download a free trial or pay for a copy at *http://www.macromates.com*.)

TextMate has language bundles that make editing in a given language—such as HTML, C, Java, Python, Ruby, and Rails—a snap. Other IDEs have similar features, for sure, and I don't spend any energy knocking them, in public or private. The difference to me is that TextMate is elegant; it doesn't overwhelm you with complex features. It's there to help without getting in your way.

Figure 1-2 shows a version of *matz.rb* open for editing in TextMate. To run this program in TextMate, I simply type Command-R, and the results appear in a separate window (RubyMate), shown in Figure 1-3.

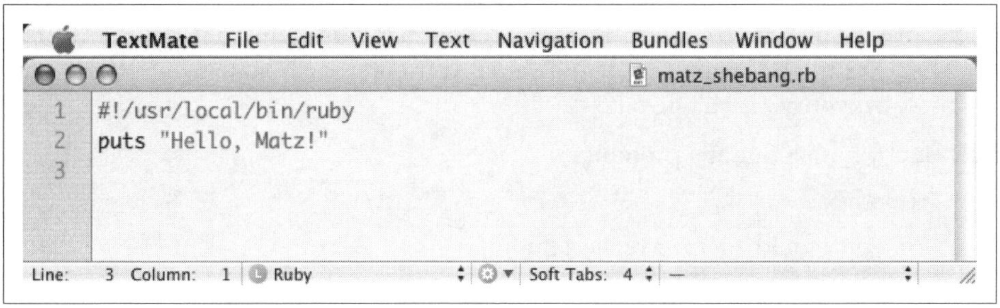

```
 TextMate   File   Edit   View   Text   Navigation   Bundles   Window   Help
                                                    matz_shebang.rb
1  #!/usr/local/bin/ruby
2  puts "Hello, Matz!"
3

Line:   3  Column:   1   Ruby                    Soft Tabs:  4   —
```

Figure 1-2. Editing a Ruby program in TextMate

```
                    RubyMate — matz_shebang.rb

RubyMate

    RubyMate r4913 running Ruby v1.8.5 (/usr/local/bin/ruby)
    >>> matz_shebang.rb

    Hello, Matz!


Program exited.
```

Figure 1-3. Results of running a Ruby program in TextMate

Here are a few of the Ruby shortcuts in TextMate:

- Insert Ruby templates to make file creation quicker.
- Insert Ruby keywords, such as `begin` or `if`, followed by a tab, and TextMate completes the typing for you.
- Execute a single line as Ruby with Control-Shift-E. This inserts the result right into the file. You can do this in other files, too (HTML files, for example).
- Validate syntax, without running the program, with Control-Shift-V.
- Place the cursor on a Ruby keyword or method name, then enter Control-H to get documentation on that term.

Interactive Ruby

Interactive Ruby, or *irb*, is an interactive command-line environment for Ruby, allowing you to see results (or errors) after you enter each statement. When you install Ruby, you get *irb* along with it.

Start out by typing this at a prompt:

```
$ irb -v
```

In return, you should get *irb*'s version number:

```
irb 0.9.5(05/04/13)
```

If *irb* is present, you are ready to go; if it isn't, go to the section "Installing Ruby," later in this chapter, and follow the instructions.

When you enter *irb* at a shell prompt, you will get the *irb* prompt. Type a Ruby statement at the prompt, and then press the Return or Enter key:

```
irb(main):001:0> puts "Hello, Matz! "
Hello, Matz!
=> nil
```

nil, set off by => in the output of *irb*, is a value returned by the method puts. nil has a special meaning in Ruby. It denotes empty and always means false.

puts prints out the string Hello, Matz!, followed by a newline character.

The newline character varies, depending on your platform. On Mac OS X and Unix/Linux systems, it is an LF (linefeed) character; on Microsoft Windows, it's CR+LF (a carriage return character followed by a linefeed).

As mentioned earlier, you can assign a string, or just about any other value, to a name (variable), and then reuse it. In the following command, Hello, Matz! is assigned to the name hi and printed by puts:

```
irb(main):002:0> hi = "Hello, Matz!"
=> "Hello, Matz! "
irb(main):003:0> puts hi
Hello, Matz!
=> nil
```

Print out hi three times:

```
irb(main):004:0> puts hi * 3
Hello, Matz! Hello, Matz! Hello, Matz!
=> nil
```

You can do some simple math:

```
irb(main):006:0> 10 + 10
=> 20
irb(main):007:0> 4 * 5
=> 20
irb(main):008:0> 100 / 5
=> 20
irb(main):009:0> 50 - 30
=> 20
irb(main):010:0> 80 % 60
=> 20
```

We could go on and on. *irb* is a great environment for playing around with Ruby and learning how it works because you always get immediate feedback with every step you take.

You'll have opportunities to fire up *irb* later in the book. In fact, you can use *irb* to run any Ruby program that you find here.

Resources

You can find a lot about Ruby at the official Ruby site, *http://www.ruby-lang.org*. There you can find news, downloads, tutorials, as well as documentation, mailing lists, and other good stuff. Ruby Central, Inc. (*http://www.rubycentral.org*) runs the annual International Ruby Conference (*http://www.rubycentral.org/conference*). It usually gets sold out way early, so plan accordingly.

Aside from the documentation page on *ruby-lang.org* (*http://www.ruby-lang.org/en/ documentation*), *http://www.ruby-doc.org* is a great place to hunt down information on all things Ruby. RDoc is a tool that generates documentation from Ruby source code. You can find the Ruby core documentation produced by RDoc at *http:// www.ruby-doc.org/core*. On the Mac (Tiger or later), a good tool for looking things up quickly is the RDoc widget for Dashboard (see Figure 1-4), thanks to Precision Information Services (*http://www.precisionis.com.au*). You can download the widget from *http://www.apple.com/downloads/dashboard/developer/rubyrdocwidget.html*.

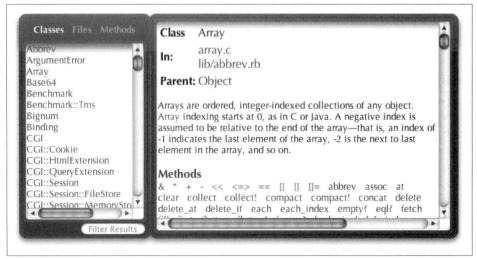

Figure 1-4. RDoc widget on Dashboard

Ruby-Talk is the most popular general Ruby mail list. To sign up (easily), go to *http://www.ruby-lang.org/en/community/mailing-lists*. You'll also see several other lists at this site. For a more complete list of mail groups, including lists in languages besides English, see *http://www.ruby-forum.com*.

RubyForge (*http://rubyforge.org*) is the host of a growing number of open source Ruby projects. Some of the more popular projects include Mongrel, a fast HTTP server (*http://rubyforge.org/projects/mongrel*), RubyGems (*http://rubyforge.org/projects/rubygems*), a dead-simple tool for installing Ruby packages, and Instant Rails (*http://rubyforge.org/projects/instantrails*), a single-step Windows installer that includes Ruby, Rails, Apache, and MySQL. The Ruby Application Archive (RAA) at *http://raa.ruby-lang.org* predates RubyForge and is still a popular site for hosting Ruby projects—more than 1,500 and counting.

For future reading, check out Dave Thomas's *Programming Ruby*, Second Edition, published by Pragmatic (see *http://www.pragmaticprogrammer.com/titles/ruby/index.html* or *http://www.oreilly.com/catalog/0974514055/index.html*). This book, often referred to as the pickaxe book (for the pickaxe on its cover), is well-written and as complete as it could possibly be. You won't be disappointed. You can also find a free, online version of the first edition at *http://www.rubycentral.com/book*.

Hal Fulton's *The Ruby Way* (Addison-Wesley) is also now in its second edition (*http://www.samspublishing.com/bookstore/product.asp?isbn=0672328844&rl=1*). It has also been well-received and is a worthwhile investment. Other books exist, and many more are on the way—too many to list (see *http://www.ruby-lang.org/en/documentation/ book-list*)—but I note Dave and Hal's books because they were in the game early, and are still in it.

Oh, and before I forget, you can't be a complete Ruby programmer until you've read *why's (poignant) guide to Ruby,* by *why the lucky stiff.* That's his moniker. (I don't know his real name. Frankly, I don't want to know his "real" name. It would spoil the fun.) why's guide is the funniest technical book I've ever read, and I highly recommend it. You'll find it at *http://poignantguide.net/ruby*.

Installing Ruby

Ruby is available on the major platforms. The following sections show you how to install Ruby on Mac OS X, Windows, and Linux. Ruby's general download page is at *http://www.ruby-lang.org/en/downloads*. Most of you could likely figure out how to install Ruby just by following the links there, but the material here provides a little extra guidance.

Installation procedures are a moving target, and print media can't keep up with electronic media. That means that some of this material may get out of sync with what's happening out there on the Web, so I'll be as generally specific as I can.

Installing Ruby on Mac OS X Tiger

As shipped, Tiger comes with an older version of Ruby. Which version depends on what release of Tiger you're dealing with. The release of Tiger on my system at the moment is 10.4.8, which comes with version 1.8.2. You'll want an updated version, as I did.

The simple way to install Ruby (and a boatload of other software) is with Locomotive (*http://locomotive.raaum.org*). For information on what comes with the Locomotive download (a *dmg* file), which includes Ruby on Rails, see *http://locomotive.raaum.org/ bundles.html*. It might be more than you want to deal with. You can find a mirror at *http://prdownloads.sourceforge.net/locomotive/Locomotive_2.0.8.dmg?download*. Select a mirror and then follow the steps just like you would when installing any other *dmg*.

The purest form of installation, at least in my mind, is to download and compile the source files. In other words, you download the file distribution for a given release, pull the files out of the release archive, compile the files (those that need compilation), and then copy those files to their proper directories. Those are the basic steps, but there are a few tools to make this job easier, like `configure` and `make`. We'll take advantage of them here as we install a new version of Ruby on Tiger (these steps could apply to a Linux installation as well).

These steps may appear daunting at first, but they really are not. Just follow along and things will come together in the end.

You can find excellent instructions on installing Ruby on Tiger in Dan Benjamin's "Building Ruby, Rails, LightTPD, and MySQL on Tiger" (*http://hivelogic.com/ articles/2005/12/01/ruby_rails_lighttpd_mysql_tiger*). He covers installing more software than you need to install now; I'll only use his steps for installing Ruby, and I'll update those steps to include the latest versions of software.

You need to have XCode installed on your Mac for this install procedure to work. XCode is a set of programming tools from Apple. You can learn about it at *http:// www.apple.com/macosx/features/xcode,* and download it from *http://developer.apple. com/tools/download*. The download instructions are easy to follow.

As shipped, Tiger has some issues with Ruby (see *http://wiki.rubyonrails.com/rails/pages/ HowtoInstallOnOSXTiger*). One way to resolve some of the problems is by downloading and installing readline (*http://tiswww.tis.case.edu/~chet/readline/readline.html*), which lets you do command-line editing (*irb* uses readline). Here are the steps for downloading and installing readline:

1. Go to *ftp://ftp.gnu.org/gnu/readline* to find the latest version (5.2 at this writing) and download it. (I put source archives in the directory */usr/local/src* on my Mac so I can keep track of them.) You can avoid using the browser or FTP. Just use curl (*http://curl.haxx.se*). The -O option takes the last part of the URL to create a desination filename.

   ```
   $ curl -O ftp://ftp.gnu.org/gnu/readline/readline-5.2.tar.gz
   ```

2. Extract the archive with tar (x means extract, z means *gunzip*, v means verbose, f means use file archive):

   ```
   $ tar xzvf readline-5.2.tar.gz
   ```

3. Change directories:

   ```
   $ cd readline-5.2
   ```

4. Run configure (generated from Autoconf, a tool that produces shell scripts for configuring software packages), replacing {$prefix} with /usr/local:

   ```
   $ ./configure --prefix=/usr/local
   ```

5. Run make, a tool for building applications. This compiles the source files, and gets things ready to install. You can test the results, too:

   ```
   $ make
   $ make test
   ```

6. Finally, install:

   ```
   $ make install
   ```

   If you have not logged in as root, you can assume superuser powers by prefixing this command with the sudo utility (*http://www.sudo.ws*), which will require a password:

   ```
   $ sudo make install
   ```

The steps to install Ruby are very similar:

1. While in /usr/local/src, grab the archive for the latest version of Ruby (1.8.6 at this writing):

    ```
    $ curl -O ftp://ftp.ruby-lang.org/pub/ruby/ruby-1.8.6.tar.gz
    ```

2. Extract the archive:

    ```
    $ tar xzvf ruby-1.8.6.tar.gz
    ```

3. Change directories:

    ```
    $ cd ruby-1.8.6
    ```

4. Run configure (enabling POSIX threads, with readline):

    ```
    $ ./configure --prefix=/usr/local --enable-pthread --with-readline-dir=/usr/local
    ```

5. Run make and then test it:

    ```
    $ make
    $ make test
    ```

6. Install the software:

    ```
    $ make install
    ```

    You may need the sudo utility (*http://www.sudo.ws*), which will require a password):

    ```
    $ sudo make install
    ```

7. Then install the documentation:

    ```
    $ make install-doc
    ```

    or:

    ```
    $ sudo make install-doc
    ```

8. Place */usr/local/bin* in the path if it is not already. If you don't know how to do this, see the sidebar "Setting Up the Path Environment," later in this chapter.

9. Now test to make sure Ruby is in place:

    ```
    $ ruby -v
    ```

10. You should get this happy reply:

    ```
    $ ruby 1.8.6 (2007-03-13 patchlevel 0) [powerpc-darwin8.9.0]
    ```

Alrighty then. You are ready to roll with Ruby on Mac OS X.

Installing Ruby on Windows with the One-Click Installer

It's easy to install Ruby on Windows with the One-Click Installer, available on Ruby-Forge at *http://rubyforge.org/projects/rubyinstaller*. Here are the steps:

1. Go to the Ruby download site and click on the link labeled "1.8.6 One-Click Installer (or later)," or go to the One-Click Installer site and click the Download link. Click on the latest executable, which is *ruby186-25.exe* at this writing.

2. Open the executable. An install wizard will appear (see Figure 1-5). You'll have a chance to include other goodies in the download, such as the SciTE editor (*http://www.scintilla.org/SciTE.html*). Also, be sure to enable RubyGems when asked, as it is installed by default, and you'll no doubt want use it later.

3. Select a destination folder (such as *C:\Ruby* or *C:\"Program Files"\Ruby*). If you try to install over an older version of Ruby, you'll be asked to uninstall the old version first.

4. Add the new Ruby *bin* directory to your path; for example, if your Ruby directory is *C:\Ruby*, add *C:\Ruby\bin* to your path (see the sidebar "Setting Up the Path Environment," later in this chapter, if you don't know how to do this; it's OK to set up the path *after* the installation).

5. After you install Ruby, open a DOS window and type this line:

```
$ ruby -v
```

You should get something like the following response:

```
$ ruby 1.8.6 (2007-03-13 patchlevel 0) [i386-mswin32]
```

6. Check your system path variable and make sure it contains the path to the Ruby binaries in the *bin* directory. The One-click installer should take care of all this for you, however.

Figure 1-5. Windows One-Click Installer

Installing Ruby on Windows with Binaries

Installing Ruby using binaries (precompiled executables) is just as easy as using the One-Click Installer. *I* think it is, anyway. Here are the steps I suggest:

1. Decide where you want to install the Ruby files—for example, *C:\Ruby* or *C:\ "Program Files"\Ruby*.

2. Download the stable binary ZIP archive for the latest release of Ruby (1.8.6 at this writing). Go to the Ruby download page at *http://www.ruby-lang.org/en/ downloads*, and find the "Ruby on Windows" section, then click the link Ruby 1.8.6 Binary. Or you can just point to *ftp://ftp.ruby-lang.org/pub/ruby/binaries/ mswin32/ruby-1.8.6-i386-mswin32.zip* (or latest version) in a browser. This will download the file archive.

3. Open the archive (*ruby-1.8.6-i386-mswin32.zip* or later) with Windows Explorer, and then extract it to the directory you set up in step 1 (see Figure 1-6).

4. Place the new Ruby *bin* directory in your path; for example, if your Ruby directory is *C:\Ruby*, add *C:\Ruby\bin* to your path (see the sidebar "Setting Up the Path Environment," later in this chapter, if you don't know how to do this).

5. After you install Ruby, open a DOS window and type:

   ```
   $ ruby -v
   ```

6. If you don't get something like the following answer, check your system path variable and make sure it contains the path to the Ruby binaries in the *bin* directory:

   ```
   $ ruby 1.8.6 (2006-08-25) [i386-mswin32]
   ```

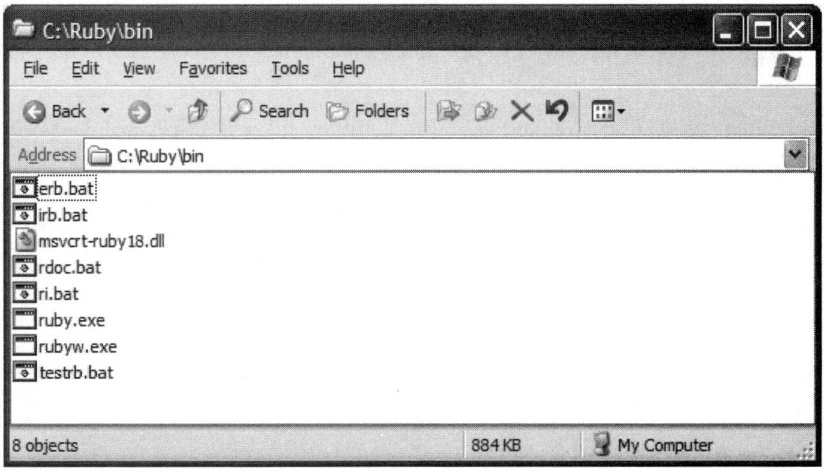

Figure 1-6. C:\Ruby\bin in Windows Explorer

Installing Ruby on Linux

The installation steps I discussed for installing Ruby on Mac OS X from source will also work for Linux, but I will just mention a few other options here. If you know Linux, you'll know what I am talking about.

- If you're running Red Hat (*http://www.redhat.com*), you can find the latest version of Ruby at RPM Find (*http://rpmfind.net/linux/rpm2html/search.php?query=Ruby*) and then use rpm to install it.

- On Debian (*http://www.debian.org*), you can use apt-get (*http://www.debian.org/doc/manuals/apt-howto*).

- On Gentoo (*http://www.gentoo.org*), use emerge (*http://www.gentoo.org/doc/en/handbook/handbook-x86.xml?part=2&chap=1*).

Permission Denied

If you are new to using the shell on Mac OS X or Linux, what do you do when you get a message like this?

```
-bash: ./matz.rb: Permission denied
```

This reply most likely means that the file is not set up as an executable. To fix this, change the access control on the file using the chmod command by typing:

```
chmod 755 matz.rb
```

755 makes the control list read `rwxr-xr-x` (where r means read, w write, and x execute). This means that the file is readable and executable by everyone (owner, group, and others, in that order), but writable only by the owner. To find out more about chmod, type `man chmod` at a shell prompt.

Associating File Types on Windows

This section is for those who use Windows and have never associated a file type before. If this is a familiar topic to you or you are on a different platform, you can skip it.

On its own, Windows doesn't know or care about shebang (#!), which allows the program to execute by merely invoking its name in a shell on Unix/Linux systems. However, you can achieve a similar effect to shebang by creating a file type association with the assoc and ftype commands on Windows.

 If you used the One-Click Ruby Installer for installing Ruby on Windows, the following was performed automatically for you, behind the scenes.

First, find out if an association exists for *.rb* with the assoc command:

```
C:\Ruby Code>assoc .rb
File association not found for extension .rb
```

It's not found, so associate the *.rb* extension with a file type:

```
C:\Ruby Code>assoc .rb=rbFile
```

Test to see if the association exists now:

```
C:\Ruby Code>assoc .rb
.rb=rbFile
```

Test to see if the file type exists:

```
C:\Ruby Code>ftype rbfile
File type 'rbfile' not found or no open command associated with it.
```

It's not found, so create it:

```
C:\Ruby Code>ftype rbfile="C:\Program Files\Ruby\bin\ruby.exe" "%1" %*
```

Be sure to put the correct path to the executable for the Ruby interpreter, followed by the substitution variables. %1 is a substitution variable for the file you want to run, and %* accepts all other parameters that may appear on the command line. Test it:

```
C:\Ruby Code>ftype rbfile
rbfile="C:\Program Files\Ruby\bin\ruby.exe" "%1" %*
```

Finally, add *.rb* to the PATHEXT environment variable. Is it there already?

```
C:\Ruby Code>set PATHEXT
PATHEXT=.COM;.EXE;.BAT;.CMD;.VBS;.VBE;.JS;.JSE;.WSF;.WSH;.tcl
```

No. What we want isn't there, so let's add it:

```
C:\Ruby Code>set PATHEXT=.rb;%PATHEXT%
```

And then test it:

```
C:\Ruby Code>set PATHEXT
PATHEXT=.rb;.COM;.EXE;.BAT;.CMD;.VBS;.VBE;.JS;.JSE;.WSF;.WSH;.tcl
```

Very good. Now run a Ruby program by entering the program's filename at the command prompt, without the file extension:

```
C:\Ruby Code> matz
Hello, Matz!
```

To preserve these settings, you can add these commands to your *autoexec.bat* file or set the environment variables by selecting Start → Control Panel → System, clicking on the Advanced tab, and then clicking the Environment Variables button.

Review Questions

1. What is the nickname of the inventor of Ruby?
2. Ruby came out in 1995. What other programming language was released to the public that year?
3. Is everyone who writes a programming book morally or otherwise obligated to write a "Hello, World!" program?
4. What does the abbreviation *irb* stand for?
5. What is Ruby's killer app?
6. What is the name of the funny book on Ruby?
7. Who wrote the pickaxe book?
8. What's one of the author's favorite programming environments on the Mac?

## CHAPTER 2

A Quick Tour of Ruby

Without going into all the details, this chapter introduces you to the fundamentals of Ruby: classes and modules, including the Object class and the Kernel module, reserved words (keywords), comments, variables, methods, and so forth. Most topics will be dealt with elsewhere in the book in more detail. Some topics merit entire chapters, others only sections (found in Chapter 10). I'll always tell you where else to look for more information on a topic. This book's most detailed discussions on methods and blocks are found in this chapter.

Ruby Is Object-Oriented

Matz, the creator of Ruby, had wanted to create his own programming language since he was in high school. He wanted to create a scripting language, but he also wanted it to be object-oriented.

Ruby goes beyond mere scripting, though its programs may look like shell scripts. It is not just a procedural language, but it can be used like one.

Ruby has *classes*. Classes hold data—in the form of variables and constants—and methods, which are compact collections of code that help you perform operations on data. Classes can inherit information from each other, but only one at a time. This allows you to reuse code—which means you'll spend less time fixing or debugging code—and intermix the code through inheritance.

A class is like a blueprint; with a new method, this blueprint can be assigned to a variable or become instantiated, and thereby become an *object*. In Ruby, almost everything is an object; in fact, everything that Ruby can bind to a variable name is an object.

There's lots more to learn about classes, and you'll find a lot more information on classes in Chapter 9. For right now, you can get by with the basics. Example 2-1 shows a Ruby program, *friendly.rb,* that has two classes, Hello and Goodbye. You'll find this program in the archive of Ruby programs that comes with this book (download it from *http://www.oreilly.com/catalog/learningruby*). Run this program at a shell or command prompt, in the directory where the archive was installed. If a code example is not in a file, you can type that code in *irb* to see for yourself what it does. I encourage you to run as much code as you dare.

Example 2-1. friendly.rb

```ruby
class Hello
  def howdy
    greeting = "Hello, Matz!"
    puts greeting
  end
end

class Goodbye < Hello
  def solong
    farewell = "Goodbye, Matz."
    puts farewell
  end
end

friendly = Goodbye.new
friendly.howdy
friendly.solong
```

If you run the program in Example 2-1, you'll get these messages back:

```
$ friendly.rb
Hello, Matz!
Goodbye, Matz.
```

Experienced programmers can likely tell what's happening in Example 2-1 without any tutoring. If you're not one of these, read on; otherwise, you can skip ahead to the next heading (or jump to Chapter 9 if you are eager to get the whole story on Ruby classes).

The Hello class defines the howdy method. This method prints the contents of the string associated with the greeting variable, Hello, Matz!. The Goodbye class likewise contains the definition of a method, solong, which prints a string assigned to the farewell variable, Goodbye, Matz!. The Goodbye class also inherits what's in the Hello class; that's what the < symbol is for. This means that the Goodbye class didn't have to redefine the howdy method. It just inherited it.

friendly is an object, an instance of the Goodbye class. The new method called on Goodbye comes from the Object class and creates the new instance friendly (more on the Object class in the next section). You can use the friendly object to call both the howdy and solong methods, because it inherently knows about them. It knows about the solong method because it is defined inside the Goodbye class, and it knows about the howdy method because Goodbye inherited it from Hello.

That's about as much as I am going to tell you for now. There will be information on classes spread throughout the chapters that follow. Chapter 9 spells out classes in more detail.

The Object Class and the Kernel Module

The `Object` class is the Ruby base class, the parent of all other classes in Ruby, and it is always magically present whenever you run a Ruby program. You don't have to do anything fancy to get access to its functionality in other classes. It's just there for you.

With `Object` comes a lot of functionality in the form of methods and constants. This functionality is inherited by all other Ruby programs automatically. In this section, I'll introduce you to some of this functionality.

`Object` gives you methods like `==` and `eql?`, `class`, `inspect`, `object_id`, and `to_s`. You will learn more about these methods in upcoming chapters. You can read about all of `Object`'s methods at *http://www.ruby-doc.org/core/classes/Object.html*.

`Kernel` is a Ruby *module*. A module is like a class, but you can't instantiate it as an object as you can with a class. However, when you include or mix in a module in a class, you get access to all its methods within that class. You can use methods from an included module without having to implement those methods.

`Object` includes the `Kernel` module. This means that because you always get access to `Object` in a Ruby program, you also get all the `Kernel` methods, too. You have already seen some of these methods in action, such as `print` and `puts`. A sampling of commonly used `Kernel` methods includes `eval`, `exit`, `gets`, `loop`, `require`, `sleep`, and `sprintf`. You will get to use most of these methods in later chapters of this book.

You don't have to prefix the `Kernel` methods with an object or receiver name. Just call the methods anywhere in any program, and they work. Read about `Kernel` at *http://www.ruby-doc.org/core/classes/Kernel.html*.

Ruby's Reserved Words

Every programming language has its own list of *reserved words* (aka keywords), which are reserved for its own purposes so that it can do its job. They are the words that make statements in programs, and without statements, or instructions, how could a program tell a computer what to do?

Table 2-1 lists Ruby's reserved words and briefly describes the purpose of each.

Table 2-1. Ruby's reserved words

Reserved word	Description
BEGIN	Code, enclosed in { and }, to run before the program runs.
END	Code, enclosed in { and }, to run when the program ends.
alias	Creates an alias for an existing method, operator, or global variable.
and	Logical operator; same as && except and has lower precedence. (Compare with or.)
begin	Begins a code block or group of statements; closes with end.
break	Terminates a while or until loop or a method inside a block.
\case	Compares an expression with a matching when clause; closes with end. (See when.)
class	Defines a class; closes with end.
def	Defines a method; closes with end.
defined?	A special operator that determines if a variable, method, super method, or block exists.
do	Begins a block and executes code in that block; closes with end.
else	Executes following code if previous conditional, in if, elsif, unless, or when, is not true.
elsif	Executes following code if previous conditional, in if or elsif, is not true.
end	Ends a code block (group of statements) starting with begin, def, do, if, etc.
ensure	Always executes at block termination; use after last rescue.
false	Logical or Boolean false, instance of FalseClass. (See true.)
for	Begins a for loop; used with in.
if	Executes code block if conditional statement is true. Closes with end. (Compare with unless, until.)
in	Used with for loop. (See for.)
module	Defines a module; closes with end.
next	Jumps before a loop's conditional. (Compare with redo.)
nil	Empty, uninitialized variable, or invalid, but not the same as zero; object of NilClass.
not	Logical operator; same as !.
or	Logical operator; same as || except or has lower precedence. (Compare with and.)
redo	Jumps after a loop's conditional. (Compare with next.)
rescue	Evaluates an expression after an exception is raised; used before ensure.
retry	Repeats a method call outside of rescue; jumps to top of block (begin) if inside rescue.
return	Returns a value from a method or block. May be omitted.

Table 2-1. Ruby's reserved words (continued)

Reserved word	Description
self	Current object (invoked by a method).
super	Calls method of the same name in the superclass. The *superclass* is the parent of this class.
then	A continuation for if, unless, and when. May be omitted.
true	Logical or Boolean true, instance of TrueClass. (See false.)
undef	Makes a method in current class undefined.
unless	Executes code block if conditional statement is false. (Compare with if, until.)
until	Executes code block while conditional statement is false. (Compare with if, unless.)
when	Starts a clause (one or more) under case.
while	Executes code while the conditional statement is true.
yield	Executes the block passed to the method.
__FILE__	Name of current source file.
__LINE__	Number of current line in the current source file.

Comments

A comment hides lines from the Ruby interpreter so that the lines are discarded or ignored. This allows a programmer (that's you) to insert all kinds of information in a program so that other people can figure out what's going on. There are two basic comment styles in Ruby. The hash character (#) can be at the beginning of a line:

```
# I am a comment. Just ignore me.
```

Or on the same line after a statement or expression:

```
name = "Floydene Wallup" # ain't that a name to beat all
```

You can make a comment run over several lines, like this:

```
# This is a comment.
# This is a comment, too.
# This is a comment, too.
# I said that already.
```

Here is another form. This block comment conceals several lines from the interpreter with =begin/=end:

```
=begin
This is a comment.
This is a comment, too.
This is a comment, too.
I said that already.
=end
```

A block can comment out one line or as many lines as you want.

Variables

A variable is an identifier or name that can be assigned a value, and a value has, or will have, a type at runtime (when the program runs). An example is found in the following statement, where the variable x is assigned the value 100 by the equals sign.

```
x = 100
```

Now the local variable x holds the value 100. But, hey, what type is it? Looks like an integer to me—how about you? And what does Ruby think?

Many modern programming languages, like C++ and Java, are statically typed. This basically means that a variable is assigned a type at the time it is declared, and, because these languages are also strongly typed, the variable remains that type unless it is cast into a different type, if it is possible to do so.

For example, in Java, you would declare variables with the types (int) on the left:

```
int months = 12;
int year = 2007;
```

Ruby doesn't have type declarations. It just assigns values to variables, like this:

```
months = 12
year = 2007
```

You could use a semicolon at the end of the line if you wanted, but a newline character is all you really need.

The values in x, months, and year are clearly integers, but you didn't have to give them a type because Ruby does that for you, automatically. It's called *dynamic* or *duck typing*.

This is how duck typing works: if you observe an aquatically competent bird, and it walks like a duck, quacks like a duck, flies like a duck, and swims like a duck, well, by George, it's probably a duck. Ruby likewise looks at a value assigned to a variable, and if it walks, quacks, flies, and swims like an integer, then Ruby assumes it can act *as* an integer.

Let's ask Ruby what it thinks of x—that is, whether it is an integer—with the kind_of? method (this method is from the Object class).

```
x.kind_of? Integer # => true
```

Why yes, the value of x behaves like an integer! As a matter of fact, it is an instance of the Fixnum class, which inherits the Integer class.

```
x.class # => Fixnum
```

Change the value of x from an integer to a floating point with the to_f method from the Fixnum class (it is inherited by other classes, too).

```
x.to_f # => 100.0
```

As I noted in Chapter 1, whenever you see => in a code example here, it will always follow a comment character (#). Whatever follows => is the output you can expect from the line or block of code, or from the whole program.

Local Variables

Earlier I referred to x as a local variable. What does that mean? It means that the variable has a local scope (context). For example, when a local variable is defined inside of a method or a loop, its scope is *within* the method or loop where it was defined. It doesn't have a useful life beyond that.

Local variables must start with a lowercase letter or with an underscore character (_), such as alpha or _beta. Another way you can identify a local variable in Ruby is that its name is not prefixed by a special character or symbol, other than _. There are other kinds of variables, each of which is easily recognized by its prefix character. These other kinds include global variables, instance variables, and class variables.

Instance Variables

An *instance variable* is a variable that is referenced via an instance of a class and therefore belongs to a given object. An instance variable is prefixed by a single at sign (@), like this:

```
@hello = hello
```

You can access instance variables from outside of their class only by accessor methods. You will learn about accessor methods in Chapter 9.

Class Variables

A *class variable* is shared among all instances of a class. Only one copy of a class variable exists for a given class. In Ruby, it is prefixed by two at signs (@@). You have to initialize (declare a value for) a class variable before you use it.

```
@@times = 0
```

You'll see class variables in action in Chapter 9.

Global Variables

Global variables are available globally to a program, inside any structure. Their scope is the whole program. They are prefixed by a dollar sign ($).

```
$amount = "0.00"
```

It's hard to keep track of global variables. You are better off designing your code to use class variables or constants. Matz's opinion on global variables is, and I quote, "They are ugly, so don't use them." I would take his advice. (Use a singleton instead; see Chapter 9.)

Constants

A constant holds a constant value for the life of a Ruby program. Constants are variables whose names are capitalized or all uppercase. Here is the definition of a constant named Matz:

```
Matz = "Yukihiro Matsumoto"
puts Matz # => Yukihiro Matsumoto
```

If a constant is defined within a class or module, you can access the constant from within that class or module; if it is defined outside either a class or module, the constant is available globally. Unlike other languages, a Ruby constant is mutable—that is, you can change its value.

Parallel Assignment

I like Ruby's ability to do parallel assignment (like Perl, Python, and JavaScript 1.7). What's that? It's a way to assign a group or series of variables in one statement, on one line. Often, we assign variables one per line:

```
x = 100
y = 200
z = 500
```

With parallel assignment, you do the same thing by separating the variables, then the values, with commas:

```
x, y, z = 100, 200, 500
```

You can even assign values of different kinds, such as a string, float, and integer:

```
a, b, c = "cash", 1.99, 100
```

Parallel assignment is convenient. It's just got Ruby written all over it.

Strings

A string is a sequence of letters, numbers, and other characters. There are several ways to create a string in Ruby, but probably the simplest way is just to write it out, surrounded in quotes (double or single quotes will do). Here we have a quote from Thoreau's *Walden*:

```
thoreau = "If a man does not keep pace with his companions, perhaps it is because he
hears a different drummer."
```

With String methods, you can access and manipulate the string thoreau. For example, you can retrieve part of a string with the [] method, using a range. Let's grab characters 37 through 46:

```
thoreau[37..46] # => "companions"
```

Or, starting at the end of the string using negative numbers, get the second to last character through the eighth to last:

```
thoreau[-8..-2] # => "drummer"
```

You can iterate over all the characters in the string using a block that munches on every byte (8-bit sequence) in an ASCII string and generates a character (with the chr method), separating each character with a slash:

```
thoreau.each_byte do |c|
  print c.chr, "/"
end
# => I/f/ /a/ /m/a/n/ /d/o/e/s/ /n/o/t/ /k/e/e/p/ /p/a/c/e/ /w/i/t/h/ /h/i/s/ /c/o/m/
p/a/n/i/o/n/s/,/ /p/e/r/h/a/p/s/ /i/t/ /i/s/ /b/e/c/a/u/s/e/ /h/e/ /h/e/a/r/s/ /a/ /
d/i/f/f/e/r/e/n/t/ /d/r/u/m/m/e/r/./
```

> If you want to use something beyond ASCII characters in your programs, you should read this note; otherwise, it may be more information than you need. I must admit, implying that a character is synonymous with a byte is rather old-fashioned. In the broader, Unicode-based world, characters can be represented by more than one byte. For example, the character encoding UTF-8 represents characters with one to four bytes. By default, Ruby uses ASCII character encoding, but you can change the encoding by setting (early in the program) the $KCODE variable to 'u' (for UTF-8), 'e' (for EUC), 's' (for SJIS), or 'a' or 'n' (for ASCII or NONE).

Incidentally, the chr method converts a character code (which each_byte produces) into an actual character. You should also know about the opposite method—the ? operator, which returns a character code from a character. I'll demonstrate that with *irb*:

```
irb(main):001:0> ?I
=> 73
irb(main):002:0> ?f
=> 102
irb(main):003:0> ?\  # you can't see it, but this is a space
=> 32
irb(main):004:0> ?m
=> 109
irb(main):005:0> ?a
=> 97
irb(main):006:0> ?n
=> 110
```

I won't go into more detail about strings here, but you'll learn quite a bit about them in Chapter 4.

Regular Expressions

A *regular expression* is a special sequence of characters that matches strings or a set of strings. Regular expressions, or *regexps*, are often used to find string matches so you can do something else to that string or perform some other operation. Regexps are also used to retrieve a string or substring (part of a string) for use elsewhere.

Regexps use elements (one or more characters) to instruct the regular expression engine on how to find a given string. A combination of the special characters, enclosed by a pair of slashes (//), makes up a regular expression pattern. Some examples of these elements are:

^

> Matches the beginning of a line

$

> Matches the end of a line

\w

> Matches a word character

[...]

> Matches any character in the brackets

[^...]

> Matches any characters *not* in the brackets

*

> Matches zero or more occurrences of the previous regexp

+

> Matches one or more occurrences of the previous regexp

?

> Matches zero or one occurrences of the previous regexp

Here is an example of a regular expression used to match a string with the `String` method scan.

```
hamlet = "The slings and arrows of outrageous fortune"
hamlet.scan(/\w+/) # => ["The", "slings", "and", "arrows", "of", "outrageous",
"fortune"]
```

This regexp matches one or more (+) word characters (\w), and places all the matches in an array.

I go into more detail on regexps in Chapter 4. There you'll find a table of all the regexp patterns recognized by Ruby. If you are serious about learning more about regexps in general, pick up a copy of Jeffrey E. F. Friedl's *Mastering Regular Expressions* (O'Reilly).

Numbers and Operators

In most any object-oriented programming language, numbers are considered to be fundamental atoms called *primitives*. They are not directly associated with a class; they just *are*. Not so with Ruby: even numbers are instances of classes.

For example, the number 1001, a positive integer, is an instance of the Fixnum class, which is a child class of Integer, which is a child class of Numeric. The number 1001.0, a floating point value, is an instance of the Float class, which is also a child class of Numeric. (Figure 5-1 shows the relationships between these classes.)

Along with numbers come operations on those numbers. For example, you can add, subtract, divide, multiply, raise a number to a power (exponentiation), and return the remainder of division (modulo), to name a few.

A great place to get acquainted with math operations in Ruby is with *irb*. Try these in *irb*:

```
irb(main):001:0> 3 + 4 # add
=> 7
irb(main):002:0> 7 - 3 # subtract
=> 4
irb(main):003:0> 3 * 4 # multiply
=> 12
irb(main):004:0> 12 / 4 # divide
=> 3
irb(main):005:0> 12**2 # raise to a power (exponent)
=> 144
irb(main):006:0> 12 % 7 # modulo (remainder)
=> 5
```

Here are a few of Ruby's assignment operators in action:

```
irb(main):007:0> x = 12 # assignment
=> 12
irb(main):008:0> x += 1 # abbreviated assignment add
=> 13
irb(main):009:0> x -= 1 # abbreviated assignment subtract
=> 12
irb(main):010:0> x *= 2 # abbreviated assignment multiply
=> 24
irb(main):011:0> x /= 2 # abbreviated assignment divide
=> 12
```

Ruby also has a Math module that provides all kinds of math functions (in the form of class methods), like square root, cosine, tangent, and so forth. Here is an example call to the class method sqrt from the Math module:

```
irb(main):012:0> Math.sqrt(16)
=> 4.0
```

Ruby also delivers some special math classes, such as Rational for doing fractions. You'll learn much more about numbers and operators in Chapter 5. Table 5-1 shows all of Ruby's math operators, including operator precedence.

Conditional Statements

Like any programming language, Ruby has *conditional statements* that test whether a given statement is true or false. It then runs code in a block, based on the answer. Here is a quick example of an if statement that tests whether a variable has a value of zero:

```
value = 0

if value.zero? then
    puts "value is zero. Did you guess that one?"
end
```

The zero? method returns true if the value of value is zero, which it is, so the statement following is executed (and any other statements in the code block if/end). By Ruby convention, any method in Ruby that ends with a question mark returns a Boolean, either true or false. This convention is not enforced, however.

Other conditionals include familiar ones like case and while, and less familiar ones like until and unless. Chapter 3 covers all of the conditional statements you'll find in Ruby.

Arrays and Hashes

An array is an ordered sequence of indexed values, with an index starting at zero. It is one of the most common data structures in computer science. Here is what an array looks like in Ruby:

```
pacific = [ "Washington", "Oregon", "California"]
```

The array is named pacific. It holds three strings—the names of the three states that make up the west coast of the United States. These strings are the *elements* of the array. The elements of an array can be of any Ruby kind, not just strings, of course. This is only one way to define an array. There are a number of other ways you could do this, as you'll see in Chapter 6.

If you wanted to access one of these elements, you could do it by specifying an index with a method. For example, to access the first element, whose index is zero, you could use the [ ] method.

```
pacific[0] # => "Washington"
```

Calling this method retrieves the value of element 0, Washington. You can learn all about Ruby arrays in Chapter 6.

A hash is a map of keys to values. It is also a very common data structure. Unlike an array, which indexes elements with positive integers, hashes let you choose how you will index the values with a key of your choice. Here is how you do it:

```
pacific = { "WA" => "Washington", "OR" => "Oregon", "CA" => "California" }
```

The hash definition is enclosed in curly braces, whereas an array is defined in square brackets. Also, each value is associated (=>) with a key. One of the ways you can access the values in a hash is by their keys. To access the value Oregon from the hash, you could use Hash's [ ] method.

```
pacific["OR"] # => "Oregon"
```

Using the key OR returns the value Oregon. The keys and values can be of any kind, not just strings. You can learn more about hashes in Chapter 7.

Methods

Methods provide a way to gather code (statements and expressions) into one place so that you can use it conveniently and, if necessary, repeatedly. You can define methods to do all kinds of things. In fact, most of the math operators in Ruby are actually methods.

 This is the most concentrated discussion on methods that you'll find in this book, so you may find yourself coming back to this section after you have read further.

Here is a simple definition for a method named hello, created with the keywords def and end:

```
def hello
  puts "Hello, Matz!"
end

hello # => Hello, Matz!
```

The hello method simply outputs a string with puts. On the flip side, you can undefine a method with undef.

```
undef hello # undefines the method named hello

hello # try calling this method now
NameError: undefined local variable or method 'hello' for main:Object
        from (irb):11
        from :0
```

You can also define methods that have arguments, as shown here in the repeat method:

```
def repeat( word, times )
 puts word * times
end
```

```
repeat("Hello! ", 3) # => Hello! Hello! Hello!
repeat "Good-bye! ", 4 # => Good-bye! Good-bye! Good-bye! Good-bye!
```

The repeat method has two arguments, word and times. You can call a method that has arguments with or without parentheses around the arguments. You can even define method arguments without parentheses, but I don't usually do it that way.

Because you don't have to use parentheses, it is possible to have normal-looking math equations when you use operator methods, such as +. Each line that follows is actually a valid call to the Fixnum + method:

```
10 + 2 # => 12
10.+ 2 # => 12
(10).+(2) # => 12
```

Return Values

Methods have return values. In other languages, you can explicitly deliver a return value with a return statement. In Ruby, the last value in a method is returned, with or without an explicit return statement. This is a Ruby idiom. Here's how to do it in *irb*:

1. First, define a method matz that just contains a string:

   ```
   rb(main):001:0> def matz
   irb(main):002:1>   "Hello, Matz!"
   irb(main):003:1> end
   => nil
   ```

2. Call the matz method, and you will see its output. This is available in *irb* but would not be seen if you were running this in a regular program from a shell prompt. Use puts with the method to actually see the output as you normally would:

   ```
   irb(main):004:0> matz
   => "Hello, Matz!"
   irb(main):005:0> puts matz
   Hello, Matz!
   => nil
   ```

3. Now assign method matz to the variables output and puts output:

   ```
   irb(main):006:0> output = matz
   => "Hello, Matz!"
   irb(main):007:0> puts output
   Hello, Matz!
   => nil
   ```

4. You can use a return statement explicitly if you want. Recreate matz, this time adding a return statement, and you get the same results:

   ```
   irb(main):008:0> def matz
   irb(main):009:1>   return "Hello, Matz!"
   irb(main):010:1> end
   => nil
   irb(main):011:0> matz
   => "Hello, Matz!"
   ```

```
irb(main):012:0> puts matz
Hello, Matz!
=> nil
irb(main):013:0> output = matz
=> "Hello, Matz!"
irb(main):014:0> puts output
Hello, Matz!
=> nil
```

Method Name Conventions

Ruby has conventions about the last character in method names—conventions that are broadly used but are not enforced by the language.

If a method name ends with a question mark (?), as in eql?, then the method returns a Boolean—true or false. For example:

```
x = 1.0
y = 1.0
x.eql? y # => true
```

If a method name ends in an exclamation point (!), as in delete!, it indicates that the method is "destructive"—that is, it makes changes *in place* to an object rather than to a copy. It changes the object itself. Note the difference in result between the String methods delete and delete!:

```
der_mensch = "Matz!" # => "Matz!"
der_mensch.delete( "!" ) # => "Matz"
puts der_mensch # => Matz!
der_mensch.delete!( "!" ) # => "Matz"
puts der_mensch # => Matz
```

If a method name ends in an equals sign (=), as in family_name=, then the method is a "setter," i.e., one that performs an assignment or sets a variable such as an instance variable in a class:

```
class Name
  def family_name=( family )
    @family_name = family
  end
  def given_name=( given )
    @given_name = given
  end
end

n = Name.new
n.family_name= "Matsumoto" # => "Matsumoto"
n.given_name= "Yukihiro" # => "Yukihiro"
p n # => <Name:0x1d441c @family_name="Matsumoto", @given_name="Yukihiro">
```

There is a more convenient way to create setter/getter or accessor methods in Ruby. See Chapter 9 to learn how.

Default Arguments

The repeat method, shown earlier, has two arguments. You can give those arguments default values by using an equals sign followed by a value. When you call the method without arguments, the defaults are used automatically.

Redefine repeat with default values: Hello for word, and 3 for times. Then call it first without arguments, then with them.

```
def repeat( word="Hello! ", times=3 )
 puts word * times
end

repeat # => Hello! Hello! Hello!

repeat( "Goodbye! ", 5 ) # => Goodbye! Goodbye! Goodbye! Goodbye! Goodbye!
```

When you call the new call to repeat without arguments, the default values for the arguments are used; but if you call repeat with arguments, the defaults are discarded and replaced by the values of the arguments.

Variable Arguments

Sometimes you don't know how many arguments a method will have. You can be flexible about that, because Ruby lets you pass a variable number of arguments to a method just by prefixing an argument with a splat (*). Example 2-2 shows a simple program that does this.

Example 2-2. num_args.rb

```
def num_args( *args )
  length = args.size
  label = length == 1 ? " argument" : " arguments"
  num = length.to_s + label + " ( " + args.inspect + " )"
  num
end

puts num_args

puts num_args(1)

puts num_args( 100, 2.5, "three" )
```

This program uses the ternary operator (?:) to determine if the noun argument should be singular or plural. (You'll learn more about the ternary operator in the next chapter.)

When you use this syntax for a variable number of arguments, the arguments are stored in an array, as shown by the inspect method. The three calls to num_args are preceded by puts so you can see the return value of the method on standard output.

```
0 arguments ( [] )
1 argument ( [1] )
3 arguments ( [100, 2.5, "three"] )
```

You can have set arguments along with variable arguments. The trick is that the variable list of arguments (the one that starts with *) always comes at the end of the argument list. Example 2-3 is an example of a method that has two regular arguments, plus room for more.

Example 2-3. two_plus.rb

```
def two_plus( one, two, *args )
  length = args.size
  label = length == 1 ? " variable argument" : " variable arguments"
  num = length.to_s + label + " (" + args.inspect + ")"
  num
end
puts two_plus( 1, 2 )

puts two_plus( 1000, 3.5, 14.3 )

puts two_plus( 100, 2.5, "three", 70, 14.3 )
```

Here is the output (it only shows how many variable arguments you get; it ignores the regular ones):

```
0 variable arguments ([])
1 variable argument ([14.3])
3 variable arguments (["three", 70, 14.3])
```

Try calling two_plus without any arguments and see what response you get from the interpreter.

Aliasing Methods

Ruby has a keyword alias that creates method aliases. Aliasing means that you in effect create a copy of the method with a new method name, though both method invocations will point to the same object. Using alias (or Module's method alias_method) gives you a way to have access to methods that have been overridden.

The following example in *irb* illustrates how to create an alias for the method greet:

```
irb(main):001:0> def greet
irb(main):002:1>   puts "Hello, baby!"
irb(main):003:1> end
=> nil
irb(main):004:0> alias baby greet # alias greet as baby
=> nil
irb(main):005:0> greet # call it
Hello, baby!
=> nil
irb(main):006:0> baby # call the aliased version
Hello, baby!
=> nil
irb(main):007:0> greet.object_id # what's the object id?
Hello, baby!
=> 4
```

```
irb(main):008:0> baby.object_id # points at the same object
Hello, baby!
=> 4
```

Blocks

A *block* in Ruby is more than just a code block or group of statements. In a certain context, a block has a special meaning. This kind of block is always invoked in conjunction with a method, as you will see. In fact, it is referred to as a *nameless function*.

A block in Ruby is often (but not always) an idiom for getting all the values out of a data structure by iterating over the structure. It sort of means, "give me everything you've got in there, one at a time." I'll show you a common use of the block.

Remember the array `pacific`? Here it is again:

```
pacific = [ "Washington", "Oregon", "California" ]
```

You can call a block on `pacific` to retrieve all of its elements, one at a time, with the each method. Here is one way to do it:

```
pacific.each do |element|
  puts element
end
```

The name between the pipe characters (`|element|`) can be any name you want. The block uses it as a local variable to keep track of every element in the array, and later uses it to do something with the element. This block uses `puts` to print each element in the array:

```
Washington
Oregon
California
```

You can replace do/end with a pair of braces, as is commonly done, to make things a bit tighter (by the way, braces actually have a higher precedence than do/end):

```
pacific.each { |e| puts e }
```

Many dozens of classes have each methods in them, such as `Array`, `Hash`, and `String`. But don't get the wrong idea. Iterating over data structures isn't the only way to use blocks. Let me give you a simple example using `yield`, a Ruby keyword.

The yield Statement

First, define a tiny little method `gimme` that contains nothing more than a `yield` statement:

```
def gimme
  yield
end
```

To find out what yield does, call gimme alone and see what happens:

```
gimme
LocalJumpError: no block given
        from (irb):11:in `gimme'
        from (irb):13
        from :0
```

You get an error here because the job of yield is to execute the code block that is associated with the method. That was missing in the call to gimme. We can avoid this error by using the block_given? method from Kernel. Redefine gimme with an if statement:

```
def gimme
  if block_given?
    yield
  else
    puts "I'm blockless!"
  end
end
```

The if statement is a *conditional statement*. If there is a block given with the method call, block_given? will return true, and yield will execute the block; otherwise, if there is no block given, it will execute the code in else.

Let's try again with and without a block.

```
gimme { print "Say hi to the people." } # => Say hi to the people.

gimme # => I'm blockless!
```

When you supply it a block, gimme yields the code in the block, printing the string Say hi to the people; when you don't, gimme gives you back the string I'm blockless. Just for fun, redefine gimme to contain two yields, then call it with a block. It executes the block twice.

```
def gimme
  if block_given?
    yield
    yield
  else
    puts "I'm blockless!"
  end
end

gimme { print "Say hi again. " } # => Say hi again. Say hi again.
```

Another thing you ought to know is that after yield executes, control comes back to the next statement immediately following yield. To illustrate this, let's define gimme one more time.

```
def gimme
  if block_given?
    yield
  else
```

```
      puts "Oops. No block."
    end
    puts "You're welcome." # executes right after yield
  end

  gimme { print "Thank you. " } # => Thank you. You're welcome.
```

I'm sure you can recognize, with this little bit of coding, how versatile blocks are. In my mind, I can see a little mushroom cloud over your head as it explodes with ideas on how to use blocks.

To fully understand what blocks are capable of, though, you need to learn something about procs.

Blocks Are Closures

Do you know what a closure is? If you do, I'm impressed—you probably learned it as a computer science major. If you don't know what one is, but are curious now, read on. A closure is a nameless function or method. It is like a method within a method, that refers to or shares variables with the enclosing or outer method. In Ruby, the closure or block is wrapped by curly braces ({}) or do/end, and depends on the associated method (such as each) in order to work.

Procs

Ruby lets you store procedures—or *procs,* as they're called—as objects, complete with their context. You can do this several ways. One way is to invoke new on the Proc class; another way is to call either the lambda or proc method from Kernel. (By the way, calling lambda or proc is preferred over Proc.new because lambda and proc do parameter checking.)

Example 2-4 demonstrates how to create a proc both ways.

Example 2-4. proc.rb

```
#!/usr/bin/env ruby

count = Proc.new { [1,2,3,4,5].each do |i| print i end; puts }
your_proc = lambda { puts "Lurch: 'You rang?'" }
my_proc = proc { puts "Morticia: 'Who was at the door, Lurch?'" }

# What kind of objects did you just create?
puts count.class, your_proc.class, my_proc.class

# Calling all procs
count.call
your_proc.call
my_proc.call
```

After letting you know that each of the objects you created are `Proc` objects, the program gives you this output as it calls each of the procs with the `call` method:

```
12345
Lurch: 'You rang?'
Morticia: 'Who was at the door, Lurch?'
```

A method may be called with a block, and it will return the result of the block, even though the method has no arguments. Remember, a block must always be associated with a method call.

You can also coax a method to convert an associated block to a proc on the fly. To do this, you need to create an argument to the method that is proceeded by an ampersand (&). I'll walk you through how to do it in Example 2-5.

Example 2-5. return_block_proc.rb

```
#!/usr/local/bin/ruby

def return_block
  yield
end

def return_proc( &proc )
  yield
end

return_block { puts "Got block!" }
return_proc { puts "Got block, convert to proc!" }
```

Here is the output:

```
Got block!
Got block, convert to proc!
```

The method `return_block` has no arguments. All it has is a `yield` statement in its body. The `yield` statement's purpose, once again, is to execute a block when the block is passed to a method. This can make a plain old method wildly versatile.

The next method, `return_proc`, has one argument, &proc. When a method has an argument preceded by an ampersand, it will accept the block—when one is submitted—and convert it to a `Proc` object. With `yield` in the body, the method executes the block *cum* proc, without having to bother with the `Proc` call method.

Symbols

Ruby has a special object called a *symbol*. All you really need to remember about symbols at this point is that they are like placeholders for identifiers and strings. You can recognize symbols because they are always prefixed by a colon (:).

You don't directly create a symbol by assigning a value to it. You create a symbol by calling the to_sym or intern methods on a string or by assigning a symbol to a symbol. To understand this better, let's take a string on a roundtrip from a string to a symbol and back to a string.

```
name = "Matz"
name.to_sym # => :Matz
:Matz.id2name # => "Matz"
name == :Matz.id2name # => true
```

Are your palms getting sweaty? I know symbols may look a little confusing. They are somewhat abstract, because you don't really see what is going on under the Ruby interpreter's hood. On the surface you see that the content of the string name is magically transformed into the label of a symbol. So what?

The "so what" is that once a symbol is created, *only one copy* of the symbol is held in a single memory address, as long as the program is running. Because of this, rather than making copy after copy, Ruby keeps referring back to that single memory address. This makes Ruby programs more efficient because they don't gobble up as much memory.

Ruby on Rails uses lots of symbols, and it's likely that as you become better acquainted with them, you will use lots of symbols, too. In fact, Ruby uses tons of symbols internally. To prove it, execute this line of Ruby code:

```
Symbol.all_symbols
```

You'll get more than 1,000 symbols in your lap!

 If you are an experienced Java or C# programmer, this analogy will help: symbols in Ruby are like interned strings, held in a string intern pool.

Exception Handling

Like Java, C++, and other languages, Ruby offers exception handling. An exception occurs when a program commits a transgression, and the normal flow of that program is interrupted. Ruby is prepared to handle such problems, but you can manage them in your own way using Ruby's exception handling.

Java and C++ have try blocks; in Ruby, you would just use a begin block. catch statements in Java and C++ are used where Ruby has rescue statements. Where Java uses a finally clause, Ruby uses ensure.

You will learn how to use exception handling in Chapter 10.

Ruby Documentation

When I say "Ruby documentation," I am mostly referring to the documentation that is generated by RDoc (*http://rdoc.sourceforge.net*), a program that extracts documentation from Ruby source files, both C and Ruby files.

The documentation is stored in comments in the source files, and encoded so that RDoc can easily find it. For example, equals signs (such as ===) on the left margin set off a heading, and indented text is formatted as code. RDoc can generate output as HTML, XML, *ri* (Ruby information), or Windows help (*chm*) files.

To view the RDoc-generated HTML documentation for Ruby, go to *http://www. ruby-doc.org/core*. If you have Ruby documentation installed on your system, which you likely do if you followed the installation instructions in Chapter 1, you can type something like the following at a shell prompt to get formatted documentation in return. Type:

```
ri Kernel.print
```

and you will get output that looks like:

```
-------------------------------------------------------- Kernel#print
    print(obj, ...)     => nil
----------------------------------------------------------------------
    Prints each object in turn to +$stdout+. If the output field
    separator (+$,+) is not +nil+, its contents will appear between
    each field. If the output record separator (+$\+) is not +nil+, it
    will be appended to the output. If no arguments are given, prints
    +$_+. Objects that aren't strings will be converted by calling
    their +to_s+ method.

        print "cat", [1,2,3], 99, "\n"
        $, = ", "
        $\ = "\n"
        print "cat", [1,2,3], 99

    _produces:_

        cat12399
        cat, 1, 2, 3, 99
```

In Chapter 10, you'll find a tutorial on creating documentation with RDoc.

Review Questions

1. What is one of the main differences between a class and a module?
2. What module does the Object class include?
3. What syntax do you use to form block comments?

4. What special character begins an instance variable? A class variable? A global variable?

5. What is the main feature that distinguishes a constant?

6. When a method ends with a ?, what does that signify by convention?

7. A block is a sort of nameless _____.

8. What is a proc?

9. What is the most important characteristic of a symbol?

10. What is RDoc?

## CHAPTER 3

Conditional Love

Many of Ruby's control structures, such as `if` and `while`, are standard fare and quite familiar to programmers, while others, like `unless` and `until`, are not. Think of control structures, which contain conditional statements, as lie detector tests. In every instance, when you use a control structure with a conditional, you are asking if something is true or false. When you get the desired answer—true or false depending on how you've designed your code—the code block associated with the control is executed.

 Two related structures, `rescue` and `ensure`, which are used for exception handling, are not explained here. They are discussed in Chapter 10.

This chapter introduces you to Ruby's control structures with plenty of examples, as usual. We'll start out with the `if` statement—one of the most common structures in just about any programming language.

The if Statement

Let's start out really simple and build from there.

```
if 1 == 1 then
  print "True!"
end
```

If it's true that 1 equals (==) 1, which it does, then the `if` statement returns true, and the code block, consisting only of a `print` statement, will execute. (This `if` statement, by the way, could be typed out on one line.)

Now you'll create a variable and compare it with a number. If the variable and number are equal, the code is executed.

```
x = 256
if x == 256
```

```
    puts "x equals 256"
end
# => x equals 256
```

Notice that we dropped then from the if statement. You don't have to use it in this instance. In addition, you don't have to use end if you write this code all on one line, like so:

```
x = 256
if x == 256 then puts "x equals 256" end
```

In fact, you can change the order of things, placing if after puts, and you can drop then and end.

```
x = 256
puts "x equals 256" if x == 256
```

When you change the order like this, the if is referred to as a *statement modifier*. You can do this with other control structures, as you will see later on.

Another way you can lay out an if statement is by replacing the then with a colon (:), like this:

```
x = 256
if x == 256: puts "x equals 256" end
```

Play with that code a little bit. Change the value of x so that it won't return true when fed to if. Change the text that the statement outputs. Put something else in the block. Do this until you feel the code in your soul.

Now I'll show you some other operators for testing the truth or falsehood of a statement or set of statements. For example, the && operator means "and."

```
ruby = "nifty"
programming = "fun"

if ruby == "nifty" && programming == "fun"
    puts "Keep programming!"
end
# => Keep programming!
```

In other words, if *both* these statements are true, execute the code in the block. You can have more than two statements separated by &&:

```
if a == 10 && b == 27 && c == 43 && d == -14
    print sum = a + b + c + d
end
```

If *all* these statements are true, sum will be printed.

You can also use the keyword and instead of &&.

```
if ruby == "nifty" and programming == "fun" and weather == "nice"
    puts "Stop programming and go outside for a break!"
end
```

Another choice is the || operator; a synonym for this operator is or. When you use || or or, if any of the statements are true, the code executes:

```
if ruby == "nifty" or programming == "fun"
  puts "Keep programming!"
end
```

If either of the two statements is true, the string Keep programming! will print. Are more than two statements OK? Of course:

```
if a == 10 || b == 27 || c = 43 || d = -14
  print sum = a + b + c + d
end
```

|| and or, and && and and, are considered logical operators. Lots of other operators are possible, too, such as:

```
delete_record if record != 0x8ff # not equal to

if amt > 1.00 then desc = "dollars" end # greater than

desc = "cents" if amt < 1.00 # less than

if height >= 6 then print "L or XL" end # greater than or equal to

print "shrimpy" if weight <= 100 # less than or equal to
```

Two other operators reverse the meaning of a test. They are ! and not.

```
if !queue then print "The queue is empty." end
```

What this is saying is that if queue is *not* equal to true, the statement evaluates as true and the print statement prints The queue is empty!. An alternative to ! is the not keyword.

```
if not queue then print "The the queue is empty." end
```

Using else and elsif

Sometimes you set flags in programming in order to tell a program to carry out a task. A flag usually just carries a value of true or false. For example, let's say your program had queue and print flags. If the flag is true, then the code in the block is executed; if false, the block is ignored.

```
if queue
  pr = true
else
  pr = false
end

start_printer if pr # starts if pr is is true
```

The else keyword gives if an escape hatch. In other words, if the if statement does not evaluate true, the code after else will be executed, and if if evaluates false, the code after else is ignored.

I didn't have to use a logical operator with pr or queue because the actual values were either true or false, and that's all the answer that the Ruby interpreter needs from if in order to act.

There are no quotes around the words true or false because they are not strings. true is actually the only instance of TrueClass. Its counterpart, false, is the only instance of FalseClass. true and false are also considered *pseudovariables*, which look like variables, and behave like constants, but cannot be assigned a value.

The elsif keyword provides you with one or more intermediate options after the initial if, where you can test various statements.

Notice that elsif has only one *e*, not two. My fingers forget that all the time, which sends me into debug mode.

The following if statement contains several elsif statements; they are testing to see which language is currently in use via symbols—English (:en), Spanish (:es), French (:fr), and German (:de)—to decide how to render dog:

```
lang = :es
if lang == :en
  print "dog"
elsif lang == :es
  print "perro"
elsif lang == :fr
  print "chien"
elsif lang == :de
  print "Hund"
else
  puts "No language set; default = 'dog'."
end
# "perro" is assigned to dog
```

You can also write this statement a little tighter by using colons after the symbols:

```
if lang == :en: print "dog"
  elsif lang == :es: print "perro"
  elsif lang == :fr: print "chien"
  elsif lang == :de: print "Hund"
  else puts "No language set; default = 'dog'."
end
```

Don't follow the else (the last statement) with a colon.

The Ternary Operator

The ternary or base-three operator (?:) is a concise structure that descended from C to Ruby. In the C language, it was called the "conditional expression" (see *The C Programming Language*, by Brian W. Kernigan and Dennis M. Ritchie (Prentice-Hall)). The conditional expression is broken into three parts.

Here is an example of something useful you can do with the ternary operator:

```
label = length == 1 ? " argument" : " arguments"
```

This expression assigns a string value to label based on the value of length. If the value of length is 1, then the string value argument (singular) will be assigned to label; but if it is not true—that is, if length has a value other than 1—then the value of label will be the string arguments (plural).

Once you get the hang of it, the conditional expression or ternary operator is a great way to express concise logic on a single line.

The case Statement

Ruby's case statement provides a way to express conditional logic in a succinct way. It is similar to using elsifs with colons, but you use case in place of if, and when in place of elsif.

Here is an example similar to what you saw earlier using lang with the possible symbols :en, :es, :fr, and :de:

```
lang = :fr

dog = case lang
  when :en: "dog"
  when :es: "perro"
  when :fr: "chien"
  when :de: "Hund"
  else      "dog"
end
# "chien" is assigned to dog
```

case/when is more convenient and terse than if/elsif/else because the logic of == is assumed—you don't have to keep retyping == or the variable name:

Ruby's case is similar to the switch statement, a familiar C construct, but case is more powerful. One of the annoying things to me about switch statements in C, C++, and Java, is that you can't switch on strings in a straightforward way (though you can in C#).

If the lang variable held a string instead of symbols, your code would look like this:

```
lang = "de"

dog = case lang
  when "en": "dog"
  when "es": "perro"
  when "fr": "chien"
  when "de": "Hund"
  else       "dog"
end
# "Hund" is assigned to dog
```

The next example uses several *ranges* to test values. A range is a range of numbers.

```
scale = 8
case scale
  when    0: puts "lowest"
  when 1..3: puts "medium-low"
  when 4..5: puts "medium"
  when 6..7: puts "medium-high"
  when 8..9: puts "high"
  when   10: puts "highest"
  else       puts "off scale"
end
# => high
```

The range 1..3 means a range of numbers from 1 to 3, inclusive. Because scale equals 8, scale matches the range 8..9 and case returns the string high. However, when you use three dots as in the range 1...5, the ending value 5 is excluded. The sets of dots, .. and ..., are called *range operators*; two dots includes all the numbers in the range, and three dots excludes the last value in the range. Underneath the hood, case uses the === operator from Range to test whether a value is a member of or included in a range.

The while Loop

A while loop executes the code it contains as long as its conditional statement remains true. The following piece of code initializes a counter i to 0 and sets up an array containing four elements called breeds (horse breeds). It also creates a temporary array named temp. (You'll learn more about arrays in Chapter 6.)

The following few paragraphs are fairly fundamental, and are provided for beginning programmers. If you already have plenty of programming under your belt, skip ahead to the code itself.

The while loop will execute as long as its conditional (i < breeds.size) is true. The i variable starts out its little life equaling 0, and the size or length of the breeds array is 4.

As you come to the end of the loop, i is incremented by 1, and then control returns to the top of the loop. In the first loop, i equals 0, and is fed as 0 as an argument to breeds[i], which retrieves the first element (numbered 0). This is the string value quarter. That element is appended via << to the temp array. The capitalize method from String changes quarter to Quarter. At this point, 1 is added to i by the += operator, so i equals 1. And we take it again from the top.

This continues until i equals 4, whereupon the conditional test for while fails. The Ruby interpreter moves to the next valid statement, that is, temp.sort!, which sorts the new array alphabetically. It does not make a copy but changes the array in place. You know this by the tell-tale ! at the end of the method name (sort!). Then the contents of temp replace breeds, and we have cleaned up the array.

```ruby
i = 0
breeds = [ "quarter", "arabian", "appalosa", "paint" ]
puts breeds.size # => 4
temp = []

while i < breeds.size do
  temp << breeds[i].capitalize
  i +=1
end

temp.sort! # => ["Appalosa", "Arabian", "Paint", "Quarter"]
breeds.replace( temp )
p breeds # => ["Appalosa", "Arabian", "Paint", "Quarter"]
```

By the way, the do is optional here, so this form of the loop is legitimate, too:

```ruby
while i < breeds.size
  temp << breeds[i].capitalize
  i +=1
end
```

Another form you can use is with begin/end:

```ruby
temp = 98.3

begin
  print "Your temperature is " + temp.to_s + " Fahrenheit. "
  puts "I think you're okay."
  temp += 0.1
end while temp < 98.6

puts "Your temperature is " + temp.to_s + " Fahrenheit. Are you okay?"
```

When you use while like this, with while at the end, the statements in the loop are evaluated once *before* the conditional is checked. This is like the do/while loop from C.

Also, like if, you can use while as a statement modifier, at the end of a statement:

```ruby
cash = 100_000.00
sum = 0

cash += 1.00, sum while cash < 1_000_000.00 # underscores ignored
```

So cash just keeps adding up until it equals $1,000,000.00. I like that!

Give me a break

You can break out of a while loop with the keyword break. For example, let's say you were just looping along as before, but you wanted to stop processing once you got to a certain element in the array. You could use break to bust out, like this:

```
while i < breeds.size
  temp << breeds[i].capitalize
  break if temp[i] == "Arabian"
  i +=1
end
p => temp # => ["Quarter", "Arabian"]
```

When the if modifier following break found Arabian in the temp array, it broke out of the loop right then. The next statement (which calls the p method) shows that we didn't get very far appending elements to the temp array.

unless and until

The unless and until statements are similar to if and while, except they are executed while their conditionals are false, whereas if and while statements are executed while their conditionals are true. Of course, if and while are used more frequently than unless and until, but the nice thing about having them is that Ruby offers you more expressiveness.

An unless statement is really like a negated if statement. I'll show you an if statement first:

```
if lang == "de"
  dog = "Hund"
else
  dog = "dog"
end
```

Now I'll translate it into unless:

```
unless lang == "de"
  dog = "dog"
else
  dog = "Hund"
end
```

This example is saying, in effect, that unless the value of lang is de, then dog will be assigned the value of dog; otherwise, assign dog the value Hund.

See how the statements are reversed? In the if statement, the assignment of Hund to dog comes first; in the unless example, the assignment of dog to dog comes first.

Like if, you can also use unless as a statement modifier:

```
puts age += 1 unless age > 29
```

As unless is a negated form of if, until is really a negated form of while. Compare the following statements. The first is a while loop:

```
weight = 150
while weight < 200 do
  puts "Weight: " + weight.to_s
  weight += 5
end
```

Here is the same logic expressed with until:

```
weight = 150
until weight == 200 do
  puts "Weight: " + weight.to_s
  weight += 5
end
```

And like while, you have another form you can use with until—that is, with begin/end:

```
weight = 150

begin
  puts "Weight: " + weight.to_s
  weight += 5
end until weight == 200
```

In this form, the statements in the loop are evaluated once before the conditional is checked.

And finally, like while, you can also use until as a statement modifier:

```
puts age += 1 until age > 28
```

The loop Method

The loop method comes from Kernel. It lets you run a loop continuously—like running for(;;) in C—until you or the program does something to break out of the loop.

Run the code in Example 3-1.

Example 3-1. loop.rb

```
loop do
  print "Type something: "
  line = gets
  break if line =~ /q|Q/
  puts line
end
```

You will see a prompt, Type something:. The gets method (also from Kernel) retrieves what you type, and it is assigned to the line variable. However, if line matches q or Q, you will break out of loop then and there; otherwise, puts prints the contents of line to standard output. When you hit end, control returns to the top of the loop again.

The for loop

The for loop is a familiar structure to experienced programmers. This example of for uses a range (1..5) to print out a list of numbers from 1 to 5.

```
for i in 1..5 do
  print i, " "
end
# => 1 2 3 4 5
```

Notice the do and end. You can drop the do. It isn't required, but you have to keep end:

```
for i in 1..5
  print i, " "
end
# => 1 2 3 4 5
```

If you want to do the for loop on one line, you have to throw in the do again:

```
for i in 1..5 do print i, " " end # => 1 2 3 4 5
```

Here is an example of a for loop that prints out a times table (from 1 to 12) for the number 2:

```
for i in 1..12
  print "2 x " + i.to_s + " = ", i * 2, "\n"
end
# =>
2 x 1 = 2
2 x 2 = 4
2 x 3 = 6
2 x 4 = 8
2 x 5 = 10
2 x 6 = 12
2 x 7 = 14
2 x 8 = 16
2 x 9 = 18
2 x 10 = 20
2 x 11 = 22
2 x 12 = 24
```

With nested for loops, you can easily print out times tables from 1 to 12:

```
for i in 1..12
  for j in 1..12
    print i.to_s + " x " + j.to_s + " = ", j * i, "\n"
  end
end
```

Here is just part of the output:

```
1 x 1 = 1
1 x 2 = 2
1 x 3 = 3
1 x 4 = 4
```

```
1 x 5 = 5
1 x 6 = 6
1 x 7 = 7
1 x 8 = 8
1 x 9 = 9
1 x 10 = 10
1 x 11 = 11
1 x 12 = 12
2 x 1 = 2
2 x 2 = 4
2 x 3 = 6
...
```

This is all very nice, but for has some competition in the form of the times, upto, and downto methods.

The times Method

The times method (from Integer) is convenient and concise. Compare this for loop:

```
for i in 1..10
  print i, " "
end
# => 1 2 3 4 5 6 7 8 9 10
```

with this call to times:

```
10.times { |i | print i, " " } # => 0 1 2 3 4 5 6 7 8 9
```

Both pieces of code produce the same output. times, as you can see, takes a block and is slightly easier to type. It is used a lot, and it is Ruby-esque—classy, intuitive, succinct. Can you guess which form I prefer?

The upto Method

The upto method is a convenience method that does the same thing as a for loop but is a little more concise to write. The Integer, String, and Date classes all have upto methods, but I'll show only the Integer version here (you'll see the String version in Chapter 4).

For example, here is a for loop that prints out a list of numbers, like you saw earlier:

```
for i in 1..10
  print i, " "
end
# => 1 2 3 4 5 6 7 8 9 10
```

Compare this with upto, which does exactly the same thing:

```
1.upto(10) { |i| print i, " " } # => 1 2 3 4 5 6 7 8 9 10
```

upto uses a block to do its magic. for is there for you, but I prefer upto. It's just a little snappier.

Here is another example of upto that prints out a times table for 2:

```
1.upto(12) { |i| print "2 x " + i.to_s + " = ", i * 2, "\n"}
# =>
2 x 1 = 2
2 x 2 = 4
2 x 3 = 6
2 x 4 = 8
2 x 5 = 10
2 x 6 = 12
2 x 7 = 14
2 x 8 = 16
2 x 9 = 18
2 x 10 = 20
2 x 11 = 22
2 x 12 = 24
```

That was easy to throw together. What if you wanted to do all the times tables from 1 to 12? Try this one:

```
1.upto(12) { |i| 1.upto(12) { |j| print i.to_s + " x " + j.to_s + " = ", j * i,
"\n"} }
```

This example uses a nested pair of uptos to do its job. upto seems a little more concise than for to my taste.

The downto Method

The downto method is similar to upto but counts in the other direction. Both the Integer and Date classes have downto methods, but I'll just show you the Integer version (String does not have a downto method). Like upto, it uses a block:

```
5.downto(1) { |i| print i, " " } # => 5 4 3 2 1
```

The program *timer.rb*, shown in Example 3-2, contains a method named timer. The argument to this method equals the number of minutes you want to count down.

Example 3-2. timer.rb

```
def timer( start )
  puts "Minutes: " + start.to_s
  start_time = Time.now
  puts start_time.strftime("Start to_time: %I:%M:%S %p")
  start.downto(1) { |i| sleep 60 }
  end_time = Time.now
  print end_time.strftime("Elapsed time: %I:%M:%S %p")
end

timer 10
```

The timer method uses the Kernel method sleep in the downto method's block. The Time class is one of Ruby's built-in classes. Time's now method takes a snapshot of the current time, and the strftime method returns a formatted string using formatting directives: %I for hour, %M for minutes, and %S for seconds. (You can find a complete list of formatting directives for Time in Table A-13 in Appendix A.) The output of this program is:

```
Minutes: 10
Start to_time: 09:40:00 AM
Elapsed time: 09:50:00 AM
```

Execution Before or After a Program

Finally, I want to mention two other control structures, BEGIN and END. These structures allow code to execute before and after a program runs. Both BEGIN and END are followed by blocks enclosed by braces ({}), as in Example 3-3.

Example 3-3. bmi.rb

```
BEGIN { puts "Date and time: " + Time.now.to_s }

def bmi( weight, height )
  703.0*( weight.to_f/(height.to_f**2))
end

my_bmi = bmi( 196, 73 )

puts "Your BMI is: " + x = sprintf( "%0.2f", my_bmi )

END { puts "You've got some work ahead of you." }
```

Review Questions

1. Why is case/when somewhat more convenient than if/elsif/else?
2. What is the ternary operator?
3. What is a statement modifier?
4. Why is upto or downto more convenient than a regular for loop?
5. An unless statement is the negated form of what other control structure?
6. What are the synonyms for && and ||?
7. What is probably the most common control structure used in Ruby and other languages?
8. What is the benefit of using begin/end with a while statement?

CHAPTER 4

Strings

In the simplest terms, a string in a programming language is a sequence of one or more characters and usually represents some human language, whether written or spoken. You are probably more likely to use methods from the String class than from any other class in Ruby. Manipulating strings is one of the biggest chores a programmer has to manage. Fortunately, Ruby offers a lot of convenience in this department.

For more information on string methods, go to *http://www.ruby-doc.org/core/classes/String.html*. You can also use the command line to get information on a method. For example, to get information on the String instance method chop, type:

```
ri String#chop [or] ri String.chop
```

You can use # or . between the class and method names when returning two methods with *ri*. This, of course, assumes that you have the Ruby documentation package installed and that it is in the path (see "Installing Ruby," in Chapter 1).

Creating Strings

You can create strings with the new method. For example, this line creates a new, empty string called title:

```
title = String.new # => ""
```

Now you have a new string, but it is only filled with virtual air. You can test a string to see if it is empty with empty?:

```
title.empty? # => true
```

You might want to test a string to see if it is empty before you process it, or to end processing when you run into an empty string. You can also test its length or size:

```
title.length [or] title.size # => 0
```

The length and size methods do the same thing: they both return an integer indicating how many characters a string holds.

The new method can take a string argument:

```
title = String.new( "Much Ado about Nothing" )
```

Now check title:

```
title.empty? # => false
title.length # => 22
```

There we go. Not quite so vacuous as before.

Another way to create a string is with Kernel's String method:

```
title = String( "Much Ado about Nothing" )
puts title # => Much Ado about Nothing
```

But there is an even easier way. You don't have to use the new or String methods to generate a new string. Just an assignment operator and a pair of double quotes will do fine:

```
sad_love_story = "Romeo and Juliet"
```

You can also use single quotes:

```
sad_love_story = 'Romeo and Juliet'
```

The difference between using double quotes versus single quotes is that double quotes *interpret* escaped characters and single quotes *preserve* them. I'll show you what that means. Here's what you get with double quotes (interprets \n as a newline):

```
lear = "King Lear\nA Tragedy\nby William Shakespeare"
puts lear # => King Lear
          #     A Tragedy
          #     by William Shakespeare
```

And here's what you get with single quotes (preserves \n in context):

```
lear = 'King Lear\nA Tragedy\nby William Shakespeare'
puts lear # => King Lear\nA Tragedy\nby William Shakespeare
```

For a complete list of escape characters, see Table A-1 in Appendix A.

General Delimited Strings

Another way to create strings is with *general delimited strings*, which are all preceded by a % and then followed by a matched pair of delimiter characters, such as !, {, or [(must be nonalphanumeric). The string is embedded between the delimiters. All of the following examples are delimited by different characters (you can even use quote characters):

```
comedy = %!As You Like It!
history = %[Henry V]
tragedy = %(Julius Ceasar)
```

You can also use %Q, which is the equivalent of a double-quoted string; %q, which is equivalent to a single-quoted string; or %x for a back-quoted string (`) for command output.

Here Documents

A *here document* allows you to build strings from multiple lines on the fly, while preserving newlines. A here document is formed with a << and a delimiting character or string of your choice. I'll save Shakespeare's 29th sonnet as a here document, with 29 as the delimiter:

```
sonnet = <<29
When in disgrace with fortune and men's eyes
I all alone beweep my outcast state,
And trouble deaf heaven with my bootless cries,
And look upon myself, and curse my fate,
Wishing me like to one more rich in hope,
Featured like him, like him with friends possessed,
Desiring this man's art, and that man's scope,
With what I most enjoy contented least;
Yet in these thoughts my self almost despising,
Haply I think on thee, and then my state,
Like to the lark at break of day arising
From sullen earth, sings hymns at heaven's gate;
For thy sweet love remembered such wealth brings
That then I scorn to change my state with kings.
29
```

This document is stored in the string sonnet, but you can create a here document without placing it in a string. Wherever the line breaks, a record separator (such as \n) is inserted at that place. Now use:

```
puts sonnet
```

You'll see for yourself how the lines break.

You can also "delimit the delimiter" for various effects:

```
sonnet = <<hamlet # same as double-quoted string
O my prophetic soul! My uncle!
hamlet

sonnet = <<"hamlet" # again as double-quoted string
O my prophetic soul! My uncle!
hamlet

sonnet = <<'ghost' # same as single-quoted string
Pity me not, but lend thy serious hearing
To what I shall unfold.
ghost

my_dir = <<`dir` # same as back ticks
ls -l
dir

ind = <<-hello # for indentation
    Hello, Matz!
hello
```

Concatenating Strings

In Ruby, you can add on to an existing string with various concatenation techniques. With Ruby, you don't have to jump through the hoops that you might if you were using a language with immutable strings.

Adjacent strings can be concatenated simply because that they are next to each other:

```
"Hello," " " "Matz" "!" # => "Hello, Matz!"
```

You can also use the + method:

```
"Hello," + " " + "Matz" + "!" # => "Hello, Matz!"
```

You can even mix double and single quotes, as long as they are properly paired.

Another way to do this is with the << method. You can add a single string:

```
"Hello, " << "Matz!" # => Hello, Matz!
```

Or you can chain them together with multiple calls to <<:

```
"Hello," << " " << "Matz" << "!" # => Hello, Matz!
```

An alternative to << is the concat method (which does not allow you to chain):

```
"Hello, ".concat "Matz!"
```

Or you can do it this way:

```
h = "Hello, "
m = "Matz!"
h.concat(m)
```

You can make a string immutable with Object's freeze method:

```
greet = "Hello, Matz!"
greet.freeze

# try to append something
greet.concat("!") # => TypeError: can't modify frozen string

# is the object frozen?
greet.frozen? # => true
```

Accessing Strings

You can extract and manipulate segments of a string using the String method []. It's an alias of the slice method: any place you use [], you can use slice, with the same arguments. slice! performs in-place changes and is a counterpart to []=.

We'll access several strings in the examples that follow:

```
line = "A horse! a horse! my kingdom for a horse!"
cite = "Act V, Scene IV"
speaker = "King Richard III"
```

If you enter a string as the argument to [], it will return that string, if found:

```
speaker['King'] # => "King"
```

Otherwise, it will return nil—in other words, it's trying to break the news to you: "I didn't find the string you were looking for." If you specify a Fixnum (integer) as an index, it returns the decimal character code for the character found at the index location:

```
line[7] # => 33
```

At the location 7, [] found the character 33 (!). If you add the chr method (from the Integer class), you'll get the actual character:

```
line[7].chr # => "!"
```

You can use an offset and length (two Fixnums) to tell [] the index location where you want to start, and then how many characters you want to retrieve:

```
line[18, 23] # => "my kingdom for a horse!"
```

You started at index location 18, and then scooped up 23 characters from there, inclusive. You can capitalize the result with the capitalize method, if you want:

```
line[18, 23].capitalize # => "My kingdom for a horse!"
```

(More on capitalize and other similar methods later in the chapter.)

Enter a range to grab a range of characters. Two dots (..) means include the last character:

```
cite[0..4] # => "Act V"
```

Three dots (...) means *exclude* the last value:

```
cite[0...4] # => "Act "
```

You can also use regular expressions (see the end of the chapter), as shown here:

```
line[/horse!$/] # => "horse!"
```

The regular expression /horse!$/ asks, "Does the word horse, followed by ! come at the end of the line ($)?" If this is true, this call returns horse!; nil if not. Adding another argument, a Fixnum, returns that portion of the matched data, starting at 0 in this instance:

```
line[/^A horse/, 0] # => "A horse"
```

The index method returns the index location of a matching substring. So if you use index like this:

```
line.index("k") # => 21
```

21 refers to the index location where the letter k occurs in line.

See if you get what is going on in the following examples:

```
line[line.index("k")] # => 107
line[line.index("k")].chr # => "k"
```

If you figured out these statements, you are starting to catch on! It doesn't take long, does it? If you didn't understand what happened, here it is: when `line.index("k")` was called, it returned the value 21, which was fed as a numeric argument to []; this, in effect, called `line[21]`.

Comparing Strings

Sometimes you need to test two strings to see if they are the same or not. You can do that with the `==` method. For example, you might want to test a string before printing something:

```
print "What was the question again?" if question == ""
```

Also, here are two versions of the opening paragraph of Abraham Lincoln's Gettysburg Address, one from the so-called Hay manuscript, the other from the Nicolay (see *http://www.loc.gov/exhibits/gadd/gadrft.html*):

```
hay = "Four score and seven years ago our fathers brought forth, upon this continent,
a new nation, conceived in Liberty, and dedicated to the proposition that all men are
created equal."

nicolay = "Four score and seven years ago our fathers brought forth, upon this
continent, a new nation, conceived in liberty, and dedicated to the proposition that
\"all men are created equal\""
```

The strings are only slightly different (for example, *Liberty* is capitalized in the Hay version). Let's compare these strings:

```
hay == nicolay # => false
```

The result is `false`, because they must match exactly. (We'll let the historians figure out how to match them up.) You could also apply the `eql?` method and get the same results, though `eql?` and `==` are slightly different:

- `==` returns true if two objects are `Strings`, false otherwise.
- `eql?` returns true if two strings are equal in length and content, false otherwise.

Here `eql?` returns false:

```
hay.eql? nicolay # => false
```

Yet another way to compare strings is with the `<=>` method, commonly called the *spaceship operator*. It compares the character code values of the strings, returning -1 (less than), 0 (equals), or 1 (greater than), depending on the comparison, which is case-sensitive:

```
"a" <=> "a" # => 0
"a" <=> 97.chr # => 0
"a" <=> "b" # => -1
"a" <=> "`" # => 1
```

A case-insensitive comparison is possible with casecmp, which has the same possible results as <=> (-1, 0, 1) but doesn't care about case:

```
"a" <=> "A" # => 1
"a".casecmp "A" # => 0
"ferlin husky".casecmp "Ferlin Husky" # => 0
"Ferlin Husky".casecmp "Lefty Frizzell" # => -1
```

Manipulating Strings

Here's a fun one to get started with. The * method repeats a string by an integer factor:

```
"A horse! " * 2 # => "A horse! A horse! "
```

You can concatenate a string to the result:

```
taf = "That's ".downcase * 3 + "all folks!" # => "that's that's that's all folks!"
taf.capitalize # => "That's that's that's all folks!"
```

Inserting a String in a String

The insert method lets you insert another string at a given index in a string. For example, you can correct spelling:

```
"Be carful.".insert 6, "e" # => "Be careful."
```

or add a word (plus a space):

```
"Be careful!".insert 3, "very " # => "Be very careful!"
```

or even throw the * method in just to prove that you can:

```
"Be careful!".insert 3, "very " * 5 # => "Be very very very very very careful!"
```

Changing All or Part of a String

You can alter all or part of a string, in place, with the []= method. (Like [], which is the counterpart of slice, []= is an alias of slice!, so anywhere you use []=, you can use slice!, with the same arguments.)

Given the following strings (some scoundrel has been editing our Shakespeare text):

```
line = "A Porsche! a Porsche! my kingdom for a Porsche!"
cite = "Act V, Scene V"
speaker = "King Richard, 2007"
```

enter a string as the argument to []=, and it will return the new, corrected string, if found; nil otherwise.

```
speaker[", 2007"]= "III" # => "III"
p speaker # => "King Richard III"
```

That's looking better.

If you specify a Fixnum (integer) as an index, it returns the corrected string you placed at the index location. (String lengths are automatically adjusted by Ruby if the replacement string is a different length than the original.)

```
cite[13]= "IV" # => "IV"
p cite # => "Act V, Scene IV"
```

At the index 13, []= found the substring V and replaced it with IV.

You can use an offset and length (two Fixnums) to tell []= the index of the substring where you want to start, and then how many characters you want to retrieve:

```
line[39,8]= "Porsche 911 Turbo!" # => "Porsche 911 Turbo!"
p line # => "A Porsche! a Porsche! my kingdom for a Porsche 911 Turbo!"
```

You started at index 39, and went 8 characters from there (inclusive).

You can also enter a range to indicate a range of characters you want to change. Include the last character with two dots (..):

```
speaker[13..15]= "the Third" # => "the Third"
p speaker # => "King Richard the Third"
```

You can also use regular expressions (see "Regular Expressions," later in this chapter), as shown here:

```
line[/Porsche!$/]= "Targa!" # => "Targa!"
p line # => "A Porsche! a Porsche! my kingdom for a Targa!"
```

The regular expression /Porsche!$/ matches if Porsche! appears at the end of the line ($). If this is true, the call to []= exchanges Porsche! with Targa!.

The chomp and chop Methods

The chop (or chop!) method chops off the last character of a string, and the chomp (chomp!) method chomps off the record separator ($/)—usually just a newline—from a string. Consider the string joe, a limerick created as a here document:

```
joe = <<limerick
There once was a fellow named Joe
quite fond of Edgar Allen Poe
   He read with delight
   Nearly half the night
When his wife said "Get up!" he said "No."
limerick # => "There once was a fellow named Joe\nquite fond of Edgar Allen Poe\n
He read with delight\n   Nearly half the night\nWhen his wife said \"Get up!\" he
said \"No.\"\n"
```

Apply chomp! to remove the last record separator (\n):

```
joe.chomp! # => "There once was a fellow named Joe\nquite fond of Edgar Allen Poe\n
He read with delight\n   Nearly half the night\nWhen his wife said \"Get up!\" he
said \"No.\""
```

Now apply it again, and chomp! returns nil without altering the string because there is no record separator at the end of the string:

```
joe.chomp! # => nil
```

chop, chomp's greedy twin, shows no mercy on the string, removing the last character (a quote) with abandon:

```
joe.chop! = "There once was a fellow named Joe\nquite fond of Edgar Allen Poe\n   He
read with delight\n   Nearly half the night\nWhen his wife said \"Get up!\" he said \
"No"
```

The delete Method

With delete or delete!, you can delete characters from a string:

```
"That's call folks!".delete "c" # => "That's all folks"
```

That looks easy, because there is only one occurrence of the letter *c* in the string, so you don't see any interesting side effects, as you would in the next example. Let's say you want to get rid of that extra *l* in *alll*:

```
"That's alll folks".delete "l" # => "That's a foks"
```

Oh, boy. It cleaned me out of all *l*s. I can't use delete the way I want, so how do I fix call*l*? What if I use two *l*s instead of one?

```
"That's alll folks".delete "ll" # => "That's a foks"
```

I got the same thing. (I knew I would.) That's because delete uses the *intersection* (what intersects or is the same in both) of its arguments to decide what part of the string to take out. The nifty thing about this, though, is you can also negate all or part of an argument with the caret (^), similar to its use in regular expressions:

```
"That's all folks".delete "abcdefghijklmnopqrstuvwxyz", "^ha" # => "haa"
```

The caret negates both the characters in the argument, not just the first one (you can do "^h^a", too, and get the same answer).

Substitute the Substring

Try gsub (or gsub!). This method replaces a substring (first argument) with a replacement string (second argument):

```
"That's alll folks".gsub "alll", "all" # => "That's all folks"
```

Or you might do it this way:

```
"That's alll folks".gsub "lll", "ll" # => "That's all folks"
```

The replace method replaces a string wholesale. Not just a substring, the whole thing.

```
call = "All hands on deck!"
call.replace "All feet on deck!" # => "All feet on deck!"
```

So why wouldn't you just do it this way?

```
call = "All hands on deck!"
call = "All feet on deck!"
```

Wouldn't you get the same result? Not exactly. When you use `replace`, `call` remains the same object, with the same object ID, but when you assign the string to `call` twice, the object and its ID will change. Just a subtlety you ought to know.

```
# same object
call = "All hands on deck!" # => "All hands on deck!"
call.object_id # => 1624370
call.replace "All feet on deck!" # => "All feet on deck!"
call.object_id # => 1624370

# different object
call = "All hands on deck!" # => "All hands on deck!"
call.object_id # => 1600420
call = "All feet on deck!" # => "All feet on deck!"
call.object_id # => 1009410
```

Turn It Around

To reverse the characters means to alter the characters so they read in the opposite direction. You can do this with the reverse method (or reverse! for permanent damage). Say you want to reverse the order of the English alphabet:

```
"abcdefghijklmnopqrstuvwxyz".reverse # => "zyxwvutsrqponmlkjihgfedcba"
```

Or, maybe you'd like to reverse a palindrome:

```
palindrome = "dennis sinned"
palindrome.reverse! # => "dennis sinned"
p palindrome
```

Not much harm done, even though reverse! changed the string in place. Think about that one for a while.

From a String to an Array

Conveniently, split converts a string to an array. The first call to split is without an argument:

```
"0123456789".split # => ["0123456789"]
```

That was easy, but what about splitting up all the individual values and converting them into elements? Do that with a regular expression (//) that cuts up the original string at the junction of characters.

```
"0123456789".split( // ) # => ["0", "1", "2", "3", "4", "5", "6", "7", "8", "9"]
```

In the next example, the regular expression matches a comma and a space (/, /):

```
c_w = "George Jones, Conway Twitty, Lefty Frizzell, Ferlin Husky"
# => "George Jones, Conway Twitty, Lefty Frizzell, Ferlin Husky"
c_w.split(/, /) # => ["George Jones", "Conway Twitty", "Lefty Frizzell", "Ferlin
Husky"]
```

Case Conversion

You can capitalize a word, sentence, or phrase with `capitalize` or `capitalize!`. (By now you should know the difference between the two.) Here is a pair of sentences that are under the influence of `capitalize`:

```
"Ruby finally has a killer app. It's Ruby on Rails.".capitalize # => "Ruby finally
has a killer app. it's ruby on rails."
```

Notice that the second sentence is not capitalized, which doesn't look so good. Now you can see that `capitalize` only capitalizes the first letter of the string, not the beginning of succeeding sentences. Plan accordingly.

Iterating Over a String

To get the effect you want, you may have to split strings up. Here is a list of menu items, stored in a string. They are separated by \n. The each method (or its synonym each_line) iterates over each separate item, not just the first word in the overall string, and capitalizes it:

```
"new\nopen\nclose\nprint".each { |item| puts item.capitalize }# =>
# New
# Open
# Close
# Print
```

By the way, there is one other each method: each_byte. It takes a string apart byte by byte, returning the decimal value for the character at each index location. Print each character as a decimal, separated by /:

```
"matz".each_byte { |b| print b, "/" } # => 109/97/116/122/
```

 This example assumes that a character is represented by a single byte, which is not always the case. The default character set for Ruby is ASCII, whose characters may be represented by bytes. However, if you use UTF-8, characters may be represented in one to four bytes. You can change your character set from ASCII to UTF-8 by specifying `$KCODE = 'u'` at the beginning of your program.

Convert each decimal to its character equivalent with Integer's chr method:

```
"matz".each_byte { |b| print b.chr, "/" } # => m/a/t/z/
```

Or append the output to an array—out:

```
out = [] # create an empty array
"matz".each_byte { |b| p out << b} # =>
[109]
[109, 97]
[109, 97, 116]
[109, 97, 116, 122]
p out # => [109, 97, 116, 122]
```

You'll learn more about arrays in Chapter 6.

---

downcase, upcase, and swapcase

YOU KNOW IT CAN BE ANNOYING TO READ SOMETHING THAT IS ALL IN UPPERCASE LETTERS! It's distracting to read. That's one reason it's nice that Ruby has the downcase and downcase! methods.

```
"YOU KNOW IT CAN BE ANNOYING TO READ SOMETHING THAT IS IN ALL UPPERCASE LETTERS!".
downcase # => "you know it can be annoying to read something that is all in uppercase
letters!"
```

There, that's better. But now the first letter is lowercase, too. The grammar police will be on our case. Fix this by adding a call to capitalize onto the statement.

```
"YOU KNOW IT CAN BE ANNOYING TO READ SOMETHING THAT IS ALL IN UPPERCASE LETTERS!".
downcase.capitalize # => "You know it can be annoying to read something that is all
in uppercase letters!"
```

Good. That took care of it.

What if you want to go the other way and change lowercase letters to uppercase? For example, you may want to get someone's attention by turning warning text to all uppercase. You can do that with upcase or upcase!.

```
"warning! keyboard may be hot!".upcase # => WARNING! KEYBOARD MAY BE HOT!
```

Sometimes you may want to swap uppercase letters with lowercase. Use swapcase or swapcase!. For example, you can switch an English alphabet list that starts with lowercase first to a string that starts with uppercase first:

```
"aAbBcCdDeEfFgGhHiI".swapcase # => "AaBbCcDdEeFfGgHhIi"
```

Managing Whitespace, etc.

You can adjust whitespace (or other characters) on the left or right of a string, center a string in whitespace (or other characters), and strip whitespace away using the following methods. First, create a string—the title of a Shakespeare play:

```
title = "Love's Labours Lost"
```

How long is the string? This will be important to you (length and size are synonyms).

```
title.size # => 19
```

The string title is 19 characters long. With that information in tow, we can start making some changes. The ljust and rjust methods pad a string with whitespace or, if specified, some other character. The string will be right justified, and the number of characters, whitespace or otherwise, must be greater than the length of the string. Make sense? I hope so. Let's go over an example or two.

Let's call these two methods with an argument (an integer) that is less than or equal to the length of the string.

```
title.ljust 10 # => "Love's Labours Lost"
title.rjust 19 # => "Love's Labours Lost"
```

What happened? Nothing! That's because the argument must be greater than the length of the string in order to do anything. The added whitespace is calculated based on the length of the string *plus* the value of the argument. Watch:

```
title.ljust 20 # => "Love's Labours Lost "
title.rjust 25 # => "      Love's Labours Lost"
```

See how it works now? In the call to ljust, one space character is added on the right (20 – 19 = 1), and the call to rjust adds six characters to the left (25 – 19 = 6). If it seems backward, just remember that the string is always *right* justified. Still confused? So am I, but we'll go on. You can use another character besides the default space character if you'd like:

```
title.rjust( 21, "-" ) # => "--Love's Labours Lost"
```

or use more than one character—the sequence will be repeated:

```
title.rjust 25, "->" # => "->->->Love's Labours Lost"
```

OK, now let's really mess with your head:

```
title.rjust(20, "-").ljust(21, "-") # => "-Love's Labours Lost-"
```

You might want to do something like that someday.

If you want to play both ends to the middle, we are be better off using center instead:

```
title.center 23 # => "  Love's Labours Lost  "
title.center 23, "-" # => "--Love's Labours Lost--"
```

With one more tip of the hat, I'll use center to create a comment:

```
filename = "hack.rb" # => "hack.rb"
filename.size # => 7
filename.center 40-7, "#" # => "################hack.rb################"
```

We've been adding whitespace and other characters. What if you just want to get rid of it? Use lstrip, rstrip, and strip (lstrip!, rstrip!, and strip!). Suppose you have a string surrounded by whitespace:

```
fear = "           Fear is the little darkroom where negatives develope. -- Michael
Pritchard          "
```

Oops. Fell asleep with my thumb on the space bar—twice! I can fix it easily now, starting with the left side (make the change stick to the original string with lstrip!):

```
fear.lstrip! # => "Fear is the little darkroom where negatives develope. -- Michael
Pritchard          "
```

Now the right side:

```
fear.rstrip! # => "Fear is the little darkroom where negatives develope. -- Michael
Pritchard"
```

Or do the whole thing at once:

```
fear.strip! # => "Fear is the little darkroom where negatives develope. -- Michael
Pritchard"
```

strip removes other kinds of whitespace, too:

```
"\t\tBye, tabs and line endings!\r\n".strip # => "Bye, tabs and line endings!"
```

Incrementing Strings

The Ruby String class has several methods that let you produce successive strings—that is, strings that increment, starting at the rightmost character. You can increment strings with next and next! (or succ and succ!). I prefer to use next. (The methods ending in ! make in-place changes.) For example:

```
"a".next [or] "a".succ # => "b"
```

Remember, next increments the rightmost character:

```
"aa".next # => "ab"
```

It adds a character when it reaches a boundary, or adds a digit or decimal place when appropriate, as shown in these lines:

```
"z".next # => "aa" # two a's after one z
"zzzz".next # => "aaaaa" # five a's after four z's
"999.0".next # => "999.1" # increment by .1
"999".next # => "1000" # increment from 999 to 1000
```

We're not just talking letters here, but any character, based on the character set in use (ASCII in these examples):

```
" ".next # => "!"
```

Chain calls of next together—let's try three:

```
"0".next.next.next # => "3"
```

As you saw earlier, next works for numbers represented as strings as well:

```
"2007".next # => "2008"
```

Or you can get it to work when numbers are *not* represented as strings, though the method will come from a different class, not String. For example:

```
2008.next # => 2009
```

Instead of from String, this call actually uses the next method from Integer. (The Date, Generator, Integer, and String classes all have next methods.)

You can even use a character code via chr with next:

```
120.chr # => "x"
120.chr.next # => "y"
```

The upto method from String, which uses a block, makes it easy to increment. For example, this call to upto prints the English alphabet:

```
"a".upto("z") { |i| print i } # => abcdefghijklmnopqrstuvwxyz
```

You could also do this with a for loop and an inclusive range:

```
for i in "a".."z"
  print i
end
```

You decide what's simpler. The for loop takes only slightly more keystrokes (29 versus 31, including whitespace). But I like upto.

Converting Strings

You can convert a string into a float (`Float`) or integer (`Fixnum`). To convert a string into a float, or, more precisely, an instance of the `String` class into an instance of `Float`, use the to_f method:

```
"200".class # => String
"200".to_f # => 200.0
"200".to_f.class # => Float
```

Likewise, to convert a string to an integer, use to_i:

```
"100".class # => String
"100".to_i # => 100
"100".to_i.class # => Fixnum
```

To convert a string into a symbol (`Symbol` class), you can use either the to_sym or intern methods.

```
"name".intern # => :name
"name".to_sym # => :name
```

The value of the string, not its name, becomes the symbol:

```
play = "The Merchant of Venice".intern # => :"The Merchant of Venice"
```

Convert an object to a string with to_s. Ruby calls the to_s method from the class of the object, not the `String` class (parentheses are optional).

```
(256.0).class # => Float
(256.0).to_s # => "256.0"
```

Regular Expressions

You have already seen regular expressions in action. A regular expression is a special sequence of characters that helps you match or find other strings or sets of strings, using a specialized syntax held in a pattern. The syntax for regular expressions was invented by mathematician Stephen Kleene in the 1950s.

I'll spend a little time demonstrating some patterns to search for strings. In this little discussion, you'll learn the fundamentals: how to use basic string patterns, square brackets, alternation, grouping, anchors, shortcuts, repetition operators, and braces. Table 4-1 lists the syntax for regular expressions in Ruby.

We need a little text to munch on. Here are the opening lines of Shakespeare's 29th sonnet:

```
opening = "When in disgrace with fortune and men's eyes\nI all alone beweep my
outcast state,\n"
```

Note that this string contains two lines, set off by the newline character \n.

You can match the first line just by using a word in the pattern:

```
opening.grep(/men/) # => ["When in disgrace with fortune and men's eyes\n"]
```

By the way, grep is not a String method; it comes from the Enumerable module, which the String class includes, so it is available for processing strings. grep takes a pattern as an argument, and can also take a block (see *http://www.ruby-doc.org/core/classes/Enumerable.html*).

When you use a pair of square brackets ([ ]), you can match any character in the brackets. Let's try to match the word *man* or *men* using [ ]:

```
opening.grep(/m[ae]n/) # => ["When in disgrace with fortune and men's eyes\n"]
```

It would also match a line with the word *man* in it:

Alternation lets you match alternate forms of a pattern using the pipe character (|):

```
opening.grep(/men|man/) # => ["When in disgrace with fortune and men's eyes\n"]
```

Grouping uses parentheses to group a subexpression, like this one that contains an alternation:

```
opening.grep(/m(e|a)n/) # => ["When in disgrace with fortune and men's eyes\n"]
```

Anchors anchor a pattern to the beginning (^) or end ($) of a line:

```
opening.grep(/^When in/) # => ["When in disgrace with fortune and men's eyes\n"]
opening.grep(/outcast state,$/) # => ["I all alone beweep my outcast state,\n"]
```

The ^ means that a match is found when the text When in is at the beginning of a line, and $ will only match outcast state if it is found at the end of a line.

One way to specify the beginning and ending of strings in a pattern is with *shortcuts*. Shortcut syntax is brief—a single character preceded by a backslash. For example, the \d shortcut represents a digit; it is the same as using [0-9] but, well, shorter. Similarly to ^, the shortcut \A matches the beginning of a string, not a line:

```
opening.grep(/\AWhen in/) # => ["When in disgrace with fortune and men's eyes\n"]
```

Similar to $, the shortcut \z matches the end of a string, not a line:

```
opening.grep(/outcast state,\z/) # => ["I all alone beweep my outcast state,"]
```

The shortcut \Z matches the end of a string before the newline character, assuming that a newline character (\n) is at the end of the string (it won't work otherwise).

Let's figure out how to match a phone number in the form (555)123-4567. Supposing that the string phone contains a phone number like this, the following pattern will find it:

```
phone.grep(/[\(\d\d\d\)]?\d\d\d-\d\d\d\d/) # => ["(555)123-4567"]
```

The backslash precedes the parentheses (\(...\)) to let the regexp engine know that these are literal characters. Otherwise, the engine will see the parentheses as enclosing a subexpression. The three \ds in the parentheses represent three digits. The hyphen (-) is just an unambiguous character, so you can use it in the pattern as is.

The question mark (?) is a *repetition operator*. It indicates zero or one occurrence of the previous pattern. So the phone number you are looking for can have an area code in parentheses, or not. The area-code pattern is surrounded by [and] so that the ?

operator applies to the entire area code. Either form of the phone number, with or without the area code, will work. Here is a way to use ? with just a single character, u:

```
color.grep(/colou?r/) # => ["I think that colour is just right for you office."]
```

The plus sign (+) operator indicates one or more of the previous pattern, in this case digits:

```
phone.grep(/[\(\d+\)]?\d+-\d+/) # => ["(555)123-4567"]
```

Braces ({}) let you specify the exact number of digits, such as \d{3} or \d{4}:

```
phone.grep(/[\(\d{3}\)]?\d{3}-\d{4}/)# => ["(555)123-4567"]
```

 It is also possible to indicate an "at least" amount with {m,}, and a minimum/maximum number with {m,n}.

The String class also has the =~ method and the !~ operator. If =~ finds a match, it returns the offset position where the match starts in the string:

```
color =~ /colou?r/ # => 13
```

The !~ operator returns true if it *does not* match the string, false otherwise:

```
color !~ /colou?r/ # => false
```

Also of interest are the Regexp and MatchData classes. The Regexp class (*http://www.ruby-doc.org/core/classes/Regexp.html*) lets you create a regular expression object. The MatchData class (*http://www.ruby-doc.org/core/classes/MatchData.html*) provides the special $- variable, which encapsulates all search results from a pattern match.

This discussion has given you a decent foundation in regular expressions (see Table 4-1 for a listing). With these fundamentals, you can define most any pattern.

Table 4-1. Regular expressions in Ruby

Pattern	Description
/pattern/options	Pattern *pattern* in slashes, followed by optional *options*, i.e., one or more of: i for case-insensitive; o for substitute once; x for ignore whitespace, allow comments; m for match multiple lines, newlines as normal characters
%r!*pattern*!	General delimited string for a regular expression, where ! can be an arbitrary character
^	Matches beginning of line
$	Matches end of line
.	Matches any character
\1...\9	Matches *n*th grouped subexpression
\10	Matches *n*th grouped subexpression, if already matched; otherwise, refers to octal representation of a character code
\n, \r, \t, etc.	Matches character in backslash notation

Table 4-1. Regular expressions in Ruby (continued)

Pattern	Description
\w	Matches word character, as in [0-9A-Za-z_]
\W	Matches nonword character
\s	Matches whitespace character, as in [\t\n\r\f]
\S	Matches nonwhitespace character
\d	Matches digit, same as [0-9]
\D	Matches nondigit
\A	Matches beginning of a string
\Z	Matches end of a string, or before newline at the end
\z	Matches end of a string
\b	Matches word boundary outside [ ], or backspace (0x08) inside [ ]
\B	Matches nonword boundary
\G	Matches point where last match finished
[..]	Matches any single character in brackets, such as [ch]at
[^..]	Matches any single character *not* in brackets
*	Matches 0 or more of previous regular expressions
*?	Matches zero or more of previous regular expressions (nongreedy)
+	Matches one or more of previous regular expressions
+?	Matches one or more of previous regular expressions (nongreedy)
{m}	Matches exactly *m* number of previous regular expressions
{m,}	Matches at least *m* number of previous regular expressions
{m,n}	Matches at least *m* but at most *n* number of previous regular expressions
{m,n}?	Matches at least *m* but at most *n* number of previous regular expressions (nongreedy)
?	Matches zero or one of previous regular expressions
|	Alternation, such as color|colour
( )	Grouping regular expressions or subexpression, such as col(o|ou)r
(?#..)	Comment
(?:..)	Grouping without back-references (without remembering matched text)
(?=..)	Specify position with pattern
(?!..)	Specify position with pattern negation
(?>..)	Matches independent pattern without backtracking
(?imx)	Toggles i, m, or x options on
(?-imx)	Toggles i, m, or x options off
(?imx:..)	Toggles i, m, or x options on within parentheses
(?-imx:..)	Toggles i, m, or x options off within parentheses
(?ix-ix:)	Turns on (or off) i and x options within this noncapturing group

1.9 and Beyond

In the versions of Ruby that follow, String will likely:

- Add the start_with? and end_with? methods, which will return true if a string starts with or ends with a given prefix or suffix of the string.
- Add a clear method that will turn a string with a length greater than 1 to an empty string.
- Add an ord method that will return a character code.
- Add the partition and rpartition methods to partition a string at a given separator.
- Add a bytes method that will return the bytes of a string, one by one.
- Return a single character string instead of a character code when a string is indexed with [].
- Consider characters to be more than one byte in length.

Review Questions

1. How do chop and chomp differ?
2. Name two ways to concatenate strings.
3. What happens when you reverse a palindrome?
4. How do you iterate over a string?
5. Name two or more case conversion methods.
6. What methods would you use to adjust space in a string?
7. Describe alternation in a regular expression pattern?
8. What does /\d{3}/ match?
9. How do you convert a string to an array?
10. What do you think is the easiest way to create a string?

## CHAPTER 5

Math

In other programming languages, numbers are primitives, or basic building blocks, that are used by other objects to create logic. In Ruby, everything (almost) is an object, even numbers. For example, here are some numbers that are considered primitives by other languages. What classes do they come from?

```
2.class # => Fixnum
2.0.class # => Float
2_000_000_000.class # => Bignum
```

There's the proof in living code: Ruby does turn almost everything into an object. (The underscores in the last number, by the way, are just there for readability; the Ruby interpreter ignores them.)

Ruby has a number of classes and modules related to numbers. Here are the more important ones:

Numeric
> The base class for numbers

Integer
> The basic integer class, and the basis for the Fixnum class

Float
> The class for real or floating-point numbers, based on the computer's native capacity to represent double-precision

Fixnum
> The main integer class, based on what the computer can hold in a native machine word, such as 32 bits or 64 bits, minus 1

Bignum
> The class of integers outside the range of the basic, native machine word

Math
> A module that holds math functions (as methods)

`Precision`
A module for approximating the precision of real numbers

`Rational`
A class that represents fractional numbers

`Complex`
A class that represents complex numbers, which extend real numbers with imaginary numbers ($x + iy$)

`Matrix`
A class for creating mathematical matrixes

A hierarchy of the math classes, along with modules, is shown in Figure 5-1.

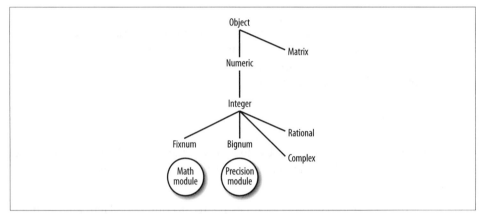

Figure 5-1. Math class and module hierarchy

Class Hierarchy and Included Modules

By the way, a handy way to quickly determine the hierarchy of a math class (or any other Ruby class) is with the ancestors method, one of Ruby's reflection methods. (*Reflection* is a term that describes a programming language's ability to observe itself and report on what it sees. Ruby is good at reflection, and you'll learn more about it in Chapter 10.) Call ancestors on a class name to see its inheritance hierarchy, like this:

```
Fixnum.ancestors # => [Fixnum, Integer, Precision, Numeric, Comparable, Object,
Kernel]
```

The names of included modules `Precision`, `Comparable`, and `Kernel` are also in the genealogy. In addition, you can use the `included_modules` method to discover what modules a class uses:

```
Object.included_modules # => [Kernel]
Numeric.included_modules # => [Comparable, Kernel]
Integer.included_modules # => [Precision, Comparable, Kernel]
Fixnum.included_modules # => [Precision, Comparable, Kernel]
```

Converting Numbers

You can convert a number from another form into an integer with the Integer method from Kernel. Let's call it a few times in *irb*.

```
irb(main):001:0> Integer(1.4) # convert a floating-point number
=> 1
irb(main):002:0> Integer("256") # convert a string
=> 256
irb(main):002:0> Integer("0b11110010") # convert a binary number from a string
=> 242
irb(main):003:0> Integer(0177) # convert an octal number
=> 127
irb(main):004:0> Integer(0x20) # convert a hexadecimal number
=> 32
irb(main):005:0> Integer(?z) # convert a character code
=> 122
```

Floating-point numbers are rounded down; for example, 1.9999 becomes 1. Integer honors the 0 (octal), 0b (binary), and 0x (hexadecimal) prefixes, whether they're in strings or not.

You can also create or convert floating-point numbers with Kernel's Float method. Use *irb* again to see how it works.

```
irb(main):001:0> Float(167) # convert an integer
=> 167.0
irb(main):002:0> Float("77") # convert a string
=> 77.0
irb(main):003:0> Float(?a) # convert a character code
=> 97.0
```

Basic Math Operations

The easiest way to show you the basic math operations is with *irb*. Fire up *irb* again and type in some basic expressions, like these:

```
irb(main):001:0> 7 + 5 # add
=> 12
irb(main):002:0> 20 - 8 # subtract
=> 12
irb(main):003:0> 2 * 6 # multiply
=> 12
irb(main):004:0> 144 / 12 # divide
=> 12
irb(main):005:0> 12**2 # exponent
=> 144
irb(main):006:0> 12 % 5 # modulo (remainder of division)
=> 2
```

Don't forget the unary operators, + and -, which indicate negative and positive numbers:

```
irb(main):007:0> +7 + -5
=> 2
```

```
irb(main):008:0> -20 + 32
=> 12
irb(main):009:0> -20 - +32
=> -52
irb(main):010:0> 20 * -8
=> -160
```

If there is no sign immediately before the number, it is positive.

You can also do some of these operations with named methods such as div, modulo, divmod, quo, and remainder. Method calls are shown with integer, float, and parentheses so you can see the differences they make.

```
irb(main):011:0> 24.div 2 # division
=> 12
irb(main):012:0> (25.0).div(2.0) # result is integer
=> 12
irb(main):013:0> 12.modulo 5 # modulo
=> 2
irb(main):014:0> 12.modulo(5.0) # modulo with float
=> 2.0
irb(main):015:0> 12.divmod 5 # return array with quotient, modulus
=> [2, 2]
irb(main):016:0> 12.0.divmod 5.0 # with float
=> [2, 2.0]
irb(main):017:0> 12.quo 5 # return the quotient
=> 2.4
irb(main):018:0> 12.remainder 5 # return the remainder
=> 2
```

Many of these methods started life as methods of the Numeric class, but were overridden or redefined in other subclasses. You will find versions of div, for example, in Numeric, Fixnum, and Bignum.

Division and Truncation

Division presents a little problem. When you do integer division in Ruby, any fractional part in the result will be truncated, and you may not realize it.

```
irb(main):019:0> 24 / 2 # no problem
=> 12
irb(main):020:0> 25 / 2 # uh-oh, truncation
=> 12
irb(main):021:0> 25.0 / 2 # using a float as at least one operand solves it
=> 12.5
irb(main):022:0> 25.0 / 2.0 # same when both operands are floats
=> 12.5
```

Just keep in mind that in order to get a fractional result, you must use at least one float as an operand. See the section "Rational Numbers," later in the chapter, for more on fractions.

Also, be careful when you use the div method:

```
irb(main):005:0> 24.div 2 # division method
=> 12
irb(main):006:0> (25.0).div(2.0) # returns result as integer, truncates
=> 12
```

div returns only the integral part as a result, truncating the decimal part, even if one or more of the operands are floats.

Equality, Less Than, or Greater Than

Test two numbers for equality with ==, eql?, or <=>:

```
irb(main):007:0> 12 == 24/2
=> true
irb(main):008:0> 24.eql?(12*2)
=> true
irb(main):009:0> 12 == 14
=> false
irb(main):010:0> 12 <=> 12
=> 0
irb(main):011:0> 12 <=> 10
=> 1
irb(main):012:0> 12 <=> 14
=> -1
```

The == and eql? return true or false; the <=> (spaceship operator) returns -1, 0, or 1, depending on whether the first value is equal to the second (0), less than the second (-1), or greater than the second (1).

Test if two numbers are equal, less than, or greater than each other:

```
irb(main):013:0> 12 < 14 #less than
=> true
irb(main):014:0> 12 < 12
=> false
irb(main):015:0> 12 <= 12 # less than or equal to
=> true
irb(main):016:0> 12.0 > 11.9
=> true
irb(main):017:0> 12.0 >= 12 # greater than or equal to
=> true
```

Abbreviated Assignment Operators

Ruby offers abbreviated assignment operators that perform operations on variables without an added operand. I'll show you what this means. Given that x equals 5, you could add a value to x the normal way:

```
x = x + 1
```

or the abbreviated way:

```
x += 1
```

Which way do you prefer? Probably, like me, the one with 33 percent fewer keystrokes. Either operation results in 6. Here are the abbreviated assignment operators in action in *irb*:

```
irb(main):001:0> x = 12 # regular assignment
=> 12
irb(main):002:0> x += 6 # addition
=> 18
irb(main):003:0> x -= 12 # subtraction
=> 6
irb(main):004:0> x *= 4 # multiplication
=> 24
irb(main):005:0> x /= 8 # division
=> 3
irb(main):006:0> x **= 2 # power (exponentiation)
=> 9
irb(main):007:0> x %= 3 # modulo
=> 0
irb(main):008:0> x # return the variable's value
=> 0
```

> Ruby does not have the increment (++) or decrement (--) operators that C and other languages have.

You can also do bitwise operations in Ruby. A *bitwise operation* operates on each bit, bit for bit, rather than on the numeral as a single unit. Bitwise operations are often faster than regular arithmetic operations. Here are a few examples in *irb*:

```
irb(main):001:0> ~1011 # bitwise not or complement
=> -1012
irb(main):002:0> 1011 | 1010 # bitwise or
=> 1011
irb(main):003:0> 1011 & 1010 # bitwise and
=> 1010
irb(main):004:0> 1011 ^ 1010 # bitwise exclusive or
=> 1
irb(main):005:0> 1011 << 1 # shift left
=> 2022
irb(main):006:0> 1011 >> 1 # shift right
=> 505
```

The bitwise operators also include abbreviated assignment operators such as &=, ^=, or ||=, to name a few.

Operators

Table 5-1 lists all of Ruby's operators in the order of precedence. If the operator is defined as a method, it is indicated in the Method column, and may be overridden.

Table 5-1. Ruby operators

Operator	Description	Method
::	Scope resolution	
[] []=	Reference, set	✓
**	Raise to power (exponentiation)	✓
+ - ! ~	Positive (unary), negative (unary), logical negation, complement	✓ (but not !)
* / %	Multiplication, division, modulo (remainder)	✓
+ -	Addition, subtraction	✓
<< >>	Shift left, shift right	✓
&	Bitwise *and*	✓
| ^	Bitwise *or*, bitwise exclusive *or*	✓
> >= < <=	Greater than, greater than or equal to, less than, less than or equal to	✓
<=> == === != =~ !~	Equality comparison (spaceship), equality (e.g., range), not equal to, match, not match	✓ (but not != or !~)
&&	Logical *and* (also keyword and, which has lower precedence)	
||	Logical *or* (also keyword or, which has lower precedence)	
.. ...	Range inclusive, range exclusive	✓ (but not ...)
?:	Ternary operator	
= += -= *= /= %= **= <<= >>= &= |= ^= &&= ||=	Assignment, abbreviated assignment	
not	Logical negation	
and or	Logical composition	
defined?	Special operator (no precedence)	

Ranges

As discussed earlier, Ruby has *ranges*, with *range operators* and a Range class. Ranges are intervals with a start value and an end value, separated by a range operator. There are two range operators, .. (two dots) and ... (three dots). The range operator .. means an inclusive range of numbers. For example, 1..10 means a range of numbers from 1 to 10, including 10 (1, 2, 3, 4, 5, 6, 7, 9, 10). The range operator ... means an exclusive range of numbers that exclude the last in the series; in other words, 1...10 means a range of numbers from 1 to 9, as the 10 at the end of the range is excluded (1, 2, 3, 4, 5, 6, 7, 9).

The === method determines if a value is a member of, or included in, a range, as you can see in these lines of code:

```
(1..25) === 14 # => true, in range
(1..25) === 26 # => false, out of range
(1...25) === 25 # => false, out of range if ... used
```

When a range is used as an iterator, each value in the sequence is returned. So you can use a range to do things like create an array of digits:

```
(1..9).to_a # => [1, 2, 3, 4, 5, 6, 7, 8, 9]
```

With the Range class, you can also create a range like this:

```
digits = Range.new(1, 9)
digits.to_a # => [1, 2, 3, 4, 5, 6, 7, 8, 9]
```

Inquiring About Numbers

At times you need to find out things about a number or variable. Is it an integer? A zero? A number at all? Ruby's math methods can handle that. These methods come from all kinds of classes.

Let's start things out simple. Let's ask if a value is a zero or not.

```
op = 0
op.zero? # => true
op.nonzero? # => false
```

That was a little too obvious. (But that's what I like about Ruby.) Try something more meaningful:

```
op = 0

if !op.zero? # not a zero?
  puts 12 / op
else
  puts "Can't divide by zero."
end

op = 2

if op.nonzero? # is it nonzero?
  puts 12 / op
else
  puts "Can't divide by zero."
end
```

Both if statements mean essentially the same thing: divide 12 by op if it isn't a zero.

The integer? method comes from the Numeric class:

```
12.integer? # => true
12.0.integer? # => false
-1.integer? # => true
-12.integer? # => true
```

This method needs a little more meaning in its life.

```
num = 4 # => 4

if num.integer?
  puts "Invited guests: " + num.to_s
else
  puts "Only whole persons can come to this party."
end
```

Check whether a number is finite or infinite with the `finite?` and `infinite?` Float methods (in fact, these methods only work for floats):

```
0.0.finite? # => true
(-1.0/0.0).finite? # => false
(+1.0/0.0).finite? # => false

0.0.infinite? # => nil
(-1.0/0.0).infinite? # => -1
(+1.0/0.0).infinite? # => 1
```

Check whether a floating-point value is a number at all with Float's `nan?`:

```
val = 1.0
val.nan? # => false
val = 0.0/0.0
val.inspect # => "NaN"
val.nan? # => true
```

Iterating Through Blocks

Starting with zero, the `times` method iterates *value* times. Here, *value* is 10:

```
10.times { |i| print i, " " } # => 0 1 2 3 4 5 6 7 8 9
```

You also get the ability to do something like this:

```
10.times { |i| print 5*i, " " } # => 0 5 10 15 20 25 30 35 40 45
```

You can rewrite the block this way:

```
10.times do |i|
  puts 5*i
end
```

or this way:

```
10.times do |i| print 5*i, " " end
```

The block can be opened and closed with do/end or {and }. The braces are a little more concise and more common.

Integer also has the downto and upto methods, which were already demonstrated and compared to the for loop in Chapter 3, but I'll show them again here for a brief refresher. First, the downto method:

```
100.downto(1) { |c| print c, " "; sleep 1 }
```

This method prints out the numbers from 100 down to 1, sleeping for 1 second before each number is printed. The upto method goes the other direction:

```
1.upto(100) { |c| print c, " "; sleep 1 }
```

More Math Methods

Following are just a few common math instance methods. Get the absolute value of a number (Bignum, Complex, Fixnum, Float, Numeric, Rational):

```
-40.abs # => 40
40.abs # => 40
```

Get the ceiling or floor of a number (from Float, Integer, or Numeric):

```
4.65.ceil # => 5
4.65.floor # => 4
```

Or round a number up or down (Float, Integer, or Numeric):

```
100.45.round # => 100
100.49.round # => 100
100.5.round # => 101
100.6.round # => 101
```

Get the next integer with next (or its alias succ):

```
-24.next # => -23
1.next # => 2
999.next # => 1000
```

Get the character value of an integer with chr:

```
97.chr # => "a"
98.chr # => "b"
125.chr # => "}"
126.chr # => "~"
127.chr # => "\177"
```

For a nonprinting character, chr outputs an octal representation of that character (for example, \177 is the octal representation of DEL).

Math Functions

The Math module provides a number of math functions (via class methods). I'll show you how to use a few of them, so you can get started.

Math also has two constants, along with its methods. To find out what constants Math (or any other module or class) has defined, use reflection by invoking the constants method:

```
Math.constants # => ["E", "PI"]
```

Let's check what the values of these constants, Euler and π, are.

```
print Math::E # => 2.71828182845905
print Math::PI # => 3.14159265358979
```

The Math.exp function returns Euler to the power of *x*.

```
Math.exp(1) # => 2.71828182845905
Math.exp(11) # => 59874.1417151978
```

The Math.sqrt method returns the square root of *x*.

```
Math.sqrt(4) # => 2.0
Math.sqrt(16) # => 4.0
Math.sqrt(144) # => 12.0
```

You can do natural logarithms (base E or Euler) and base-10 logarithms.

```
Math.log(Math::E) # => 1.0
Math.log(1) # => 0.0
Math.log(0) # => -Infinity
Math.log10(100.0) # => 2.0
```

Table 5-2 shows all the math functions (all class methods) available from the Math module. By convention, remember that Ruby methods ending in ! mean that the method makes in-place, or destructive, changes to an object, not to a copy of it.

Table 5-2. Math functions (methods)

Method(s)	Description
Math.acos, Math.acos!	Arc cosine
Math.acosh, Math.acosh!	Hyperbolic arc cosine
Math.asin, Math.asin!	Arc sine
Math.asinh, Math.asinh	Hyperbolic arc sine
Math.atan, Math.atan!, Math.atan2, Math.atan2!	Arc tangent; atan takes an x argument; atan2 takes an x and a y argument
Math.atanh, Math.atanh!	Hyperbolic arc tangent
Math.cos, Math.cos!	Cosine
Math.cosh, Math.cosh	Hyperbolic cosine
Math.sin, Math.sin!	Sine
Math.erf	Error function
Match.erfc	Complementary error function
Math.exp, Math.exp!	Base *x* of Euler
Math.frexp	Normalized fraction and exponent
Math.hypot	Hypotenuse
Math.ldexp	Floating-point value corresponding to a given mantissa and exponent
Math.sinh, Math.sinh!	Hyperbolic sine
Math.sqrt, Math.sqrt!	Square root
Math.tan, Math.tan!	Tangent
Math.tanh, Math.tanh!	Hyperbolic tangent

Rational Numbers

A rational number is a number that can be expressed as a fraction of integers. Ruby supports the use of rational numbers via the Rational class. To use the Rational class, you must require it in the program. If you also require the mathn library, the Rational library works better. Now, briefly, I'll show you how to play with fractions in Ruby.

You usually create a rational number with the Rational method. It reduces the fraction in its argument down to its lowest terms. (You can use Rational.new!, but it doesn't reduce to lowest terms.)

Rational expects you to use integers, by the way. It will generate errors if you use floats.

Example 5-1 demonstrates how to use fractions in Ruby, including how to create a fraction; how to add (+), subtract (-), multiply (*), and divide (/) fractions; how to perform modulo (%), power (**), and equality (== or <=>); and how to produce a string or a float representation of a fraction (inspect).

Example 5-1. fractions.rb

```
require 'rational'
require 'mathn'

rat = Rational(25/100) # => 1/4 -- lowest terms

rat + Rational(1/4) # =>  1/2 -- add
rat + 1/4 # => 1/2

rat - Rational(1/8) # => 1/8 -- subtract
rat - 1/8 # => 1/8

rat * 3 # => 3/4 -- multiply
rat / 2 # => 1/8 -- divide

rat % Rational(1/2) # => 1/4 -- modulo or remainder

rat**2 # => 1/16 -- exponent or power

rat == 1/8 # => false -- equality
rat == 1/4 # => true
rat <=> 1/4 # => 0
rat <=> 1/8 # => 1
rat <=> 1/2 # => -1

rat.inspect # => "1/4"
rat.to_s # => "1/4"
rat.to_f # => 0.25
p rat # => 1/4
```

When you use `Rational`, all operations on numbers in the program will likely create rational results.

Prime Numbers

The `mathn` library, which helps math classes get along a little better, has a `Prime` class that allows you to successively generate prime numbers, starting from 2. Actually, it starts from 1 as the seed, but it calculates the first prime as 2, as it must. `Prime` has four methods: `new`, which creates a new `Prime` object; `next` and `succ` (synonyms), which produce the next prime number; and `each`, which lists prime numbers until something halts it.

The program in Example 5-2 shows you how to generate primes one by one.

Example 5-2. prime.rb

```
require 'mathn'

prime_number = Prime.new # instantiate a Prime object
prime_number.next # => 2 # return the next prime number (seed = 1)
prime_number.succ # => 3 # succ works, too

# print the next prime number as a string
puts "The next prime number is " + prime_number.next.to_s + "."
# => The next prime number is 5.
```

The code in Example 5-3 generates 25 prime numbers—all the prime numbers from 2 to 97:

Example 5-3. prime_each.rb

```
require 'mathn'

list_primes = Prime.new

list_primes.each { |prime| print prime, " "; break unless prime < 90 }
# => 2 3 5 7 11 13 17 19 23 29 31 37 41 43 47 53 59 61 67 71 73 79 83 89 97
```

Just for Fun

Here's a sentence that can help you remember the first seven prime numbers: "In the early morning astronomers spiritualized nonmathematicians." (See *http://mathworld. wolfram.com/PrimeNumber.html*.) The number of letters of each word in the sentence add up to a prime number, in succession.

This line of Ruby code analyzes the sentence, returning the length of each word so you can see the underlying prime number (punctuation has been removed to get the counting right):

```
"In the early morning astronomers spiritualized nonmathematicians".split.each { |p|
  print p.length, " " } # => 2 3 5 7 11 13 17
```

The split method is from the String class. It splits the string at the spaces (by default), returning each word as an element of an array. Then the length (number of characters) of each string element is printed, yielding the first seven prime numbers.

Review Questions

1. In Ruby, are numbers primitives or objects?
2. What method can you use to discover what modules a Ruby class includes?
3. What is the possible range of numbers represented by the Fixnum class?
4. How can you avoid truncating the result of division?
5. Rational numbers are another name for _____.
6. If a unary operator is absent, what is the sign of the number that follows?
7. What are the two constants in the Math module?
8. What method can you use to convert an integer into a character representation?

## CHAPTER 6

Arrays

The `Array` class is one of Ruby's built-in classes. Arrays are compact, ordered collections of objects. Ruby arrays can hold objects such as `String`, `Integer`, `Fixnum`, `Hash`, `Symbol`, even other `Array` objects—you name it. Any object that Ruby can create, it can hold in an array.

Each element in an array is associated with and referred to by an *index* (also known as a *subscript* in other languages). Array elements are automatically indexed (numbered) with an integer (`Fixnum`), starting with 0, then numbered consecutively, adding 1 for each additional element. In certain instances, you can refer to the last element of an array with –1, the second to last with –2, and so forth. That's handy.

Ruby arrays are not as rigid as arrays in other languages. In static, compiled programming languages, you have to guess the ultimate size of the array at the time it is created. If an array grows beyond that size, you must copy the array into a temporary one and then create a new, larger array, copying the temporary array into it. Ruby is a dynamic language—as are Perl, Python, and PHP, among others—and therefore lets you grow an array at will, adding elements while it automatically increases the size. Another interesting distinction is that Ruby can hold arrays with objects of all different types, not just one type, as is common in static languages. You'll see this in action later in this chapter.

Remember that, by convention, any Ruby method that ends with an exclamation point (!), like `sort!`, changes an object in place. It doesn't make a copy. In other words, it's destructive. Well, not in the same way that Caligula was destructive, but it will change an array for good. Also, any method ending with a question mark (?), such as `eql?`, returns either `true` or `false`.

This chapter shows you by example how to create and manipulate arrays. It's my same old pattern. Type in the examples in *irb*, or type the examples in files and then run them as Ruby programs, and you'll learn as you go along. This chapter introduces you to many of `Array`'s methods—not all, but many.

Creating Arrays

There are many ways to create or initialize an array. One way is with the new class method:

```
months = Array.new
```

This creates an empty array, represented as [], named months. Not much to it, is there? In fact, you test whether an array is empty or not with the empty? method (returns true if the array is truly and madly empty, false otherwise):

```
months.empty? # => true
```

This isn't very exciting. Let's improve on this a little. You can set the size of an array (the number of elements in an array) like this:

```
months = Array.new(12)
```

or like this:

```
months = Array.new 12
```

The array months now has a size (or length) of 12 elements. You can return the size of an array with either the size or length method:

```
months.size # => 12
```

or:

```
months.length # => 12
```

But what elements are in months so far? They are all nil, because no one (that would be me) has bothered to specify what they are. At this point, the months array contains 12 nils. To inspect the array—that is, to look at the array as an array—use:

```
puts months.inspect
```

or:

```
p months
```

I usually use p—you can probably guess why. Either of these methods return:

```
[nil, nil, nil, nil, nil, nil, nil, nil, nil, nil, nil, nil]
```

Not very exciting, frankly. But we can fix that. Another form of new lets you assign an object (such as a string) to each element in the array:

```
month = Array.new(12, "month")
```

month now appears like this:

```
["month", "month", "month", "month", "month", "month", "month", "month",
"month", "month", "month"]
```

Clear the Deck

Slightly better, but we're not there yet. You know, if you don't like what you got, you can always ream out an array with `clear`:

```
month.clear # => []
month.empty? # => true
```

Don't use `clear` in a fit of anger. You might be sorry.

Creating an Array with a Block

You can also use a block with `new`, populating each element with what the block evaluates to:

```
num = Array.new(10) { |e| e = e * 2 }
```

giving you an array like this:

```
[0, 2, 4, 6, 8, 10, 12, 14, 16, 18]
```

That's a little better. We've got things more under control now.

There's an Easier Way

There is another method of `Array`, `[]`. It works like this:

```
month_abbrv = Array.[]( "jan", "feb", "mar", "apr", "may", "jun",
"jul", "aug", "sep", "oct", "nov", "dec" )
```

or like this, dropping the dot (.) and parentheses (( )), which is possible because of Ruby's flexible method syntax:

```
month_abbrv = Array[ "jan", "feb", "mar", "apr", "may", "jun",
"jul", "aug", "sep", "oct", "nov", "dec" ]
```

This keeps getting easier. An even simpler method for creating an array is by just using the square brackets:

```
months = [ nil, "January", "February", "March", "April", "May", "June",
"July", "August", "September", "October", "November", "December" ]
```

 Why does this array begin with `nil`? It's just an artificial filler. It is the first element in the array `months`, and, as such, is associated with the index 0. I want to associate the first month of the year with index 1, not 0, so I prepended a `nil` as the first element. It's just my preference, but it doesn't have to be yours.

It Gets Even Easier

Here is one easier way to create an array. The Kernel module, included in Object, has an Array method, which only accepts a single argument. Here, the method takes a range as an argument to create an array of digits.

```
digits = Array(0..9) # => [1, 2, 3, 4, 5, 6, 7, 8, 9]
```

But if you submit a set of strings, Array accepts them as a single, concatenated element.

```
donald_duck_nephews = Array( "Huey" "Dewey" "Louie" )
=> ["HueyDeweyLouie"]
```

Not what you wanted, eh? Well, an even easier way to define an array of strings is with the %w notation. It assumes that all elements are strings (even nil), but it sure saves keystrokes (no typing quotes or commas):

```
months = %w[ nil January February March April May June July August September October
November December ]
```

This produces the array months:

```
["nil", "January", "February", "March", "April", "May", "June", "July", "August",
"September", "October", "November", "December"]
```

But I don't want nil represented as a string. How do I use my favorite notation (%w) and fix this problem? Like this:

```
months[0] = nil;
```

I accessed the array with [0] and assigned a new value to the element with =. Look at the array and notice the change:

```
[nil, "January", "February", "March", "April", "May", "June", "July", "August",
"September", "October", "November", "December"]
```

Now for another conundrum. If I fill an array with numbers using %w, like the following:

```
year = %w[ 2000 2001 2002 2003 2004 2005 2006 2007 2008 2009 ]
```

it treats those numbers as strings:

```
["2000", "2001", "2002", "2003", "2004", "2005", "2006", "2007", "2008", "2009"]
```

You can check an element of this array to see its class:

```
year[0].class # => String
```

This may be an unintended consequence. To correct this so that the elements are numbers, avoid %w and use one of the other methods for creating an array:

```
year = [2000, 2001, 2002, 2003, 2004, 2005, 2006, 2007, 2008, 2009]
```

Check the element's class again, and you'll see that you're in good shape:

```
year[0].class # => Fixnum
```

You can even have an array that contains objects from different classes, not all just one type. For example, here's an array that contains four elements, each a different kind of object:

```
hodge_podge = ["January", 1, :year, [2006,01,01]]
```

Use each to iterate over the array, and class to find what kind of object each element is:

```
hodge_podge.each {|e| print e.class, " " } # => String Fixnum Symbol Array
```

Accessing Elements

You just saw that you can access elements with the [ ] method. Given the q1 array:

```
q1 = %w[ January February March ]
```

you can access the first element of the array, element 0, with the 0 index:

```
q1[0] # => January
```

Access the last element of the array, element 2, with:

```
q1[2] # => March
```

You can also use the at method, like so:

```
q1.at(0) # => January
```

The at method is supposed to be slightly faster than [ ], according to the Ruby documentation for at. I'll just use [ ] from now on, but at will work, too.

Access elements for use in a string in this way:

```
print "The event is scheduled for " + months[3] + " " + years[8] + "."
# => The event is scheduled for March 2008.
```

Good work. Index 3 matches March, the third month of the year, and the index 8 matches 2008.

You can access the last element in the array with:

```
q1[-1] # => March
```

With -1, you access the last element in an array by looping back around with a negative number. What about the second element (1)? How do you get that? You could use as an index either:

```
q1[1]
```

or:

```
q1[-2]
```

Another way to get the first and last elements of an array is with the `first` and `last` methods:

```
q1.first # => January
q1.last # => March
```

Both `first` and `last` take integer arguments, indicating the number of elements to return:

```
q1.first 2 # => ["January", "February"]
q1.last 0 # => [] not particularly useful
```

You can get the flip side with `index`. This method returns an index, not an element, based on the argument (an object). It returns the index of the *first* element that matches the object:

```
q1.index "March" # => 2
```

Similarly, `rindex` matches the *last* element that matches the object.

I'll use a longer array for the next few methods:

```
year = [2000, 2001, 2002, 2003, 2004, 2005, 2006, 2007, 2008, 2009]
```

This time, specify where to start in the array and how many elements you want:

```
year[0, 3] # => [2000, 2001, 2002]
```

The 0 is the `start` parameter. It says to start at 0, or the beginning of the array. The second is the `length` parameter, which tells how many elements you want. (You can't do this with the `at` method.) You can also use a range:

```
year[7..9] # => [2007, 2008, 2009]
```

Remember that two dots means "include both elements," and three dots means "don't include the last element." (By the way, you can't use ranges with the `at` method.)

Instead of [], you can also use the `slice` method, another alias:

```
year.slice(1) # => 2001
year.slice(0,4) # => [2000, 2001, 2002, 2003]
year.slice(0..2) # => [2000, 2001, 2002]
year.slice(0...2) # => [2000, 2001]
```

It's a matter of taste, but I'd stick with the [] notation myself.

I'll show you one last method—`include?`. It tests to see if an array includes an element with a given value, returning `true` or `false`:

```
year.include? 2004 # => true
year.include?( 2010 ) # => false
```

Concatenation

Let's play a little bit with the following arrays:

```
q1 = %w[ January February March ]
q2 = %w[ April May June ]
q3 = %w[ July August September ]
q4 = %w[ October November December ]
```

You can concatenate these arrays in several ways. One way is with the + operator or method:

```
half1 = q1 + q2
half2 = q3 + q4
yr = half1 + half2
```

Inspecting these new arrays yields the following results, respectively:

```
["January", "February", "March", "April", "May", "June"]
["July", "August", "September", "October", "November", "December"]
["January", "February", "March", "April", "May", "June", "July", "August",
"September", "October", "November", "December"]
```

Another way to concatenate is with the << method, like this:

```
yrs = [1999]
yrs << 2000 # => [1999, 2000]
```

You can chain these, too:

```
yrs << 2001 << 2002 << 2003 # => [1999, 2000, 2001, 2002, 2003]
```

Static languages, such as Java and C, require you to grow the size of the array in order to add elements to it. A Java `ArrayList` collection eliminates this need, but if you try to add the 11th element onto a plain old 10-element array in Java, you'll get an exception. Programmers usually copy arrays and create a new one with a higher index. I like the Ruby way of doing things better.

As with +, you can concatenate one array onto another with concat:

```
last_part = q3.concat( q4 )
```

This concatenated q3 and q4, making a new array, last_part. concat always returns a new array; it does not add elements to an existing array the way << does.

Set Operations

Ruby can do several set operations on arrays, such as:

- Intersection with &
- Difference with -
- Union with |

Intersection (&) creates a new array, merging the common elements of two arrays but removing uncommon elements and duplicates.

```
tue = [ "shop", "make pie", "sleep" ]
wed = [ "shop", "make pie", "read", "sleep" ]
tue & wed # => ["shop", "make pie", "sleep"]
```

The result tells what things I plan to do on both days (I won't be reading).

Difference (-) creates a new array, removing elements that appear in both arrays:

```
wed - tue # => ["read"]
```

Union (|) joins two arrays together, removing duplicates:

```
tue | wed # => ["shop", "make pie", "read", "sleep"]
```

You can also do set operations with arrays and other objects using the Ruby Set class (see *http://www.ruby-doc.org/core/classes/Set.html* or do *ri* Set).

Unique Elements

Vaguely related to the set operations, the uniq method also removes duplicates from a single array, creating a new array. Its next-door neighbor uniq! changes the array itself, in place.

```
shopping_list = %w[ cheese bread crackers potatoes carrots cheese ]
=> ["cheese", "bread", "crackers", "potatoes", "carrots", "cheese"]

shopping_list.uniq!=> ["cheese", "bread", "crackers", "potatoes", "carrots"]
```

Blow Your Stack

If you have ever eaten at a cafeteria, you might remember the stack of warm plates that were held in a rack with a spring in the bottom of it. The first plate in was also the last one out.

This is similar to a stack structure in computer science. A stack is a LIFO (last in, first out) structure. You can use an array like a stack by using the push and pop methods from the Array class. Here's how:

```
fruit = %w[ apple orange banana ]
fruit.pop # => "banana"
p fruit # => ["apple", "orange" ]
fruit.push "mango"
p fruit # => ["apple", "orange", "mango"]
```

Comparing Arrays

Three methods allow you to compare arrays to see if they are equal. Those methods are ==, <=>, and eql?. Consider these arrays. Each is named for an employee and answers whether they work full time or part time (full or part), how many hours per week they work, and whether or not they have benefits (yes or no).

```
bob = [ "full", 40, "yes" ]
lou = ["part", 23, "no"]
schlomo = [ "full", 40, "yes" ]
```

The == method compares two arrays to test if they are equal. Two arrays are considered equal if (1) they contain the same number of elements, and (2) each element is equal to the corresponding element in the other array (compare with Object#==).

Compare these arrays with ==:

```
lou == lou # => true
bob == schlomo # => true
schlomo == lou # => false
```

Closely related is eql?. This method will return true if the objects are the same or if their content is the same. What's the difference between == and eql?. eql? checks to see if the values are equal (as in ==), but also checks if the values are of the same type.

```
bob == schlomo # => true
bob.eql?( "full", 40, yes" ) # => false, bob is not a string
```

Another way to compare arrays is with <=> (spaceship operator). When it compares two arrays, it compares each object in the arrays. The two arrays are considered equal if they are the same length and if the value of each element is equal to the value of the corresponding element in the other array. When a comparison is made, it determines whether the values of the compared elements are greater than, lesser than, or equal to each other. Rather than true or false, the comparison returns an integer: -1 for less than, 0 for equal, and 1 for greater than.

```
lou <=> lou # => 0
bob <=> lou # => -1
lou <=> schlomo # => 1
```

Changing Elements

Ruby give you lots of ways to manipulate the elements in arrays—e.g., ways to change their values, ways to change the way they are represented. We'll start out with some simple changes. Let's go back to our months array:

```
months = %w[ nil January February March April May June July August September October
November December ]
```

This creates an array that looks like:

```
["nil", "January", "February", "March", "April", "May", "June", "July", "August",
"September", "October", "November", "December"]
```

Look familiar? There's the nil again, shown as a string, in index 0. That's not what we want. Let's change that with insert:

```
months.insert( 0, nil )
```

This fixes that problem:

```
[nil, "January", "February", "March", "April", "May", "June", "July", "August",
"September", "October", "November", "December"]
```

Let's say you wanted to change three of the elements to have German rather than English spelling. Here are several ways you could do it. This example uses a range to change elements 5 through 7 to hold the strings Mai, Juni, and Juli instead of May, June, and July.

```
months[5..7] = "Mai", "Juni", "Juli" # => [nil, "January", "February", "March",
"April", "Mai", "Juni", "Juli", "August", "September", "October", "November",
"December"]
```

You can also do this with start and length parameters (going back to English):

```
months[5, 3] = "May", "June", "July" # => [nil, "January", "February", "March",
"April", "May", "June", "July", "August", "September", "October", "November",
"December"]
```

As a String

You can extract the elements of an array as a single string using to_s. to_s is common to many classes.

```
greeting = [ "Hello! ", "Bonjour! ", "Guten Tag!" ]
puts greeting.to_s # => Hello! Bonjour! Guten Tag!
```

Use join to smash all the elements together into a single string:

```
months.join # =>
"JanuaryFebruaryMarchAprilMayJuneJulyAugustSeptemberOctoberNovemberDecember"
```

Not exactly what you had in mind? Let's throw in a comma and a space between each of the elements:

```
months.join ", " # => " , January, February, March, April, May, June, July, August,
September, October, November, December"
```

Looks better, but what about that comma at the beginning? Yuck. How do you get rid of that? For one, you can use the compact method, which removes all nils from an array.

```
months.compact.join( ", " ) # => "January, February, March, April, May, June, July,
August, September, October, November, December"
```

There you go. Much better.

Using shift and unshift

Another way to remove an element from an array is with the `shift` method. This method returns the first element of an array (`nil` if the array is empty), and then removes the element, shifting all other elements down by one. It is sort of like a pop method except it works on the frontend of the array rather than the backend (FIFO—first in, first out).

```
dates = [ 4, 5, 6, 7 ] # => [4, 5, 6, 7]
dates.shift # => 4
p dates # => [5, 6, 7]
```

Related to `shift` is `unshift`, which prepends objects (one or more) to an array. It is like push but works on the beginning of an array, not the end.

```
dates.unshift 4 # => [4, 5, 6, 7]
dates.unshift(2,3) # => [2, 3, 4, 5, 6, 7]
```

Deleting Elements

The delete method removes a matching object from an array, returning the deleted object if found. Given the following array:

```
month_a = %w[ nil jan feb mar apr may jun jul aug sep oct nov dec ] # => ["nil",
"jan", "feb", "mar", "apr", "may", "jun", "jul", "aug", "sep", "oct", "nov", "dec"]
```

The following call deletes the string `nil` from `month_a`:

```
month_a.delete "nil"
```

This method also takes a block. The result of the block is returned if the object is not found:

```
month_a.delete("noon") {"noon wasn't found. What are you going to do about it?"}
```

With `delete_at`, you can also delete an element based on its index (the example assumes you are working with the original array):

```
month_a.delete_at( 12 ) # => "dec"
p month_a # ["nil", "jan", "feb", "mar", "apr", "may", "jun", "jul", "aug", "sep",
"oct", "nov"]
```

Arrays and Blocks

Array has an each method, too—just like lots of other Ruby classes. each lets you iterate over every element in an array and do something to it. This call capitalizes the names of all the abbreviations in `month_a` (no `nil` at 0):

```
month_a.each { |e| print e.capitalize + " " }
```

yielding the following string, not an array:

```
Jan Feb Mar Apr May Jun Jul Aug Sep Oct Nov Dec
```

The map method (and its synonym collect) is similar to each, but it returns a new array instead of a string.

```
month_a_2007 = month_a.map { |e| e.capitalize + " 2007" }
```

This gives you:

```
p month_a_2007 # => ["Jan 2007", "Feb 2007", "Mar 2007", "Apr 2007", "May 2007", "Jun
2007", "Jul 2007", "Aug 2007", "Sep 2007", "Oct 2007", "Nov 2007", "Dec 2007"]
```

Sorting Things and About Face

You've added number objects to an array in a higgledy-piggledy fashion. It's time to straighten things out. Given x:

```
x = [ 2, 5, 1, 7, 23, 99, 14, 27 ]
```

apply the sort (or sort!, for in-place changes), and your wayward array will line up its elements in numeric order:

```
x.sort! # => [1, 2, 5, 7, 14, 23, 27, 99]
```

 In order for an array to be sorted, its elements must be comparable (greater than, less than, or equal). That's easy to do with strings and numbers. But because Ruby arrays can hold objects of any type, it is possible that the elements won't be comparable, and in that case, you won't be able to sort the elements with sort or sort!.

The reverse method reverses the order of the elements in an array, returning a new array of elements, reversed:

```
%w[ one two three four five six seven eight nine ten ].reverse # => ["ten", "nine",
"eight", "seven", "six", "five", "four", "three", "two", "one"]
```

Multidimensional Arrays

A multidimensional array is an array of arrays. You create such an array by giving array elements that are themselves arrays. This is a two-dimensional array:

```
d2 = [ ["January", 2007],
       ["February", 2007],
       ["March", 2007] ]
```

The array d2's elements are also arrays. Here is an example of how to form a three-dimensional array (it's a hummer):

```
yrs = [ 2007, 2008, 2009 ]
days = [ 31, [28, 29], 31, 30, 31, 30, 31, 31, 30, 31, 30, 31 ]
months = [ "Jn", "Fb", "Mr", "Ap", "Ma", "Ju", "Jl", "Au", "Sp", "Oc", "Nv", "Dc" ]
d3 = [ yrs, days, months ] # => => [[2007, 2008, 2009], [31, [28, 29], 31, 30, 31,
30, 31, 31, 30, 31, 30, 31], ["Jn", "Fb", "Mr", "Ap", "Ma", "Ju", "Jl", "Au", "Sp",
"Oc", "Nv", "Dc"]]
```

On second thought, let's turn d2 into a one-dimensional array with flatten.

```
d2.flatten # => ["January", 2007, "February", 2007, "March", 2007]
```

Nice! That saved me a little typing.

A two-dimensional array is like a table, with rows and columns. Let's try the transpose method on d2, turning this:

```
d2 = [ ["January", 2007], ["February", 2007], ["March", 2007] ]
```

into this:

```
d2.transpose # => => [["January", "February", "March"], [2007, 2007, 2007]]
```

1.9 and Beyond

These may be added for 1.9:

- The Array class may have a new method: nitems. This method will return the size of the resulting array, after the conditions of the block have been met.
- The index and rindex methods will take a block.
- The pop method will take an argument, allowing it to pop more than one item off an array at a time.
- You will be able to assign nil to existing array elements, thus deleting them.
- Like Hash, the to_s method will have the same result as the inspect method.

Other Array Methods

To get a list of all the Array methods, type:

```
ri Array
```

For more information on any method via *ri*, type something like this at a command line:

```
ri Array#map [or] ri Array.map [or] ri "Array.&"
```

You can look up any of these methods in Ruby's online documentation at *http://www.ruby-doc.org/core/classes/Array.html*.

Review Questions

1. Name the class methods for Array. Come on, there's only two of them.
2. Show three ways to create an array.
3. Use two methods to access the last element in an array.
4. True or false: shift and unshift perform reverse stack operations.

5. What is the difference between delete and delete_at?

6. Multiple choice: You need to add an object to every element in an array. Where do you turn?

    a. value_at

    b. length

    c. map

    d. []=

7. What are two methods for comparing arrays for equality?

8. What method can you use to remove nils from an array?

## CHAPTER 7

Hashes

A hash is an unordered collection of key-value pairs that look like this: `"storm" => "tornado"`. A hash is similar to an `Array` (see Chapter 6), but instead of a default integer index starting at zero, the indexing is done with keys that can be made up from any Ruby object. In other words, you can use integer keys just like an `Array`, but you also have the option of using any Ruby object as a key, even an `Array`! (Hashes are actually implemented as arrays in Ruby.)

Hashes can be accessed by keys or by values, but usually by keys, which must be unique. If you attempt to access a hash with a key that does not exist, the method will return `nil` (unless the hash has a default value). The key-value pairs in a hash are not stored in the same order that they are inserted (the order you placed them in the hash), so don't be surprised if the contents of a hash look different from what you put in—the contents are not ordered the same way as in an array.

Creating Hashes

Like arrays, there are a variety of ways to create hashes. You can create an empty hash with the new class method.

```
months = Hash.new
```

You can test to see if a hash is empty with `empty?`:

```
months.empty? # => true
```

or how big it is with `length` or `size`:

```
months.length
months.size # => 0
```

You can also use new to create a hash with a default value—which is otherwise just `nil`—like this:

```
months = Hash.new( "month" )
```

or like this:

```
months = Hash.new "month"
```

When you access any key in a hash that has a default value, if the key or value doesn't exist, accessing the hash will return the default value:

```
months[0]
```

or:

```
months[72]
```

or:

```
months[234] # => "month"
```

Hash also has a class method [ ], which is called in either one of two ways: with a comma separating the pairs, like this:

```
christmas_carol = Hash[ :name, "Ebenezer Scrooge", :partner, "Jacob Marley", :
employee, "Bob Cratchit", :location, "London", :year, 1843 ] # => {:name=>"Ebenezer
Scrooge", :employee=>"Bob Cratchit", :year=>1843, :partner=>"Jacob Marley", :
location=>"London"}
```

Or with =>:

```
christmas_carol = Hash[ :name => "Ebenezer Scrooge", :partner => "Jacob Marley", :
employee => "Bob Cratchit" =>:location, "London", :year => 1843 ] # => {:name=>
"Ebenezer Scrooge", :employee =>"Bob Cratchit", :year=>1843, :partner=>"Jacob
Marley", :location=>"London"}
```

The easiest way to create a hash, I think, is with curly braces, like this:

```
months = { 1 => "January", 2 => "February", 3 => "March", 4 => "April", 5 => "May",
6 => "June", 7 => "July", 8 => "August", 9 => "September", 10 => "October", 11 =>
"November", 12 => "December" }
```

But that looks just like an array we created in the last chapter. What else could you do? Instead of integers, you could use strings for the keys:

```
month_a = { "jan" => "January", "feb" => "February", "mar" => "March", "apr" =>
"April", "may" => "May", "jun" => "June", "jul" => "July", "aug" => "August", "sep"
=> "September", "oct" => "October", "nov" => "November", "dec" => "December" }
```

So far I've used symbols, integers (Fixnums), and strings as keys. You can use any Ruby object as a key or value, even an array. So this will work, for example: [1,"jan"] => "January".

Accessing Hashes

Here's a hash that associates zip codes with the names of towns in Wyoming that start with the letter *T* (had to limit it somehow):

```
zip = { 82442 => "Ten Sleep", 83025 => "Teton Village", 83127 => "Thayne", 82443 =>
"Thermopolis", 82084 => "Tie Siding", 82336 => "Tipton", 82240 => "Torrington", 83110
=> "Turnerville", 83112 => "Turnerville" }
```

There are tons of ways to access keys and/or values from a hash. You can pick what works for you—what works for the task at hand.

You can test to see if the hash zip has a given key with any of the following methods, which are all synonyms of each other: key?, has_key?, member?, or include?:

```
zip.has_key? 82442 # => true
```

Or you can do the flip side, and see if it has a given value with value? or has_value?:

```
zip.has_value? "Ten Sleep" # => true
```

Let's start pulling stuff out of zip. Here is a simple way of grabbing a value: the [] method. It retrieves a single hash value based on a key:

```
zip[82442] # => "Ten Sleep"
```

Then we have the methods keys and values. Return an array containing all the keys in a hash with keys:

```
zip.keys # => [83110, 83127, 82336, 83112, 82084, 83025, 82442, 82443, 82240]
```

Get an array with all the values from a hash with values:

```
zip.values # => ["Turnerville", "Thayne", "Tipton", "Turnerville", "Tie Siding",
"Teton Village", "Ten Sleep", "Thermopolis", "Torrington"]
```

Retrieve the values out of a hash based on one or more keys with values_at, also placing the value or values in an array:

```
zip.values_at 82084 # => ["Tie Siding"]
zip.values_at 82442, 82443, 82240 # => ["Ten Sleep", "Thermopolis", "Torrington"]
```

Now return a value for a given key (one key only) with the index method:

```
zip.index "Thayne" # => 83127
```

The select method uses a block to return a new, multidimensional array of key-value pairs:

```
zip.select { |key,val| key > 83000 } # => [[83110, "Turnerville"], [83127, "Thayne"],
[83112, "Turnerville"], [83025, "Teton Village"]]
```

Iterating over Hashes

Like you have seen before, Ruby does a good job of handing you easy ways to munch on an object. You can iterate over hashes with each, each_key, each_value, or each_pair. Here are the differences.

The each method calls a block once for each key in a hash, letting you take a swipe at each pair:

```
zip.each {|k,v| puts "#{k}/#{v}" } # =>
83110/Turnerville
83127/Thayne
82336/Tipton
83112/Turnerville
82084/Tie Siding
83025/Teton Village
```

```
82442/Ten Sleep
82443/Thermopolis
82240/Torrington
```

each may take one or two parameters, which are passed to the block as two-element arrays. The each_pair method is similar to each except it must take two parameters and is somewhat more efficient than each when using both parameters.

The each_key method passes only the keys to the block:

```
zip.each_key { |key| print key, " " } # => 83110 83127 82336 83112 82084 83025 82442
82443 82240
```

Compare this with the keys method, which returns all the keys in an array. The each_value method passes all the values to a block:

```
zip.each_value { |value| print value, " " } # => Turnerville Thayne Tipton
Turnerville Tie Siding Ten Sleep Teton Village Thermopolis Torrington
```

Changing Hashes

Hash's []= method replaces or adds key-value pairs to an existing hash. For example:

```
rhode_island = { 1 => "Bristol", 2 => "Kent", 3 => "Newport", 4 => "Providence",
5 => "Washington" }
```

By the way, this hash uses integers as keys, similar to the way an array is indexed, but it doesn't use 0, which is the first index of an array.

You can use []= to add a pair to this array:

```
rhode_island[6]= "Dunthorpe"
```

This adds the value "Dunthorpe" with a key 6. Or you can use []= to change a value:

```
rhode_island[2]= "Bent"
```

This changes the value associated with the key 2 to "Bent". Similarly, you can use the store method to add a pair to the rhode_island array:

```
rhode_island.store(6, "Dunthorpe")
```

Merging Hashes

In addition to rhode_island, you also have a hash listing the counties in Delaware. There are only three:

```
delaware = { 1 => "Kent", 2 => "New Castle", 3 => "Sussex" }
```

Look again at the Rhode Island hash:

```
rhode_island = { 1 => "Bristol", 2 => "Kent", 3 => "Newport", 4 => "Providence",
5 => "Washington" }
```

The merge method merges two hashes together, producing a copy of the hashes that removes duplicate keys by overwriting the key-value pairs from the merged array. To see what I mean by all that, run the example:

```
rhode_island.merge delaware # => {5=>"Washington", 1=>"Kent", 2=>"New Castle", 3=>
"Sussex", 4=>"Providence"}
```

Do you see what happened in the result? The keys and values from delaware took over the pairs with the same keys in rhode_island, making Bristol, Kent, and Newport disappear.

You can also cherry-pick your values by using merge with a block:

```
rhode_island.merge( delaware ){|key,old,new| new = old + "_new" } # => {5=>
"Washington", 1=>"Bristol_new", 2=>"Kent_new", 3=>"Newport_new", 4=>"Providence"}
```

The merge! method makes the changes in place to the hash in the first argument. It works with a block as well; you can also use its synonym, update.

Sorting a Hash

When you sort a hash with the sort method, you get a multidimensional array of two-element arrays in return. Remember, when you create a hash, the key-value pairs are not stored in the order they were added. Ruby orders them however it wants to, most likely because the values can be accessed or retrieved via the keys, not by sequence, as with an array. So order is of no moment to a hash. But it might be to you. If it is, try sort:

```
rhode_island = { 1 => "Bristol", 2 => "Kent", 3 => "Newport", 4 => "Providence", 5 =>
"Washington" }
p rhode_island # => {5=>"Washington", 1=>"Bristol", 2=>"Kent", 3=>"Newport", 4=>
"Providence"}
rhode_island.sort # => [[1, "Bristol"], [2, "Kent"], [3, "Newport"], [4,
"Providence"], [5, "Washington"]]
```

Hash does not have a sort! method, to change the contents of the hash in place.

Deleting and Clearing a Hash

You can delete key-value pairs from a hash with the delete method. The delete method uses a key to find the pair and then destroy it. Back to our Rhode Island hash:

```
rhode_island = { 1 => "Bristol", 2 => "Kent", 3 => "Newport", 4 => "Providence", 5 =>
"Washington" }
```

I'll delete the pair identified by key 5:

```
rhode_island.delete( 5 ) # => "Washington"
```

Now if you look at the hash again, you'll see that the deleted pair has been removed.

```
p rhode_island # => {1=>"Bristol", 2=>"Kent", 3=>"Newport", 4=>"Providence"}
```

You can pass a block to your call to delete. If the key you're wanting to delete is not found, the block runs, and its return value will be returned by delete.

```
rhode_island.delete( 6 ) { |key| puts "not found, bubba" }
```

The delete_if method also uses a block, but in a different way. It removes the key-values from the hash for which the block evaluates to true. Restoring the Rhode Island hash:

```
rhode_island = { 1 => "Bristol", 2 => "Kent", 3 => "Newport", 4 => "Providence", 5 =>
"Washington" }
```

With delete_if, I'll remove all pairs whose key values are less than 3:

```
rhode_island.delete_if { |key, value| key < 3 } # => {5=>"Washington", 3=>"Newport",
4=>"Providence"}
```

delete_if passes all pairs into the block, so you can delete based on a key or a value. Here is an example of a deletion based on value:

```
rhode_island.delete_if { |key, value| value == "Kent" } # => {5=>"Washington", 1=>
"Bristol", 3=>"Newport", 4=>"Providence"}
```

The key-value pair 2=>"Kent" has now been removed from the hash.

Hash's reject method works just like delete_if, but it returns a copy of the hash with the indicated pairs removed, and doesn't actually change the original. The reject! method makes its changes in place and is the equivalent of delete_if.

Maybe you are feeling ruthless. The clear method will help you. It removes all the key-value pairs from a hash, leaving it empty:

```
counties = { "Delaware" => 3, "Rhode Island" => 5 }
counties.clear # bye-bye
counties.empty? # => true
```

Use clear at your own risk!

Replacing a Hash

In order to completely replace the contents of a hash, use the replace method. This example replaces the contents of the counties hash with those of temp:

```
temp = {"Delaware" => 3 }
counties.replace( temp )
```

You can also do it this way with an anonymous hash, so to speak:

```
counties.replace( { "Delaware" => 3 } )
```

Converting Hashes to Other Classes

You can convert a hash into an array with to_a. Let's say you have a hash that contains a few novels written by F. Scott Fitzgerald (no relation):

```
fitzgerald = { 1920 => "This Side of Paradise", 1925 => "The Great Gatsby", 1934 =>
"Tender Is the Night" }
```

You can convert that to an array with to_a like this:

```
fitzgerald.to_a # => [[1925, "The Great Gatsby"], [1920, "This Side of Paradise"],
[1934, "Tender Is the Night"]]
```

to_a converts a hash into a multidimensional array, where each key-value pair is a two-element array within an array.

You can also convert this hash to a string with to_s:

```
novels = fitzgerald.to_s # => "1925The Great Gatsby1920This Side of
Paradise1934Tender Is the Night"
```

Whoa. That's ugly. Let's clean it up a bit with the String function gsub:

```
novels.gsub(/\d{4}/, " " ) { |token| print token } # => " The Great Gatsby This Side
of Paradise Tender Is the Night"
```

When you convert a hash to a hash (self) with to_hash, it may not seem like you are accomplishing much on the surface, but you are getting a benefit.

```
fitz = fitzgerald.to_hash # => {1925=>"The Great Gatsby", 1920=>"This Side of
Paradise", 1934=>"Tender Is the Night"}
fitz.object_id # => 1745050
fitzgerald.object_id # => 1745050
```

Notice that both fitz and fitzgerald have the same object ID of 1745050, but different names.

1.9 and Beyond

In version 1.9, Hash will have the following changes:

- The output of inspect and to_s in Hash will be the same.
- Two instance methods will be added—compare_by_identity and compare_by_identity?. With compare_by_identity, the Hash can compare keys by identity—in other words, by using equal? instead of eql?; compare_by_identity? returns true if the hash compares its keys by their identity.

Other Hash Methods

For more information on Hash, type this at a command line:

```
ri Hash
```

For information on a class method, type:

```
ri Hash::new
```

or:

```
ri Hash::[]
```

For more information on an instance method, type something like:

```
ri Hash.keys
```

or:

```
ri Hash#keys
```

ri only works if you installed the Ruby documentation at the time you installed Ruby (see "Installing Ruby" in Chapter 1). If Ruby documentation is not installed locally, you can look up any Hash method online at *http://ruby-doc.org/core/classes/Hash.html*.

Review Questions

1. What is the difference between a hash and an array?
2. Why would you choose a hash over an array?
3. How would you check to see if a hash has a given key, or a given value?
4. The Hash class is based on what other class?
5. What is the benefit of converting a hash to a hash?
6. What is the difference between has_key? and key??
7. Show how to create a hash with Hash[].
8. What is the result of sorting a hash?

## CHAPTER 8

Working with Files

You can manipulate file directories (folders) and files from within Ruby programs using methods from the `Dir` and `File` classes. There are other related classes, such as `FileUtils`, with lots of interesting methods, but we'll narrow our focus to methods from `Dir` and `File`.

Most of the methods I'll show you are class methods—that is, the method name is prefixed by the class name, as in `File.open` and `File::open` (you can use either `::` or `.` to separate the class and method names).

Ruby uses a number of global constants (for a complete list, see Appendix A). Two global constants that are important in working with files are `ARGV` (or `$*`) and `ARGF` (or `$<`). Like Perl's `@ARGV`, Ruby's `ARGV` is an array that contains all the command-line arguments passed to a program. `ARGF` provides an I/O-like stream that allows access to a virtual concatenation of all files provided on the command line, or standard input if no files are provided. I'll demonstrate both `ARGV` and `ARGF` later in the chapter.

Let's start working with directories.

Directories

You can navigate directory structures on your computer with class methods from the `Dir` class. I'll highlight three here: `Dir.pwd`, `Dir.chdir` (or `Dir.getwd`), and `Dir.mkdir`.

First, I'll change directories (using an absolute path), and then store the value of the directory path in a variable.

```
Dir.chdir( "/Users/mikejfz" )
home = Dir.pwd # => "/Users/mikejfz/"
p home # => "/Users/mikejfz"
```

Compare a variable storing a directory path with the current directory:

```
ruby_progs = "/Users/mikejfz/Desktop/Ruby"

if not Dir.pwd == ruby_progs
  Dir.chdir ruby_progs
end
```

If you need a directory, create it with `mkdir`; later on, delete it with `rmdir` (or delete, a synonym of `rmdir`):

```
Dir.mkdir( "/Users/mikejfz/sandbox" )

Dir.rmdir( "/Users/mikejfz/sandbox" )
```

You can also set permissions on a new directory (not one that already exists) with `mkdir`:

```
Dir.mkdir( "/Users/mikejfz/sandbox", 755 )
```

755 means the owner or user of the directory can read, write, and execute; the group can read and execute; and others can read and execute as well (see Table 8-2).

Looking Inside Directories

`Dir`'s class method `entries` returns an array that contains all the entries found in a directory, including files, hidden files, and other directories, one array element per entry. I'll apply `Array`'s each method to the output of `entries`:

```
Dir.entries( "/usr/local/src/ruby-1.8.6" ).each { |e| puts e }
```

The beginning of the output from this command looks like this:

```
.
..
.cvsignore
.document
.ext
.rbconfig.time
array.c
array.o
bcc32
bignum.c
bignum.o
...
```

You can do the same thing with `Dir`'s foreach:

```
Dir.foreach( "/usr/local/src/ruby-1.8.6" ) { |e| puts e }
```

The Directory Stream

You can open a directory stream and have a look around in it with some of `Dir`'s instance methods. The class method `open` (or `new`) opens a directory stream on the given directory. `path` tells you the path of the stream. `tell` returns the current entry. `read` reads the next available entry from *dir*. `rewind` takes you back to the beginning of the stream. `each` iterates through each entry in *dir*.

```
dir = Dir.open( "/usr/local/src/ruby-1.8.6" ) # => #<Dir:0x1cd784>
dir.path # => "/usr/local/src/ruby-1.8.6"
dir.tell # => "."
dir.read # => 1
```

```
dir.tell # => ".."
dir.rewind # => rewind to beginning
dir.each { |e| puts e } # puts each entry in dir
dir.close # => close stream
```

Creating a New File

To create a new file and open it at the same time, use the File method new, like this:

```
file = File.new( "file.rb", "w" ) # => #<File:file.rb>
```

The first argument names the new file, and the second argument specifies the file mode—r for readable, w for writable, or x for executable.

Table 8-1 shows the effect of the different modes.

Table 8-1. File modes

Mode	Description
"r"	Read-only. Starts at beginning of file (default mode).
"r+"	Read-write. Starts at beginning of file.
"w"	Write-only. Truncates existing file to zero length or creates a new file for writing.
"w+"	Read-write. Truncates existing file to zero length or creates a new file for reading and writing.
"a"	Write-only. Starts at end of file if file exists; otherwise, creates a new file for writing.
"a+"	Read-write. Starts at end of file if file exists; otherwise, creates a new file for reading and writing.
"b"	(DOS/Windows only.) Binary file mode. May appear with any of the key letters listed above.

> You can also create files using new with flags and permission bits. For more information, see *http://www.ruby-doc.org/core/classes/File.html*.

Opening an Existing File

You open an existing file with the open method. Example 8-1 opens the file *sonnet_129.txt* (it comes with the code archive), prints each line of the file using each with a block, then closes it with close. (By the way, you can use file.closed? to test whether a file is closed. It returns true or false.)

Example 8-1. open.rb

```
file = File.open( "sonnet_129.txt" )

file.each { |line| print "#{file.lineno}. ", line }

file.close
```

The expression substitution syntax, that is, #{file.lineno}, inserts the line number in the output, followed by the line from the file.

 The open, each, and close methods are all from the IO class, not File. See "The IO Class," later in this chapter.

The output is:

```
 1. The expense of spirit in a waste of shame
 2. Is lust in action: and till action, lust
 3. Is perjured, murderous, bloody, full of blame,
 4. Savage, extreme, rude, cruel, not to trust;
 5. Enjoyed no sooner but despised straight;
 6. Past reason hunted; and no sooner had,
 7. Past reason hated, as a swallowed bait,
 8. On purpose laid to make the taker mad.
 9. Mad in pursuit and in possession so;
10. Had, having, and in quest to have extreme;
11. A bliss in proof, and proved, a very woe;
12. Before, a joy proposed; behind a dream.
13. All this the world well knows; yet none knows well
14. To shun the heaven that leads men to this hell.
```

I used the print method in *open.rb* because the line-end character already exists at the end of each line in the file.

ARGV and ARGF

Another interesting way to do the same procedure is with ARGV, using only two lines of code (see Example 8-2).

Example 8-2. argv.rb

```
ARGV << "sonnet_129.txt"
print while gets
```

How does that work? Remember that ARGV (or $*) is an array, and each of its elements is a filename submitted on the command line—usually. But in this case, we have appended a filename to ARGV directly with <<, an array method. Clever. You can apply any method to ARGV that you might apply to any other array. For example, try adding this command:

```
p ARGV # => ["sonnet_119.txt"]
```

or:

```
ARGV#[0] # => ["sonnet_119.txt"]
```

The gets method is a Kernel method that gets lines from ARGV, and as long as gets returns a string, that line is printed with print. Thus, this code produces:

```
Let me not to the marriage of true minds
Admit impediments. Love is not love
Which alters when it alteration finds,
Or bends with the remover to remove:
O, no! it is an ever-fixed mark,
That looks on tempests and is never shaken;
It is the star to every wandering bark,
Whose worth's unknown, although his height be taken.
Love's not Time's fool, though rosy lips and cheeks
Within his bending sickle's compass come;
Love alters not with his brief hours and weeks,
But bears it out even to the edge of doom.
If this be error and upon me proved,
I never writ, nor no man ever loved.
```

ARGF ($<) is, once again, a virtual concatenation of all the files that appear on the command line. Compare the program *argf.rb* in Example 8-3 with the *argv.rb*.

Example 8-3. argf.rb

```
while line = ARGF.gets
 print line
end
```

While there is a line to be retrieved from files on the command line, *argf.rb* prints that line to standard output. To see how it works, run the program with these three files on the command line:

```
$ argf.rb sonnet_29.txt sonnet_119.txt sonnet_129.txt
```

All three files are printed on the display, one line at a time.

Opening a URI

This is not directly related to File, but I think it is related enough and will be of keen interest to some of you. (I have Ryan Waldron to thank for pointing this out. Thanks, Ryan.)

Peter Szinek wrote a blog where he used Ruby to do some screen scraping. He is the creator of the scRubyt web scraping toolkit written in Ruby (see *http://www.scrubyt. org*). I am borrowing his simplest example (Example 8-4) to give you an idea of how it works.

Example 8-4. scrape.rb

```
require 'open-uri'

url = "http://www.google.com/search?q=ruby"

open(url) { |page| page_content = page.read() }
```

Example 8-4. scrape.rb (continued)

```
links = page_content.scan(/<a class=l.*?href=\"(.*?)\"/).flatten

links.each {|link| puts link}

}
```

Without going into a lot of detail, *scrape.rb* uses the built-in class OpenURI (*http://www.ruby-doc.org/core/classes/OpenURI.html*) to open a URI of a Google query on Ruby. The URI is read and scanned using a regular expression, looking for the value of the href attribute on a (anchor) elements. Those matched elements are stored in the links variable, and each is used to iterate over the lot of them. This is the output—a group of links to Ruby resources:

```
http://www.ruby-lang.org/
http://www.rubyonrails.org/
http://www.rubycentral.com/
http://www.rubycentral.com/book/
http://en.wikipedia.org/wiki/Ruby_programming_language
http://en.wikipedia.org/wiki/Ruby
http://www.w3.org/TR/ruby/
http://poignantguide.net/
http://www.zenspider.com/Languages/Ruby/QuickRef.html
http://www.rubys.com/
```

Try changing the value *ruby* in q=*ruby* to some other value of interest to you and see what happens. For the complete story on screen scraping with Ruby, see Peter Szinek's blog at *http://www.rubyrailways.com/data-extraction-for-web-20-screen-scraping-in-rubyrails*.

Deleting and Renaming Files

You can rename and delete files programmatically with Ruby using the rename and delete methods. Type these lines into *irb*:

```
File.new( "books.txt", "w" )
File.rename( "books.txt", "chaps.txt" )
File.delete( "chaps.txt" )
```

File Inquiries

You can make all kinds of inquires about files with File methods. These kinds of tests are often done before another file procedure is done. For example, the following command tests whether a file exists before opening it:

```
File::open("file.rb") if File::exists?( "file.rb" )
```

You can also test whether the file exists with exist? (singular), a synonym of exists?. Inquire whether the file is really a file with file?:

```
File.file?( "sonnet29.txt" ) # => true
```

Or find out if it is a directory with directory?:

```
# try it with a directory
File::directory?( "/usr/local/bin" ) # => true

# try it with a file...oops
File::directory?( "file.rb" ) # => false
```

Test if the file is readable with readable?, writable with writable?, and executable with executable?:

```
File.readable?( "sonnet_119.txt" ) # => true
File.writable?( "sonnet_119.txt" ) # => true
File.executable?( "sonnet_119.txt" ) # => false
```

You can find out if a file has a length of zero (0) with zero?:

```
system("touch chap.txt") # Create a zero-length file with a system command
File.zero?( "chap.txt" ) # => true
```

Get its size in bytes with size? or size:

```
File.size?( "sonnet_129.txt" ) # => 594
File.size( "sonnet_129.txt" ) # => 594
```

Finally, inquire about the type of a file with ftype:

```
File::ftype( "file.rb" ) # => "file"
```

The ftype method identifies the type of the file by returning one of the following: file, directory, characterSpecial, blockSpecial, fifo, link, socket, or unknown.

Find out when a file was created, modified, or last accessed with ctime, mtime, and atime, respectively:

```
File::ctime( "file.rb" ) # => Wed Nov 08 10:06:37 -0700 2006
File::mtime( "file.rb" ) # => Wed Nov 08 10:44:44 -0700 2006
File::atime( "file.rb" ) # => Wed Nov 08 10:45:01 -0700 2006
```

Changing File Modes and Owner

To change the mode (permissions or access list) of a file, use the chmod method with a mask (see Table 8-2 for a list of masks):

```
file = File.new( "books.txt", "w" )
file.chmod( 0755 )
```

or:

```
file = File.new( "books.txt", "w" ).chmod( 0755 )
system "ls -l books.txt" # => -rwxr-xr-x    1 mikejfz  mikejfz     0 Nov  8 22:13
books.txt
```

The preceding example means that only the owner can write the file, but all can read or execute it. Compare that with the following:

```
file = File.new( "books.txt", "w" ).chmod( 0644 )
system "ls -l books.txt" # => -rw-r--r--    1 mikejfz  mikejfz    0 Nov  8 22:13
books.txt
```

All can read the file, but only the owner can write the file, and none can execute it.

For documentation on how the system command chmod works on Mac OS X, see *http://www.hmug.org/man/2/chmod.php*.

Table 8-2. Masks for chmod

Mask	Description
0700	rwx mask for owner
0400	r for owner
0200	w for owner
0100	x for owner
0070	rwx mask for group
0040	r for group
0020	w for group
0010	x for group
0007	rwx mask for other
0004	r for other
0002	w for other
0001	x for other
4000	Set user ID on execution
2000	Set group ID on execution
1000	Save swapped text, even after use

You can change the owner and group of a file with the chown method, which is like the Unix/Linux command chown. You need superuser or root privileges to use this method.

```
file = File.new( "books.txt", "r" )
file.chown( 109, 3333 )
```

or:

```
file = File.new( "books.txt", "r" ).chown( 109, 3333 )
```

Now perform this system command (works on Unix-like systems only) to see the result:

```
system "ls -l books.txt" # => -rw-r--r--   1 109  3333  0 Nov  8 11:38 books.txt
```

The IO Class

The basis for all input and output in Ruby is the IO class, which represents an input/output (I/O) stream of data in the form of bytes. Standard streams include standard input stream ($stdin) or the keyboard, standard output stream ($stdout), the display or screen, and standard error output stream ($stderr), which is also the display by default. IO is closely associated with the File class, and File is the only standard subclass of IO in Ruby. I'll show you a sampling of IO code.

To create a new I/O stream named ios, use the new method. The first argument is 1, which is the *numeric file descriptor* for standard input. Standard input can also be represented by the predefined Ruby variable $stdin (see Table 8-3). The optional second argument, w, is a mode string meaning "write."

```
ios = IO.new( 1, "w" )

ios.puts "IO, IO, it's off to the computer lab I go."

$stdout.puts "Do you copy?"
```

Table 8-3. Standard streams

Stream description	File descriptor	Predefined Ruby variable	Ruby environment variable
Standard input stream	0	$stdin	STDIN
Standard output stream	1	$stdout	STDOUT
Standard error output stream	2	$stderr	STDERR

Other mode strings include r for read-only (the default), r+ for read-write, and w for write-only. For details on all available modes, see Table 8-4.

Table 8-4. I/O modes

Mode	Description
r	Read-only. Starts at the beginning of the file (default mode).
r+	Read-write. Starts at the beginning of the file.
w	Write-only. Truncates existing file to zero length or creates a new file for writing.
w+	Read-write. Truncates existing file to zero length or creates a new file for reading and writing.
a	Write-only. Starts at the end of file if the file exists, otherwise creates a new file for writing.
a+	Read-write. Starts at the end of the file if the file exists, otherwise creates a new file for reading and writing.
b	(DOS/Windows only.) Binary file mode. May appear with any of the modes listed in this table.

With the IO instance method `fileno`, you can test what the numeric file descriptor is for your I/O stream (`to_i` also works).

```
ios.fileno # => 1
ios.to_i # => 1

$stdout.fileno # => 1
```

You can also write strings to the stream (buffer) with the `<<` method, then flush the buffer with flush.

```
ios << "Ask not " << "for whom the bells toll." << " -John Donne"

ios.flush # => Ask not for whom the bells toll. -John Donne
```

Finally, close the stream with `close`. This also flushes any pending writes.

```
ios.close
```

Write characters to an I/O stream with `putc`, and retrieve those characters with `getc`.

```
ios = IO.new( 1 )
ios.putc "M"
ios.putc "a"
ios.putc "t"
ios.putc "z"
ios.getc => Matz
```

Open a file stream, and then retrieve each line in order with the IO method gets.

```
file = File.new( "sonnet_29.txt" )
file.gets # => "When in disgrace with fortune and men's eyes\n"
file.gets # => "I all alone beweep my outcast state,\n"
```

Or do it with `readline`. `readline` is slightly different from gets because it raises an `EOFError` when it reaches the end of the file.

```
file = File.new( "sonnet_119.txt" )
file.readline # => "Let me not to the marriage of true minds\n"
file.readline # => "Admit impediments. Love is not love\n"
file.readline # => "Which alters when it alteration finds,\n"
```

Review Questions

1. How is `ARGV` useful?

2. How would you obtain a file type from a file on disk with Ruby?

3. What does the mask `0700` do to a file's permissions?

4. How would you access the date and time a file was created?

5. What kind of object does the entries method from `Dir` return?

## CHAPTER 9

Classes

Finally, I'll go into classes in some detail. By now you certainly know that Ruby is an object-oriented programming (OOP) language, and that the centerpiece of OOP is the class. A class is a container of sorts that holds methods and properties such as variables and constants (collectively known as *class members*). One of the most important things about classes is that they can be reused by means of *inheritance*.

A class can inherit or derive characteristics from another class. That means that a child class or subclass can inherit the methods and data from a parent class. This parent is also referred to as the *superclass*. This parent-child chain forms a hierarchy of classes, with the *base class* at the root, top, or base of the hierarchy. For Ruby, the base class of the hierarchy is Object.

Ruby supports *single inheritance*, like Java, not *multiple inheritance*, like C++. What's the difference? With single inheritance, a class can only inherit from one other class; with multiple inheritance, a class can inherit from more than one class. The problem with multiple inheritance is that it opens up management issues such as *name collision*—that is, when classes and methods and variables have the same names but different meanings. Most programmers agree that single inheritance is less prone to headaches and avoids collision and other issues related to multiple inheritance; on the other hand, they would also like the power of multiple inheritance.

Java addresses the multiple-inheritance dilemma with *interfaces*. An interface in Java can define abstract methods but cannot implement them; a Java class can inherit an interface, then implement its abstract methods. Java also has *abstract classes* and *abstract methods* that can be inherited and then later implemented.

Ruby also offers a compromise between single and multiple inheritance: modules. Modules let you define variables, constants, and methods, but you can't use them until they are included in a class. You can include as many modules as you want in a class, and when Ruby encounters name collision, the last defined method or variable is the one used. In other words, you can override methods and member variables in Ruby.

Now, step by step, I'll show you how to define classes, instance methods and variables, class methods and variables, and how to define modules and include them. I'll also explain what it means to override a method, and what a singleton method is.

Defining the Class

A class is defined with the class keyword, followed by an end. The class identifier is a constant, so it must be capitalized (the norm), but it can also be all uppercase—Hello or HELLO instead of hello.

Example 9-1 shows the Hello class, which you saw in Chapter 1, but here I'll go into more detail about it.

Example 9-1. hello.rb

```ruby
class Hello

  def initialize( name )
    @name = name
  end

  def hello_matz
    puts "Hello, " + @name + "!"
  end

end

hi = Hello.new( "Matz" )
hi.hello_matz # => Hello, Matz!
```

The keyword class, followed by end, defines the Hello class. The initialize method defines the instance variable @name by storing a copy of the name argument passed into the initialize method.

The initialize method is a Ruby convention that acts something like a class constructor in other languages, but not completely. At this point, the instance is already there, fully instantiated. initialize is the first code that is executed *after* the object is instantiated; you can execute just about any Ruby code in initialize. initialize is always private; that is, it is scoped only to the current object, not beyond it.

You access the instance variable @name with the method hello_matz. More about instance methods are coming up in the following section.

A class is itself an object, even if you don't directly instantiate it. Classes are always open, so you can add to any class, even built-in classes like String and Array. You can open the Array class and add a method to it such as array_of_ten, as shown in Example 9-2. This feature makes the language incredibly flexible.

Example 9-2. array_of_ten.rb

```
class Array

  def array_of_ten
    (1..10).to_a
  end

end

arr = Array.new
ten = arr.array_of_ten
p ten # => [1, 2, 3, 4, 5, 6, 7, 8, 9, 10]
```

Instance Variables

In Rubyland, an *instance variable* is a variable that is available from within an instance of a class, and is limited in scope because it belongs to a given object. As already mentioned, an instance variable is prefixed by a single at sign (@), as in:

```
@name = "Easy Jet"
```

You can define an instance variable inside a method or outside of one. You can only access an instance variable from outside an object via a method. (You can, however, access an instance variable *within* the object without a method.) For example, you can define an instance variable in a class like this:

```
class Horse

  @name = "Easy Jet"

end
```

This works if you want to reference @name only from within the object, but is decidedly inadequate if you want to access it from outside of the object. You have no way to retrieve the value of @name directly from the outside. If you try to access @name from an instance of Horse—something like horse.name—the attempt generates an error. You must define a method to retrieve the value.

```
class Horse

  def name
    @name = "Easy Jet"
  end

end

h = Horse.new
h.name # => "Easy Jet"
```

The method name is the kind of method that is referred to as an *accessor method* or *getter*. It gets a property (the value of a variable) from an instance of a class.

Usually, when you have a getter, you also want a setter—an accessor method that sets the value of a variable. This version of the Horse class adds such a method and shows you another convention:

```
class Horse

  def name
    @name
  end

  def name=( value )
    @name = value
  end

end

h = Horse.new
h.name= "Poco Bueno"
h.name # => "Poco Bueno"
```

The setter method name= follows a Ruby convention: the name of the method ends with an equals sign (=). (This convention is not a requirement.) You could call name= whatever you like, as long as the characters are legal. But it is a nice convention, easy on the eyes, because name and name= look like business partners.

Here is yet another version of the class Horse that initializes the instance variable @name with the standard initialize method. Later the program creates an instance of the class by calling new, and then accesses the instance variable through the accessor method horse_name, via the instance horse.

```
class Horse

  def initialize( name )
    @name = name
  end

  def horse_name
    @name
  end

end

horse = Horse.new( "Doc Bar" )
puts horse.horse_name # => Doc Bar
```

There is a far easier way to write accessor methods, as you will see next.

Accessors

If you are accustomed to creating classes in other programming languages, you have no doubt created getter and setter methods. These methods set and get (return) properties in a class. Ruby simplifies the creation of getters and setters with a little *metaprogramming* and the methods attr, attr_reader, attr_writer, and attr_accessor, all from the Module class. Metaprogramming is a shorthand way to write a program, or part of one, with another program. By supplying the attr method, Ruby provides a way to quickly create the equivalent of six lines of code with a single line.

The method attr creates a single getter method, named by a symbol, with an optional setter method (if the second argument is true), as in Example 9-3.

Example 9-3. dog.rb

```
#!/usr/bin/env ruby

class Dog
  attr :bark, true
end

Dog.instance_methods - Object.instance_methods # => ["bark", "bark="]

dog = Dog.new

dog.bark="Woof!"
puts dog.bark # => Woof!
```

By calling attr, with :bark and true as arguments, the class Dog will have the instance methods bark and bark=. If you called attr with only the :bark argument, Dog would have only the method bark. (Notice how you can subtract out Object's instance methods when retrieving Dog's instance methods. It's the little things like this that make me really like Ruby.)

The single line attr :bark, true is equivalent to writing out the bark and bark= methods in six lines of code:

```
class Dog

  def bark
    @bark
  end

  def bark=(val)
    @bark = val
  end

end
```

You'll learn more about metaprogramming in the section "Metaprogramming" in Chapter 10.

The method attr_reader automatically creates one or more instance variables, with corresponding methods that return (get) the values of each method. The attr_writer method automatically creates one or more instance variables, with corresponding methods that set the values of each method. Example 9-4 calls these methods. It creates one getter and a corresponding setter.

Example 9-4. dogs.rb

```
class Dog
  attr_reader :bark
  attr_writer :bark
end

dog = Dog.new

dog.bark="Woof!"
puts dog.bark # => Woof!

dog.instance_variables.sort # => ["@bark"]
Dog.instance_methods.sort - Object.instance_methods # => [ "bark", "bark=" ]
```

Calling the attr_accessor method does the same job as calling both attr_reader and attr_writer together, for one or more instance methods, as shown in Example 9-5.

Example 9-5. gaits.rb

```
#!/usr/bin/env ruby

class Gaits
  attr_accessor :walk, :trot, :canter
end

Gaits.instance_methods.sort - Object.instance_methods # => ["canter", "canter=", "trot",
"trot=", "walk", "walk="]
```

Ruby's metaprogramming makes life so much easier when creating getters and setters.

Class Variables

In Ruby, a *class variable* is shared among all instances of a class, so only one copy of a class variable exists for a given class. In Ruby, a class variable is prefixed by two at signs (@@). You *must* initialize a class attribute before you use it.

```
@@times = 0
```

The Repeat class, shown in Example 9-6, uses the @@total class variable. The program instantiates the class three times, calls the repeat method for each instance, and accesses the value of @@total for each instance, too. Notice how the value stored in @@total is maintained between instances.

Example 9-6. repeat.rb

```
class Repeat
  @@total = 0
  def initialize( string, times )
    @string = string
    @times = times
  end
  def repeat
    @@total += @times
    return @string * @times
  end
  def total
    "Total times, so far: " + @@total.to_s
  end
end

data = Repeat.new( "ack ", 8 )
ditto = Repeat.new( "Again! ", 5 )
ditty = Repeat.new( "Rinse. Lather. Repeat. ", 2 )

puts data.repeat # => ack ack ack ack ack ack ack ack
puts data.total # => Total times, so far: 8

puts ditto.repeat # => Again! Again! Again! Again! Again!
puts ditto.total # => Total times, so far: 13

puts ditty.repeat # => Rinse. Lather. Repeat. Rinse. Lather. Repeat.
puts ditty.total # => Total times, so far: 15
```

Class Methods

A *class method* is a method that is associated with a class (and with a module in Ruby), not an instance of a class. You can invoke class methods by prefixing the name of the method with the name of the class to which it belongs. Class methods are also known as *static methods*.

In Ruby, you can also associate the name of a module with a method name, just like with a class, but to use such a method, you must include the module in a class. This line prefixes the name of the sqrt method with Math, from the Math module, which you read about in Chapter 5.

```
Math.sqrt(36) # => 6.0
```

To define a class method, you simply prefix the name of the method with the name of the class or module in the method definition. In Example 9-7, the area of a rectangle is calculated with the class method Area.rect.

Example 9-7. area.rb

```
class Area

  def Area.rect( length, width, units="inches" )
```

Example 9-7. area.rb (continued)

```
    area = length*width
    printf( "The area of this rectangle is %.2f %s.", area, units )
    sprintf( "%.2f", area )
  end

end

Area.rect(12.5, 16) # => The area of this rectangle is 200.00 inches.
```

Singletons

Another way you can define class methods is by using a class within a class—a *singleton* class—like the code in Example 9-8.

Example 9-8. area_singleton.rb

```
class Area

  class << self

    def rect( length, width, units="inches" )
      area = length*width
      printf( "The area of this rectangle is %.2f %s.", area, units )
      sprintf( "%.2f", area )
    end

  end

end

Area.rect(10, 10) # The area of this rectangle is 100.00 inches.=> "100.00"
```

In this form, you don't have to prefix the method with the class name in the definition. A singleton class is tied to a particular object, can be instantiated only once, and is not distinguished by a prefixed name.

The method rect is also effectively a singleton method because it is tied to the singleton class. Here is a way to define a singleton method—in this case, one that is tied to a single object:

```
    class Singleton
    end

    s = Singleton.new
    def s.handle
      puts "I'm a singleton method!"
    end

    s.handle # => I'm a singleton method!
```

The singleton design pattern comes from *Design Patterns: Elements of Reusable Object-Oriented Software,* by Erich Gamma, Richard Helm, Ralph Johnson, and John Vlissides, known as the "Gang of Four" (Addison-Wesley). In basic terms, a singleton is designed so that it can only be instantiated once. It is often used like a global variable. Ruby also has a class for defining singleton objects; see *http://www.ruby-doc.org/core/classes/Singleton.html.*

Inheritance

Ruby supports *single inheritance*, which means that a class can inherit only one other class—the parent or superclass. When a child class inherits or derives from a parent, it has access to the methods and properties of the parent class. Inheritance is accomplished with the < operator.

As mentioned earlier, Ruby does not support *multiple inheritance*, which allows a class to inherit more than one class and therefore have access to the functionality from more than one class. One problem with multiple inheritance is that some definitions of classes, methods, and properties may collide; for example, two classes may have the same name but carry entirely different meanings. There are simple reasons why multiple inheritance can be convenient, but more complex reasons why it can be a headache. Ruby manages this problem with modules and mixins, which you will read about in the next section.

Example 9-9 is an example of simple, single inheritance. The Address child class inherits (<) the methods and properties (instance variables) from the Name class, the parent. The method respond_to? tests to see whether an instance of Address has access to :given_name, inherited from the Name class. The answer is yes (true).

Example 9-9. inherit.rb

```ruby
#!/usr/bin/env ruby

class Name

  attr_accessor :given_name, :family_name

end

class Address < Name

  attr_accessor :street, :city, :state, :country

end

a = Address.new
puts a.respond_to?(:given_name) # => true
```

If the class Name were in a different file, you would just require that file first, and then the inheritance operation would work fine, as you can see in Examples 9-10 and 9-11. (The require method in *address.rb* assumes that *name.rb* is in the load path.)

Example 9-10. name.rb

```
class Name

  attr_accessor :given_name, :family_name

end
```

Example 9-11. address.rb

```
#!/usr/bin/env ruby

require 'name'

class Address < Name

  attr_accessor :street, :city, :state, :country

end

a = Address.new
puts a.respond_to?(:given_name)
```

 What is a load path? The system path is not necessarily the same thing as the Ruby path or load path. What's the difference? Here are some hints. Ruby has a predefined variable called $LOAD_PATH (which also has a Perl-like synonym, $:). $LOAD_PATH is an array that contains the names of directories and that is searched by load and require methods when loading files. Type $LOAD_PATH in *irb* to see what the array holds. Ruby can also use the environment variables PATH and RUBYPATH (if it is set). PATH is the system path and acts as a search path for Ruby programs, among other things; RUBYPATH may be the same thing as PATH, but because it takes precedence over PATH, it is likely to hold other directories beyond PATH. (See Table A-4 and Table A-5.)

Modules

In addition to classes, Ruby also has modules. A module is like a class, but it cannot be instantiated like a class. How is that useful? Well, a class can *include* a module so that when the class is instantiated, it gets the included module's goodies. The methods from an included module become instance methods in the class that includes the module. This is called *mixing in*, and a module is referred to as a *mixin*. Using mixins helps overcome the problems that stem from multiple inheritance.

A module is a form of a *namespace* in Ruby. A namespace is a set of names—such as method names—that have a scope or context. A Ruby module associates a single name with a set of method and constant names. The module name can be used in classes in other modules. Generally, the scope or context of such a namespace is the class or module where the namespace (module name) is included. A Ruby class can also be considered a namespace.

A module name must be a constant, that is, it must start with an uppercase letter. A module can contain methods, constants, other modules, and even classes. A module can inherit from another module, but it may not inherit from a class. As a class may include a module, it may also include modules that have inherited other modules.

The code in Example 9-12 demonstrates how to create a module (Dice) and then include it in a class (Game). The method roll is available from the instance of Game called g. (The Kernel method rand generates a pseudo-random number—between 0.0 and 1.0 if it has no argument, or between 0 and *argument*. The roll method uses rand with a little fancy footwork to make sure it does not return 0. Admittedly, it may not be the most efficient way to guarantee a nonzero result, but it works).

Example 9-12. mixin.rb

```ruby
#!/usr/bin/env ruby

module Dice

  # virtual roll of a pair of dice
  def roll
    r_1 = rand(6); r_2 = rand(6)
    r1 = r_1>0?r_1:1; r2 = r_2>0?r_2:6
    total = r1+r2
    printf( "You rolled %d and %d (%d).\n", r1, r2, total )
    total
  end

end

class Game
 include Dice
end

g = Game.new
g.roll
```

If the module were in a separate file (see Example 9-13), like with a class, you would simply require the file containing the module (see Example 9-14), and then it would work (again, require is expecting a name in the load path).

Example 9-13. dice.rb

```ruby
module Dice

  # virtual roll of a pair of dice
  def roll
    r_1 = rand(6); r_2 = rand(6)
    r1 = r_1>0?r_1:1; r2 = r_2>0?r_2:6
    total = r1+r2
    printf( "You rolled %d and %d (%d).\n", r1, r2, total )
    total
  end

end
```

Example 9-14. game.rb

```ruby
#!/usr/bin/env ruby

require 'dice'

class Game
 include Dice
end

g = Game.new
g.roll
```

When you define module methods as you would class methods—that is, prefixed with the module name—you can call the method from anywhere, as is the case with the Math module. Example 9-15 shows how to prefix a module method and then call it later.

Example 9-15. binary.rb

```ruby
#!/usr/bin/env ruby

module Binary

  def Binary.to_bin( num )
    bin = sprintf("%08b", num)
  end

end

Binary.to_bin( 123 ) # => "01111011"
```

public, private, or protected

The visibility or access of methods and constants may be set with the methods public, private, or protected.

- A class member marked public is accessible by anyone from anywhere; it is the default.
- private means that the receiver for the method is always the current object or self, so its scope is always the current object (often helper methods, that is, methods that get called by other methods to perform some job).
- A method marked protected means that it can be used only by instances of the class where it was defined, or by derived classes.

You can label methods as shown in Example 9-16. Methods following the keywords private or protected will have the indicated visibility until changed or until the definition ends.

Example 9-16. access.rb

```
class Names

  def initialize( given, family, nick, pet )
    @given = given
    @family = family
    @nick = nick
    @pet = pet
  end

# these methods are public by default

  def given
    @given
  end

  def family
    @family
  end

# all following methods private, until changed

  private

  def nick
    @nick
  end
```

Example 9-16. access.rb (continued)

```
# all following methods protected, until changed

  protected

  def pet
    @pet
  end

end

name = Names.new( "Klyde", "Kimball", "Abner", "Teddy Bear" )

name.given # => "Klyde"
name.family # => "Kimball"

# see what happens when you call nick or pet

name.nick
name.pet
```

When you change the access of methods as in Example 9-16, you have to define those methods after you use the `public`, `private`, or `protected` methods. You can also call the methods after a definition (you must use symbols for method names):

```
  def pet
    @pet
  end

  protected :pet
```

Review Questions

1. True or false: You cannot add methods or variables to built-in classes.
2. An instance variable is prefixed by a _____ character.
3. What is one distinguishing characteristic of a class method?
4. True or false: In Ruby, even a class is an object.
5. What is a singleton method, and how do you create one?
6. Can you instantiate a module?
7. What is the main difference between single and multiple inheritance?
8. What is Ruby's base class?
9. What is the default visibility for members of a class?

## CHAPTER 10

More Fun with Ruby

It's time to explore beyond the basics and move into some other areas of Ruby. Here you'll learn how to use the sprintf method to format output, process or generate XML with REXML or XML Builder, use reflection methods, use RubyGems, create documentation with RDoc, and do some error handling. You'll even do a little metaprogramming and embedded Ruby (ERB). The purpose of this chapter is to expand your knowledge and broaden your experience before cutting you loose. After this, only Chapter 11 remains.

Formatting Output with sprintf

The Kernel module has a method called sprintf (which also has a synonym called format) for creating formatted strings. If you have C programming in your DNA, as many programmers do, it is likely that you will want to reach for sprintf to do all kinds of string formatting chores for you. sprintf relies on a *format string*—which includes format specifiers, each preceded by a %—to tell it how to format a string. For example, let's say you wanted to print out the number 237 in binary format. Enter this:

```
sprintf( "%b", 237 ) # => "11101101"
```

The format specifier %b indicates that you want a binary result. b is the *field type* for binary, and the argument 237 is the number you want to convert to binary, which sprintf does very handsomely. sprintf doesn't actually print the return value to standard output (the screen); to do that you would have to use printf, another Kernel method:

```
printf( "%b", 237 ) # => 11101101
```

which is nearly identical to:

```
$stdout.write(sprintf( "%b", 237 )) # => 11101101
```

write is a method of the IO class that writes a string to the open I/O stream, which happens to be $stdout, the predefined variable for standard output (your display by default). You can even use puts (or print):

```
puts sprintf( "%b", 237 ) # => 11101101
```

But I wouldn't. I prefer printf over $stdout.write or puts sprintf—it's more elegant.

You can also assign the return value to a variable:

```
bin = sprintf("%b", 237)
```

Or you might use a variable as an argument:

```
to_bin = 237
sprintf("%b", to_bin) # => "11101101"
```

The result of converting 237 is a nice, eight-digit binary number string. What if you are converting a smaller number to binary—say, 14:

```
sprintf("%b", 14) # => "1110"
```

If you want eight digits, you can specify that, plus pad out the result with zeros:

```
sprintf("%08b", 14) # => "00001110"
```

That looks better. To review, a format specifier always begins with a percent sign (%) and may be followed by optional flags, which modify how the result is displayed (see Table 10-1 for a complete list of flags). The flag in this format specifier is 0, which indicates that you want to fill or pad the result with zeros instead of spaces (the default). The number 8 denotes the width of the result (eight digits). (Following the width, you can also have a precision indicator. More on that later.) The string ends with a field type character, such as b. Field type characters control how the corresponding argument is displayed in the result. See Table 10-2 for all the field type characters.

Let's make a sentence out of it by embedding more than one format specifier in the string.

```
sprintf("The integer %d is %08b in binary format.", 72, 72)
# => "The integer 72 is 01001000 in binary format."
```

Any characters other than the format specifiers are also copied over. The %d specifies a decimal number in the result. This call to sprintf includes two arguments (72, 72). It expects two arguments because there are two format strings, but that is unnecessary. OK, so delete the second argument:

```
sprintf("The integer %d is %08b in binary format.", 72)
ArgumentError: too few arguments
        from (irb):25:in `sprintf'
        from (irb):25
        from :0
```

That didn't work. We have to let sprintf know what argument you want to use, then it will be happy.

```
sprintf("The integer %1$d is %1$08b in binary format.", 72)
# => "The integer 72 is 01001000 in binary format."
```

The 1$ lets the method know you want it to look for the first argument only.

For a floating-point number, use the f field type. The following line displays dollars:

```
sprintf( "$%.2f", 100 ) # => "$100.00"
```

A precision indicator consists of a period followed by a number (.2 in this example). It follows the width indicator, if a width is used (it's not used here). A precision indicator controls the number of decimal places displayed in the result (two). The dollar sign at the beginning of the format string is copied through, so you get $100.00.

The x type converts an argument to a hexadecimal value.

```
sprintf( "%x", 30 ) # => "1e"
```

For uppercase characters in the hex value, use X.

```
sprintf( "%X", 30 ) # => "1E"
```

To prefix a hex result with 0x, use a hash or pound symbol (#).

```
sprintf( "%#x", 256 ) # => "0x100"
```

The %o field type returns an octal number. To prefix the octal result with 0, use the hash as you did with the hexadecimal.

```
sprintf( "%#o", 100 ) # => "0144"
```

Use %s to substitute a string argument into the format string.

```
sprintf( "Hello, %s", "Matz!" ) # => "Hello, Matz!"
```

This is the same as using the % method from String, as you saw in Chapter 1.

```
"Hello, %s" % "Matz!" # => "Hello, Matz!"
```

You can also feed this method an array:

```
birthdate = [ "November", 8, 2007 ]
p "He was born %s %d, %d." % birthdate
```

You can use % instead of sprintf wherever you want a formatted string.

For a string, the precision indicator sets the maximum number of characters that will be copied from the argument string. Here, only two characters are allowed from this substitution string:

```
sprintf( "Hello, %.2s", "Matz!" ) # => "Hello, Ma"
```

Table 10-1. Flag characters for sprintf

Flag	For field types	Description
[space]	bdeEfgGiouxX	Places a space at the start of a positive number.
[1–9]$	All field types	Absolute number of an argument for this field.
#	beEfgGoxX	For the field b, prefixes the result with 0b; for o, with 0; for x, with 0x; for X, with 0X. For e, E, f, g, and G, adds decimal point. For g and G, does not remove trailing spaces.
+	bdeEfgGiouxX	Adds a leading plus sign (+) to positive numbers.

Table 10-1. Flag characters for sprintf (continued)

Flag	For field types	Description
-	All field types	Left-justifies the result.
0	bdeEfgGiouxX	Pads result with zeros (0) instead of spaces.
*	All field types	Uses the next argument as the field width. If negative, left-justifies result. If asterisk (*) is followed by a number and a dollar sign ($), uses argument as width.

Table 10-2. Field types for sprintf

Field	Description
b	Converts a numeric argument to binary.
c	Converts a numeric argument (character code) to a character.
d	Converts a numeric argument to a decimal number. Same as i.
e	Converts a floating-point argument into exponential notation, using one digit before the decimal point. Defaults to six fractional digits. Compare with g.
E	Same as e, but uses E in result.
f	Converts a numeric argument to a floating-point number. Defaults to six fractional digits. Precision determines the number of fractional digits.
g	Converts a numeric argument to a floating-point number, using the exponential form if the exponent is less than -4 or greater than or equal to precision, otherwise using the form d.dddd. Compare with e.
G	Same as g, but uses E in result.
i	Converts a numeric argument to a decimal number. Same as d.
o	Converts a numeric argument to octal.
p	Same as argument.inspect where inspect gives you a printable version of the argument, with special characters escaped.
s	Substitutes an argument as a string. If the format string contains precision, at most that many characters are copied in the substitution.
u	Treats argument as an unsigned decimal. Negative integers are displayed as a 32-bit two's complement plus one for the underlying architecture (for example, $2**32+n$). Because Ruby has no inherent limit on the number of bits used to represent an integer, negative values are preceded by two leading periods, indicating an infinite number of leading sign bits.
x	Converts a numeric argument to hexadecimal with lowercase letters a through f. Negative numbers are displayed with two leading periods, indicating an infinite string of leading ffs.
X	Same as x, but uses uppercase letters A through F in the result. Negative numbers are displayed with two leading periods, indicating an infinite string of leading FFs.

Processing XML

Ruby has a growing number of XML facilities. Sean Russell's Ruby Electric XML (REXML) is built into Ruby, so it's an obvious choice for discussion (*http://www.germane-software.com/software/rexml*). Builder is built into Rails, so we will pay some attention to that as well (*http://rubyforge.org/projects/builder*).

Here are a couple more that I won't be showing you. Libxml-Ruby, a C-language Ruby binding to GNOME's libxml2 library, is a speedy alternative (see *http://libxml.rubyforge.org*). There is also XmlSimple, a Ruby translation of the Perl module `XML::Simple` (*http://xml-simple.rubyforge.org*). XmlSimple requires REXML.

The following discussions assume that you already know XML, so I won't be explaining what elements or attributes are, and so forth. There is so much I could tell you about, but I must be brief. You'll learn just enough about processing XML to be a little heady with the lunchroom crowd.

REXML

Because REXML is already part of Ruby, you get it free of charge. Example 10-1 shows a small program that creates an XML document from a here document and then writes the document out to standard output.

Example 10-1. mondo.rb

```
#!/usr/bin/env ruby

require 'rexml/document'
include REXML

address = <<XML
<address>
 <name><given>Mondo</given><family>Mangrove</family></name>
 <street>9876 Trekker St.</street>
 <city>Granola</city>
 <state>Colorado</state>
 <code>81000</code>
 <country>USA</country>
</address>
XML

document = Document.new( address )
puts document
```

You must require `rexml/document`. If you include the `REXML` namespace, you don't have to prefix the class name with `REXML` (as in `REXML::Document`). The `address` string holds the here document that contains an XML document—an address for our good friend Mondo Mangrove. The `Document` class from `REXML` represents an XML document. I use `puts` to write `document` to standard output.

```
<address>
 <name><given>Mondo</given><family>Mangrove</family></name>
 <street>9876 Trekker St.</street>
 <city>Granola</city>
 <state>Colorado</state>
 <code>81000</code>
 <country>USA</country>
</address>
```

The program shown in Example 10-2 puts together an XML document out of thin air and then displays it.

Example 10-2. mangrove.rb

```ruby
#!/usr/bin/env ruby

require 'rexml/document'
include REXML

document = Document.new

document << XMLDecl.new( "1.0", "UTF-8" )

document << Comment.new( "our good friend Mondo" )

document.add_element( "name", { "lang" => "en"})

given = document.root.add_element( "given" )
family = document.root.add_element( "family" )

given.add_attribute("nickname", "false")

given.text = "Mondo"
family.text = "Mangrove"

document.write( $stdout, 0 )
```

Document.new is called without any arguments because this program builds the XML file as it goes along. XMLDecl.new adds an XML declaration to the document, which will appear at the top. The first argument is the version information (1.0); the second is the encoding declaration (UTF-8). Without any arguments, XMLDecl.new creates a basic, default XML declaration (<?xml version='1.0'?>).

Comment.new creates a comment for insertion in the document, with the text our good friend Mondo.

The first call to the add_element method adds the root element name to the document with a lang attribute. The given and family elements are also added, and given is given an attribute called nickname with add_attribute. The text method adds text content to these new elements.

The write method pretty-prints the document to standard output (the second argument of write specifies the indentation). With write, the output appears as:

```xml
<?xml version='1.0' encoding='UTF-8'?>
<!--our good friend Mondo
-->
<name lang='en'>
  <given nickname='false'>Mondo</given>
  <family>Mangrove</family>
</name>
```

I don't want you to get the wrong idea. The way I did things in these examples is not the only way to do things. This little sampling should get you started. There are lots of things I didn't talk about, like deleting elements or attributes, stream parsing, and much more.

If you want to learn more, look at Sean Russell's tutorial on REXML at *http:// www.germane-software.com/software/rexml/docs/tutorial.html*, and also check out Koen Vervloesem's article "REXML: Processing XML in Ruby," at *http://www.xml.com/ pub/a/2005/11/09/rexml-processing-xml-in-ruby.html*. You'll find the online documentation for REXML at *http://www.ruby-doc.org/core/classes/REXML.html*.

Builder

Jim Weirich's XML Builder (*http://rubyforge.org/projects/builder*) is another way to create XML. It is currently at version 2.0.0. It first caught my attention when I found it was packaged in Rails. Personally, I find it a little easier to use than REXML, and you may, too.

Compare Example 10-2 with Example 10-3, which is in `Builder`.

Example 10-3. mondo_b.rb

```
#!/usr/bin/env ruby

require 'rubygems'
require_gem 'builder'

address = <<XML
<address>
 <name><given>Mondo</given><family>Mangrove</family></name>
 <street>9876 Trekker St.</street>
 <city>Granola</city>
 <state>Colorado</state>
 <code>81000</code>
 <country>USA</country>
</address>
XML

document = Builder::XmlMarkup.new( :target => address, :indent => 1 )
puts document.to_xs
```

In this example, you first require rubygems, then `builder` with `require_gem`. The `require_gem` method comes from the rubygems package. It can take another argument, allowing you to indicate what version of a package you want to use (see *http:// docs.rubygems.org/read/chapter/4#page71*).

The here document is saved in the string `address`, which is the target for the `XmlMarkup` object (similar to the `Document` object in REXML). You can also set the indentation of the output here. `puts` writes `document` to standard output with the help of the `to_xs` method—not that different from REXML on the surface.

Here's the output. A little to_xs tag follows the end tag of the root element:

```
<address>
 <name><given>Mondo</given><family>Mangrove</family></name>
 <street>9876 Trekker St.</street>
 <city>Granola</city>
 <state>Colorado</state>
 <code>81000</code>
 <country>USA</country>
</address>
<to_xs/>
```

Now compare Example 10-2 with Example 10-4.

Example 10-4. mangrove_b.rb

```ruby
#!/usr/bin/env ruby

require 'rubygems'
require_gem 'builder'
include Builder

document = XmlMarkup.new(:target => $stdout, :indent => 1)

document.instruct!

document.comment! "our good friend Mondo"

document.name( :lang => "en" ) {
  document.given "Mondo", :nickname => "false"
  document.family "Mangrove"
}
```

The target is standard output ($stdout). The XML declaration is formed with the instruct! method, and the comment with comment!. Notice how you use element names in the place of the method. (Would you guess there is a little metaprogramming magic going on in the background?)

I like how you can represent a parent/child relationship by enclosing the child elements in braces ({}). The output is sent to standard output.

```xml
<?xml version="1.0" encoding="UTF-8"?>
<!-- our good friend Mondo -->
<name lang="en">
 <given nickname="false">Mondo</given>
 <family>Mangrove</family>
</name>
```

REXML has more features than Builder and is built into Ruby, but Builder has a Rubyness that is hard for me to resist.

You will find a tutorial for Builder (written by yours truly) at *http://www.xml.com/pub/a/2006/01/04/creating-xml-with-ruby-and-builder.html*, and full documentation at *http://builder.rubyforge.org*.

Date and Time

Figuring out the day and time is important in daily life and in computing, so Ruby naturally offers facilities to do so. In this section, I'll talk about Ruby's Date and Time classes.

The Time Class

I cover many of the most commonly used Time methods here. See *http://ruby-doc.org/ core/classes/Time.html* for documentation on all the Time methods.

To determine the current time, use the now method (or its synonym new) from Time. Calling the method twice can help you determine how much time has elapsed in between.

```
start = Time.now # => Tue Jan 30 04:12:50 -0700 2007
stop = Time.now # => Tue Jan 30 04:13:00 -0700 2007
```

To set a given time, use the local method (mktime is a synonym):

```
local_time = Time.local( 2007, "jan", 30, 1, 15, 20 )
# => Tue Jan 30 01:15:20 -0700 2007
```

The arguments to this call to local are (in order) year, month, date, hour, minutes, seconds. You can also call local with these arguments:

```
my_time = Time.local( 20, 15, 1, 30, "jan", 2007, 2, 30, false, "MST")
# => Tue Jan 30 01:15:20 -0700 2007
```

In this call, the arguments, in order, are seconds, minutes, hour, day, month, year, day of the week, day of the year, is-it-daylight-savings-time?, and timezone.

From a Time object you can get all kinds of particulars, such as the day, the day of the week, and the day of the year:

```
stop.day # the day of the month => 30
stop.yday # how many days so far this year => 30
stop.wday # the day of the week => 2, or Tue (Sun == 0)
```

You can retrieve the year, the month, and the timezone:

```
stop.year # => 2007
stop.month # => 1 (January)
stop.zone # timezone => "MST" or Mountain Standard Time
```

You can find out the hour of the day and the number of minutes and seconds on that hour:

```
stop.hour # => 4
stop.min # => 13
stop.sec # => 0
```

Canonical refers to a standard determined by a set of rules. Ruby uses standards such as ISO 8601, "Data elements and interchange formats—Information interchange—

Representation of dates and times" (*http://www.iso.ch/iso/en/CatalogueDetailPage. CatalogueDetail?CSNUMBER=40874*), and RFC 2822, "Internet Message Format" (*http://www.ietf.org/rfc/rfc2822.txt*), to determine how to format times (though I cannot claim to know whether Ruby conforms to these specifications in every detail). You can get a canonical string for a given time using ctime (or asctime). It looks like the same time format you would see in an email message.

```
local_time.ctime # => "Tue Jan 30 01:15:20 2007"
```

Query a Time object with utc? (or gmt?) to determine whether it represents Coordinated Universal Time, or UTC (also known as Greenwich Mean Time or GMT):

```
local_time.utc? # => false
```

Check whether a time is daylight savings time or not with dst? or isdst:

```
my_time.dst? # => false
```

Check for the equality of two time objects with eql? or the spaceship operator <=>:

```
# make a new time object time
temp = stop # => Tue Jan 30 04:13:00 -0700 2007
stop.object_id # => 1667650
temp.object_id # => 1667650

# true or false
start.eql? stop # => false

# same object, so true
temp.eql? stop # => true

# start is less than stop
start <=> stop # => -1

# stop is greater than start
stop <=> start # => 1

# same object, so 0
temp <=> stop # => 0
```

You can see the difference in two Time objects by subtracting them:

```
stop - start # => 10.112668 (in seconds)
```

There is about a 10-second difference between stop and start.

Add seconds and multiples of seconds to add to a time with +:

```
stop.inspect # => "Tue Jan 30 04:13:00 -0700 2007"

# Add a minute (60 seconds)
stop + 60 # => Tue Jan 30 04:14:00 -0700 2007

# Add an hour (60*60)
stop + 60*60 # => Tue Jan 30 05:13:00 -0700 2007
```

```
# Add three hours (60*60*3)
stop + 60*60*3 # => Tue Jan 30 07:13:00 -0700 2007

# Add a day (60*60*24)
stop + 60*60*24 # => Wed Jan 31 04:13:00 -0700 2007
```

The Date Class

I'll present some of the Date methods in this section, but certainly not all. For documentation on all the Date methods, go to *http://ruby-doc.org/core/classes/Date.html*.

To create a Date object, use the new method (or its synonym civil). You must require the Date class before using it. The to_s method returns the date as a string.

```
require 'date'

date = Date.new( 2006, 11, 8 )

date.to_s # => "2006-11-08"
```

With the today class method, you can create a date based on today's date:

```
today = Date.today
today.to_s # => "2007-01-30"
```

Use expression substitution to show the date in a user-specified format. This line of code uses the month, day, and year methods from Date.

```
puts "The date was #{date.month}/#{date.day}/#{date.year}."
# => The date was 11/8/2006.
```

What's the next day?

```
date.next.to_s # => "2006-11-09"
```

next finds the next day but does not change date in-place. (A synonym for next is succ.)

Add 61 days to a date:

```
(date + 61).to_s # => "2007-01-08"
```

Subtract 61 days from a date:

```
(date - 61).to_s # => "2006-09-08"
```

Add and subtract six months using the >> and << methods.

```
(date >> 6).to_s # => "2007-05-08"
(date << 6).to_s # => "2006-05-08"
```

With Date's downto method, count down five days, displaying each date as you go (this makes in-place changes to the date):

```
date.downto( date - 5 ) { |date| puts date }
2006-11-08
2006-11-07
```

```
2006-11-06
2006-11-05
2006-11-04
2006-11-03

# date has changed
date.to_s # => "2007-11-03"
```

Now, using the upto method, add the same amount of days back, showing the dates as you progress along:

```
date.upto( date + 5 ) { |date| puts date }
2006-11-03
2006-11-04
2006-11-05
2006-11-06
2006-11-07
2006-11-08

date.to_s # => "2006-11-08"
```

Like Time, you can check for the equality of two date objects with eql? or the spaceship operator <=>:

```
# make a new date object time
temp = date
temp.object_id # => 2708130
date.object_id # => 2708130

# true or false
date.eql? today # => false

# same object, so true
temp.eql? date # => true

# date is less than today
date <=> today # => -1

# today is greater than date
today <=> date # => 1

# same object, so 0
temp <=> date # => 0
```

Calendar forms

The Gregorian calendar system (since A.D. 1582) has largely replaced the Julian system (45 B.C.), though the Julian system is still in use by Orthodox churches. One of the main reasons for this 16th-century reform was that the dates for events such as the equinox were shifting to earlier in the year. (Compare *http://en.wikipedia.org/wiki/Gregorian_calendar* with *http://en.wikipedia.org/wiki/Julian_calendar*.)

A date can conform to the Gregorian or Julian calendar by adding a fourth argument to new:

```
gdate = Date.new( 2006, 11, 8, "Gregorian" )

jdate = Date.new( 2006, 11, 8, "Julian" )
```

To see the difference between Julian and Gregorian dates (there is a difference of more than 10 days), find the Julian day with the `julian` method:

```
date.julian.to_s # => "2006-10-26"
```

Likewise, you can find the Gregorian day with `gregorian`.

```
date.gregorian.to_s # => "2006-11-08"
```

You can get the Julian day (days from January 1, 4713 B.C., starting from 0) with the `jd` instance method:

```
date.jd # => 2454048
```

You can even create a year based on the Julian day with the `jd` class method:

```
nd = Date.jd( 2454048 )
nd.to_s # => "2006-11-08"
```

The modified Julian day (days since November 17, 1858) with `mjd`:

```
date.mjd # => 54047
```

The astronomical Julian day is available via `ajd`:

```
date.ajd # => 4908095/2
```

Much more could be said about different calendar forms and conversions between them, but this section has offered a sufficient introduction. For more information, see the Date and Time class documentation at *http://www.ruby-doc.org/core*. Also of interest is the DateTime class, which represents both a date and a time; see *http://ruby-doc.org/core/classes/DateTime.html*.

Reflection

Ruby can easily tell you about itself—its programs and objects—through methods that, taken as a whole, constitute a feature called *reflection*. You've seen a few of these methods in action earlier in this book. I'll go over some of the most frequently called methods and point out some others you may find useful.

Using a here document (see Chapter 4), I'll define a string, a bit of a Walt Whitman poem, and then do some reflecting on it.

```
asiponder = <<whitman
As I ponder'd in silence,
Returning upon my poems, considering, lingering long,
A Phantom arose before me, with distrustful aspect,
Terrible in beauty, age, and power,
The genius of poets of old lands
whitman # => "As I ponder'd in silence, \nReturning upon my poems, considering,
lingering long, \nA Phantom arose before me, with distrustful aspect, \nTerrible in
beauty, age, and power, \nThe genius of poets of old lands\n"
```

asiponder is an instance of the String class. The Object class has a class method that returns the name of an instance's class:

```
asiponder.class # => String
```

The class method supercedes Object's deprecated method type, or gets the name of the class as a string with the name method:

```
asiponder.class.name # => "String"
```

To determine the name of the superclass—the parent class that is one step higher in the class hierarchy—use the superclass method from Class.

```
asiponder.class.superclass # => Object
String.superclass # => Object
```

Discover the names of any of the included modules of an instance or its class using the included_modules method from Module.

```
asiponder.class.included_modules # => [Enumerable, Comparable, Kernel]
asiponder.class.superclass.included_modules # => [Kernel]

String.included_modules # => [Enumerable, Comparable, Kernel]
Object.included_modules # => [Kernel]
```

Each object has its own numeric object ID. You can find out what this ID is with the object_id method from Object.

```
whitman = asiponder # copy one string object to another
whitman == asiponder # => true
asiponder.object_id # => 968680
whitman.object_id # => 968680
```

These objects are identical and have the same object ID, a hint that Ruby is managing resources efficiently. (The id method from Object has been deprecated; use object_id instead.)

You can also test to see if an object is an instance of a given class with the instance_of? method from Object:

```
asiponder.instance_of? String # => true
asiponder.instance_of? Fixnum # => false
```

Use instance_of? for robustness. In other words, don't do the block (do |t|...end) unless the variable asiponder is a string.

```
if asiponder.instance_of?( String )
  asiponder.split.each do |t|
    puts t
  end
end
```

Or use Object's is_a? or kind_of? methods (they are synonyms):

```
asiponder.is_a? String # => true
asiponder.kind_of? String # => true
```

Unlike instance_of?, is_of? or kind_of? also work if the argument is a superclass or module.

```
asiponder.is_a? Object # => true
asiponder.kind_of? Kernel # => true
asiponder.instance_of? Object # => false
```

Look at an object's ancestors with Module's ancestors method, which returns a list of both classes and modules:

```
asiponder.class.ancestors # => [String, Enumerable, Comparable, Object, Kernel]
String.ancestors # => [String, Enumerable, Comparable, Object, Kernel]
```

Reflection on Variables and Constants

Now let's examine variables and constants. Let's do this in *irb*. First I'll define a few variables based on some familiar elements from Joseph Conrad's *Lord Jim*:

```
irb(main):001:0> $ship = "Patna"
=> "Patna"
irb(main):002:0> @friend_1 = "Marlow"
=> "Marlow"
irb(main):003:0> @friend_2 = "Jewel"
=> "Jewel"
irb(main):004:0> bad_chap = "'Gentleman' Brown"
=> "'Gentleman' Brown"
```

Let's use some methods to find out about these variables. Do we have any local variables in the lot? Use Kernel's local_variables method to find out.

```
irb(main):005:0> local_variables
=> ["_", "bad_chap"]
```

We have bad_chap, and _, a peculiar animal that gives you the last value in *irb* (conf. last_value also returns the last value).

Return the instance variables with Object's instance_variables:

```
irb(main):006:0> instance_variables
=> ["@friend_2", "@friend_1"]
```

Kernel's method global_variables returns all the global variables, including $ship.

```
irb(main):007:0> global_variables
=> ["$-p", "$:", "$FILENAME", "$defout", "$,", "$`", "$binding", "$-v", "$stdin",
"$PROGRAM_NAME", "$\"", "$?", "$\\", "$=", "$-d", "$>", "$8", "$-F", "$-a",
"$VERBOSE", "$0", "$LOAD_PATH", "$$", "$-0", "$+", "$!", "$DEBUG", "$stderr", "$~",
"$;", "$SAFE", "$<", "$_", "$-K", "$-l", "$-I", "$-i", "$deferr", "$/", "$'", "$@",
"$-w", "$stdout", "$ship", "$*", "$LOADED_FEATURES", "$.", "$KCODE"]
```

Want to know what constants the Object class (or some other class) has? Use the constants method from Module (output is truncated):

```
irb(main):008:0> Object.constants.sort # => ["ARGF", "ARGV", "ArgumentError",
"Array", ... ]
```

I added the sort method (from Array) on the end to make the results more readable.

Reflection on Methods

The `Object` method `methods` returns a list of names of publicly accessible methods from an object, including the methods accessible from the ancestors of the object. Here is a sample call (truncated):

```
irb(main):009:0> Object.methods.sort
=> ["<", "<=", "<=>", "==", "===", "=~", ">", ">=", "__id__", "__send__", "allocate",
"ancestors", "autoload", "autoload?", "class", "class_eval", "class_variables",
"clone", ... ]
```

You can inquire after instance methods with a method from `Module`:

```
irb(main):010:0> Object.instance_methods.sort
=> ["==", "===", "=~", "__id__", "__send__", "class", "clone", "display", "dup",
"eql?", "equal?", "extend", "freeze", "frozen?", ... ]
```

You can also query about methods with the `Object` methods `private_methods`, `protected_methods`, `public_methods`, and `singleton_methods`. `Module` also has the methods `private_instance_methods`, `protected_instance_methods`, and `public_instance_methods`.

Here is a sample call to `Object`'s `private_methods` with `puts`:

```
irb(main):010:0> puts Object.private_methods.sort
Array
Float
Integer
String
...
```

The `respond_to?` method from `Object` lets you check to see if a given object responds to a given method. You have to refer to a method as a symbol.

```
Object.respond_to? :instance_methods # => true

class A
  attr_accessor :x
end

a = A.new

a.respond_to? :x # => true
a.respond_to? :x= # => true
a.respond_to? :y # => false
```

Using Tk

Back in Chapter 1, you saw a little program that created a graphical version of "Hello, Matz!" with the Tk toolkit, which comes with Ruby as part of its standard library (*http://www.ruby-doc.org/stdlib*). Tk is a library—a widget toolkit—of basic elements for creating graphical user interfaces. It works on a variety of platforms and is open source. John Ousterhout developed Tk as an extension for his Tcl scripting language. For more information on Tk, see *http://www.tcl.tk*.

Example 10-5 shows another Tk program. It manipulates the font, the size of the label, and colors. It also provides a Quit button.

Example 10-5. tk.rb

```ruby
#!/usr/bin/env ruby

require 'tk'

TkRoot.new {title "Ruby is fun!" }

TkLabel.new {
  font TkFont.new( 'mistral 42' )
  text "Ruby is fun, in case you didn't notice!"
  width 30
  height 3
  fg 'blue'
  pack
}

TkButton.new {
  text 'Quit'
  command 'exit'
  pack
}

Tk.mainloop
```

The Tk window is labeled with the title Ruby is fun!. A label containing the text Ruby is fun, in case you didn't notice! appears in the center of the pane. The font is Mistral and the font size is 42. (Mistral may not be available on your system, so you may have to change the font to run this program without an error.)

The foreground color (fg), the color of the text, is blue. The width is 30 and the height is 3. A button labeled Quit performs the exit command. The mainloop method makes everything happen.

Run the program with:

    tk.rb &

If you are on a Unix/Linux system, the & at the end of the command puts the process in the background. Don't use it if you are on Windows.

The graphic in Figure 10-1 will appear on your display. Click Quit to exit the program.

The program in Example 10-6 displays a photo of my horse, Sunrise.

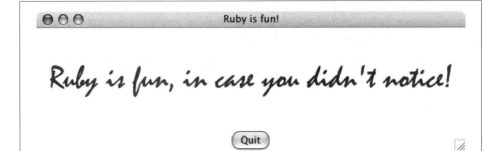

Figure 10-1. Ruby is fun!

Example 10-6. photo.rb

```ruby
#!/usr/bin/env ruby

require 'tk'
require "tkextlib/tkimg/jpeg"
require "open-uri"

photo = open("http://www.wyeast.net/images/sunrise.jpg", "rb") {|io| io.read}

TkRoot.new {title "Sunrise" }

TkLabel.new {
  image TkPhotoImage.new( :data => Tk::BinaryString( photo ) )
  width 300
  pack
}

TkLabel.new {
  font TkFont.new( 'verdana 24 bold' )
  text "Sunrise at sunset!"
  pack
}

TkButton.new {
  text 'Quit'
  command 'exit'
  pack
}

Tk.mainloop
```

This program opens a URI with a photo of my mare Sunrise in JPEG format, as shown in Figure 10-2, with the open method from the OpenURI class. The tkextlib/tkimg/jpeg or Tk::Img::JPEG library helps Tk handle JPEG images. The data from the photo is stored in photo. The title of the window is "Sunrise." The TkPhotoImage class manages the image. The label "Sunrise at sunset!" appears below the photo. A Quit button lets you exit gracefully.

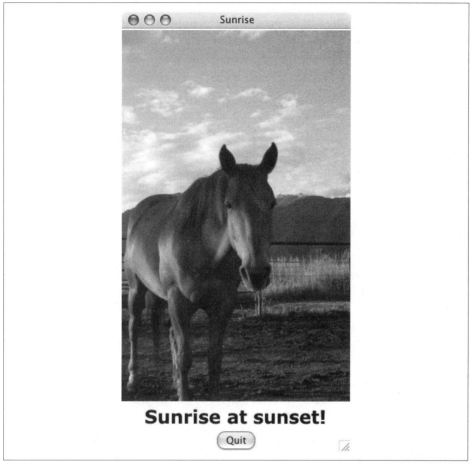

Figure 10-2. Sunrise, my quarter horse, at sunset

If you want to further explore Tk, I recommend a gallery of Ruby Tk examples at *http://pub.cozmixng.org/~the-rwiki/rw-cgi.rb?cmd=view;name=%B5%D5%B0%FA%A 4%ADRuby%2FTk*. The text is in Japanese, so if you aren't fluent in Japanese, you will only be able to read the code examples. The code is the key.

Metaprogramming

Metaprogramming is a shorthand way to write a program, or part of one, with another program. In the previous chapter, you saw metaprogramming in practice when calling the `attr` family of methods (`attr`, `attr_reader`, `attr_writer`, and `attr_ accessor` from the `Module` class) to create getter and setter methods for classes. Now you will have a chance here to do a little metaprogramming yourself.

One key is the define_method method from Module, which allows you to create methods on the fly. Have a look at the program in Example 10-7, which creates a method using the names from each element in an array.

Example 10-7. meta.rb

```ruby
#!/usr/bin/env ruby

class Meta
  %w{ jane elizabeth mary kitty lydia }.each do |n|
    define_method(n) { puts "My name is #{n.capitalize} Bennet." }
  end
end

Meta.instance_methods - Object.instance_methods #  => ["jane", "elizabeth", "mary",
"kitty", "lydia"]

meta = Meta.new

meta.elizabeth # => My name is Elizabeth Bennet.
```

Yes, the names in the string array (%w{...}) are the names of the five Bennet sisters in Jane Austen's *Pride and Prejudice*. The each method feeds all the elements of the array to the define_method method as n. Each method will output (puts) a string that contains a capitalized version of each string element by means of expression substitution (#{n.capitalize}).

When you instantiate Meta and call the instance method elizabeth, you get the output My name is Elizabeth Bennet. And that, ladies and gentlemen, is an example of metaprogramming, pure and simple.

Other reflective methods and practices could be put to good use when metaprogramming in Ruby, but you've made a fine start with define_method. Rails is full of metaprogramming, and that is one reasons it is so popular: it is smart enough to do a considerable amount of programming for you based on minimal input.

RubyGems

RubyGems is a package utility for Ruby (*http://rubyforge.org/projects/rubygems*) written by Jim Weirich. It installs Ruby software packages and keeps them up to date. RubyGems is quite easy to learn and use—even easier than tools like the Unix/Linux tar utility (*http://www.gnu.org/software/tar*) or Java's jar utility (*http://java.sun.com/ j2se/1.5.0/docs/tooldocs/windows/jar.html*).

For more information, read the RubyGems documentation at *http://docs.rubygems.org/*. The *RubyGems User Guide* (*http://docs.rubygems.org/read/book/1*) gives you most everything you need to know about using RubyGems. There is also a command Reference (*http://docs.rubygems.org/read/book/2*).

RubyGems likely was installed on your system when you installed Ruby. To make sure, type on Unix or Linux:

```
$ which gem
/usr/local/bin/gem
```

Or just check the version by typing:

```
$ gem -v
0.9.0
```

or:

```
$ gem --version
0.9.0
```

 If you don't have RubyGems installed, go to Chapter 3 of the *Ruby-Gems User Guide* at *http://rubygems.org/read/chapter/3* for complete installation instructions.

Let's start from scratch—by getting help on how to issue RubyGems commands:

```
$ gem
RubyGems is a sophisticated package manager for Ruby.  This is a
basic help message containing pointers to more information.

  Usage:
    gem -h/--help
    gem -v/--version
    gem command [arguments...] [options...]

  Examples:
    gem install rake
    gem list --local
    gem build package.gemspec
    gem help install

  Further help:
    gem help commands            list all 'gem' commands
    gem help examples            show some examples of usage
    gem help <COMMAND>           show help on COMMAND
                                   (e.g. 'gem help install')
  Further information:
    http://rubygems.rubyforge.org
```

Now let's get help on what commands are available (some output truncated).

```
$ gem help commands

GEM commands are:

  build         Build a gem from a gemspec
  ...
  specification Display gem specification (in yaml)
  uninstall     Uninstall a gem from the local repository
```

```
    unpack        Unpack an installed gem to the current directory
    update        Update the named gem (or all installed gems) in the local repository

For help on a particular command, use 'gem help COMMAND'.

Commands may be abbreviated, so long as they are unambiguous.
e.g. 'gem i rake' is short for 'gem install rake'.
```

Let's look at the help on examples (some output truncated).

```
$ gem help examples

Some examples of 'gem' usage.

* Install 'rake', either from local directory or remote server:

    gem install rake

* Install 'rake', only from remote server:

    gem install rake --remote

* Install 'rake' from remote server, and run unit tests,
  and generate RDocs:

    gem install --remote rake --test --rdoc --ri
...

* See information about RubyGems:

    gem environment
```

Select a command—why not environment—and get more help on that. You don't have to type out the full word *environment*, just enough for gem to disambiguate it (env is enough).

```
$ gem help env
Usage: gem environment [args] [options]

    Common Options:
          --source URL                 Use URL as the remote source for gems
      -p, --[no-]http-proxy [URL]      Use HTTP proxy for remote operations
      -h, --help                       Get help on this command
      -v, --verbose                    Set the verbose level of output
          --config-file FILE           Use this config file instead of default
          --backtrace                  Show stack backtrace on errors
          --debug                      Turn on Ruby debugging

    Arguments:
      packageversion  display the package version
      gemdir          display the path where gems are installed
      gempath         display path used to search for gems
      version         display the gem format version
      remotesources   display the remote gem servers
      <omitted>       display everything
```

```
Summary:
   Display RubyGems environmental information
```

Show everything on the RubyGems environment with this command:

```
$ gem env
Rubygems Environment:
  - VERSION: 0.9.0 (0.9.0)
  - INSTALLATION DIRECTORY: /usr/local/lib/ruby/gems/1.8
  - GEM PATH:
     - /usr/local/lib/ruby/gems/1.8
  - REMOTE SOURCES:
     - http://gems.rubyforge.org
```

These are the results on Mac OS X Tiger. Now just show the RubyGems installation directory:

```
$ gem env gemdir
/usr/local/lib/ruby/gems/1.8
```

Let's check to see if Ruby on Rails is present with the list command.

```
$ gem list rails

*** LOCAL GEMS ***
```

It doesn't appear to be there. Go ahead and install it with the install command and sudo (superuser), which will require a password (output truncated in the following code). I am running this command on Mac OS X. The --include-dependencies option installs Rails with all of its dependencies. The output on your system may look different; for example, Windows does not require superuser if the logged-in user has the appropriate administrative privileges, so you won't be prompted for a password in that case.

```
$ sudo gem install rails --include-dependencies
Password:
Bulk updating Gem source index for: http://gems.rubyforge.org
....
```

You can check what dependencies a gem has with the dependency command:

```
$ gem dep rails
Gem rails-1.2.3
  rake (>= 0.7.2)
  activesupport (= 1.4.2)
  activerecord (= 1.15.3)
  actionpack (= 1.13.3)
  actionmailer (= 1.3.3)
  actionwebservice (= 1.2.3)
```

To select dependencies as you install a package, skip the --include-dependencies option (this is not recommended; it is error-prone, as you have to confirm each one individually).

```
$ sudo gem install rails
```

To update all the gems on your system with all the current versions, use the update command. The `--system` flag updates the RubyGems system software (some output truncated).

```
$ sudo gem update --system
Password:
Updating RubyGems...
Need to update 2 gems from http://gems.rubyforge.org
..
complete
Attempting remote update of rubygems-update
Successfully installed rubygems-update-0.9.0
Updating version of RubyGems to 0.9.0
Installing RubyGems 0.9.0
...
  Successfully built RubyGem
  Name: sources
  Version: 0.0.1
  File: sources-0.0.1.gem
RubyGems system software updated
```

To uninstall a package with the uninstall command:

```
$ sudo gem uninstall rails
Password:
Successfully uninstalled rails version 1.1.6
Remove executables and scripts for
'rails' in addition to the gem? [Yn]
Removing rails
```

Now you know the basics of RubyGems. To learn more, consult the *RubyGems User Guide* (*http://docs.rubygems.org/read/book/1*). Go to *http://rubygems.rubyforge.org/wiki/wiki.pl?CreateAGemInTenMinutes* to learn how to create your own RubyGems package.

Exception Handling

Exceptions occur when a program gets off course and the normal program flow is interrupted. Ruby is already prepared to handle such problems with its own built-in exceptions, but you can handle them in your own way with exception handling.

Ruby's exception handing model is similar to the C++ and Java models. Table 10-3 shows a comparison of the keywords or methods used to perform exception handling in all three languages. If you are a sage programmer, this table will be a touchstone for you.

Table 10-3. C++, Java, and Ruby exception handling compared

C++	Java	Ruby
try {}	try {}	begin/end
catch {}	catch {}	rescue keyword (or catch method)
Not applicable	finally	ensure
throw	throw	raise (or throw method)

As usual, let's look at an example. If you try to divide by zero in a Ruby program, Ruby is going to complain. (Wouldn't you?) Try it in *irb*:

```
irb(main):001:0> 12 / 0
ZeroDivisionError: divided by 0
        from (irb):1:in `/'
        from (irb):1
```

Ruby knew just how to complain, so by default, it handed you a ZeroDivisionError.

You can do things Ruby's way, or you can handle this error your own way by using the rescue and ensure clauses, as shown in Example 10-8. This little program's *raison d'être* is to show you how exceptions work in Ruby.

Example 10-8. divide_by_zero.rb

```
begin
    eval "12 / 0"
rescue ZeroDivisionError
    puts "Oops. You tried to divide by zero again."
    exit 1
ensure
    puts "Tsk. Tsk."
end
```

The condescending output from this program is:

```
Oops. You tried to divide by zero again.
Tsk. Tsk.
```

Here's a brief analysis. The eval method (from Kernel) evaluates a string as a Ruby statement. The result is disastrous, as you well know, but this time the rescue clause catches the error, gives you a custom report in the form of the Oops string, and exits the program. (exit is another Kernel method; the argument 1 is a catchall for general errors.) You can have more than one ensure clause if your program calls for it.

Instead of giving its default message—that is, ZeroDivisionError: divided by 0—Ruby returns the message in rescue, plus the message in ensure. Even though the program exited at the end of the rescue clause, ensure yields its block, no matter what.

You don't have to wait for Ruby to raise an exception at you: you can raise one on your own with the raise method from Kernel (*http://www.ruby-doc.org/core/classes/Kernel.html*). If things go haywire (not to your liking) in a program, you can raise an exception with raise:

```
bad_dog = true

if bad_dog
  raise StandardError, "bad doggy"
else
  arf_arf
end
StandardError: bad doggy
```

If called without arguments, raise raises a `RuntimeError` if there was no previous exception. If raise has only a `String` argument, it raises a `RuntimeError` with the argument as a message. If the first argument is an exception, such as `StandardError`, the exception is raised with the given message, if such a message is present.

`Kernel` also has the `catch` and `throw` methods. `catch` executes a block that will properly terminate if there is no accompanying `throw`. If a `throw` accompanies `catch`, Ruby searches for a `catch` that has the same symbol as the `throw`. `catch` will then return the value given to `throw`, if present.

The program in Example 10-9 is an adaptation of an example that came with the *ri* documentation for `catch`. `throw` sends a message to `catch` if n is less than or equal to 0.

Example 10-9. catch.rb

```ruby
#!/usr/bin/env ruby

def limit( n )
  puts n
  throw :done if n <= 0
  limit( n-1 )
end

catch( :done ) { limit( 5 ) }
```

Creating Documentation with RDoc

RDoc is a tool for generating documentation from Ruby source files, whether written in Ruby or C. It was created by Dave Thomas (*http://www.pragmaticprogrammer.com*), and comes as part of the Ruby distribution. Documentation is available at *http://rdoc.sourceforge.net/doc/index.html*.

RDoc parses Ruby source code and collects information from comments, as well as information about methods, constants, and other things. It cross-references what it can before producing default XHTML output in a doc subdirectory. You can embed codes in your comments, too, allowing RDoc to format a page according to your taste.

 If you are a Java refugee, you'll be happy to know that RDoc is similar to Java's Javadoc (*http://java.sun.com/j2se/javadoc*).

RDoc Basics

I'll present the basics of RDoc here using the file *ratios.rb*, which contains the class `Ratios`. The methods in this class calculate a few financial ratios.

I first show the file piece by piece, then later, the whole file. I'll walk you through how to mark up your Ruby source files, and then show you how to process these files to get XHTML or other output. Of course, I won't show you everything you can do with RDoc, just some of the most important things.

The comments before the `class` definition begins are interpreted as general documentation for the class and are placed before any other documentation. Example 10-10 shows the beginning of *ratios.rb*.

Example 10-10. Beginning of ratios.rb

```
# This class provides a few methods for calculating financial ratios.
# So far, three ratios are available:
# 1. debt-equity ratio (_der_)
# 2. long-term debt ratio (_ltdr_)
# 3. total debt ratio (_tdr_)
#
# Author:: Mike Fitzgerald (mailto:mike@example.com)
# Copyright:: Wy'east Communications
#
# :title:Ratios

class Ratios
```

Paragraphs in the comments become paragraphs in the documentation. Numbered lists (1., 2., 3., etc.) become numbered lists. Labels followed by double colons (::) line up the text that follows in tabular form. The :title: directive lets RDoc know what you want the title of the XHTML document(s) to be (what goes inside <head> **<title></title>**</head>).

Next is some documentation for the initialize method.

```
# The +new+ class method initializes the class.
# === Parameters
# * _debt_ = long-term debt
# * _equity_ = equity
# === Example
#   ratios = Ratios.new( 2456, 9876 )

def initialize( debt, equity )
  @debt = debt
  @equity = equity
end
```

Text enclosed by plus signs (+new+) will be shown in a typewriter (constant width) font in XHTML, and text enclosed in underscores (as in _debt_) will be shown in *italic*. Lines preceded by asterisks (*) will be set off as bullets in the XHTML. Words preceded by equals signs (such as === Example) will be headings in the result, varying in font size depending on the number of equals signs (the more you use, the smaller the font of the heading; one = for a level-one heading, two == for a level two, and so forth). Text that is indented by several spaces will also show up in typewriter font.

The markup in this fragment is a little different:

```
# The <tt>ltdr</tt> method returns a long-term debt ratio.
# === Formula
#     long-term debt
#     ------------------- = long-term debt ratio
#   long-term debt/equity
# === Parameters
# The parameters are:
# * <i>debt</i> = long-term debt
# * <i>equity</i> = equity
# === Example
#   ratios = Ratios.new( 2456, 9876 )
#   ratios.ltdr # => The long-term debt ratio is 0.20.
#   ratios.ltdr 1234, 56789 # => The long-term debt ratio is 0.02.

  def ltdr( debt=@debt, equity=@equity )
    ratio = debt/(debt+equity).to_f
    printf( "The long-term debt ratio is %.2f.\n", ratio )
    ratio
  end
```

Marking up text in tt tags (`<tt>ltdr</tt>`) is the same as marking it up with plus signs (+ltdr+). Likewise, marking up text in i tags (`<i>debt</i>`) is the same as marking it up with underscores (_debt_). The indented text under the Formula heading will be displayed in typewriter font in XHTML.

The remainder of the file, shown in Example 10-11, has markup similar to what you have already seen. Figure 10-3 illustrates how the XHTML documentation will appear in a browser.

Example 10-11. Remainder of ratios.rb

```
# This class provides a few methods for calculating financial ratios.
# So far, three ratios are available:
# 1. debt-equity ratio (_der_)
# 2. long-term debt ratio (_ltdr_)
# 3. total debt ratio (_tdr_)
#
# Author:: Mike Fitzgerald (mailto:mike@example.com)
# Copyright:: Wy'east Communications
#
# :title:Ratios

class Ratios

# The +new+ class method initializes the class.
# === Parameters
# * _debt_ = long-term debt
# * _equity_ = equity
# === Example
#   ratios = Ratios.new( 2456, 9876 )
  def initialize( debt, equity )
```

Example 10-11. Remainder of ratios.rb (continued)

```
    @debt = debt
    @equity = equity
  end

# The <tt>ltdr</tt> method returns a long-term debt ratio.
# === Formula
#      long-term debt
#  -------------------- = long-term debt ratio
#  long-term debt/equity
# === Parameters
# The parameters are:
# * <i>debt</i> = long-term debt
# * <i>equity</i> = equity
# === Example
#  ratios = Ratios.new( 2456, 9876 )
#  ratios.ltdr # => The long-term debt ratio is 0.20.
#  ratios.ltdr 1234, 56789 # => The long-term debt ratio is 0.02.

  def ltdr( debt=@debt, equity=@equity )
    ratio = debt/(debt+equity).to_f
    printf( "The long-term debt ratio is %.2f.\n", ratio )
    ratio
  end

# The <tt>der</tt> method returns a debt-equity ratio.
# === Formula
#      long-term debt
#  -------------------- = debt-equity ratio
#          equity
# === Parameters
# The parameters are:
# * <i>debt</i> = long-term debt
# * <i>equity</i> = equity
# === Example
#  ratios = Ratios.new( 2456, 9876 )
#  ratios.der # => The debt-equity ratio is 0.25.
#  ratios.der( 1301, 7690 ) # => The debt-equity ratio is 0.17.

  def der( debt=@debt, equity=@equity )
    ratio = debt/equity.to_f
    printf( "The debt-equity ratio is %.2f.\n", ratio )
    ratio
  end

# The class method +tdr+ returns total debt ratio.
# === Formula
#    total liabilities
#  -------------------- = total debt ratio
#       total assets
# === Parameters
```

Example 10-11. Remainder of ratios.rb (continued)

```
# The parameters are:
# * _liabilities_ = total liabilities
# * _assets_ = total assets
# === Example
#   Ratios.tdr( 14_000, 23_000 ) # => The total debt ratio is 0.61.

 def Ratios.tdr( liabilities, assets )
   ratio = liabilities/assets.to_f
   printf( "The total debt ratio is %.2f.\n", ratio )
   ratio
 end

end
```

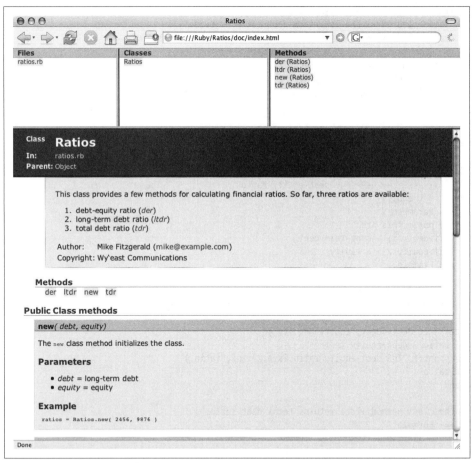

Figure 10-3. Ratios class documentation in RDoc

Processing Files with RDoc

Now that you know how to mark up files, let's talk about how to process them. Double-check to see if the rdoc command is available from a shell or command prompt. On Mac OS X and Linux systems, you can just do:

```
$ which rdoc
/usr/local/bin/rdoc
```

or run:

```
$ rdoc --version
RDoc V1.0.1 - 20041108
```

or:

```
$ rdoc -v
RDoc V1.0.1 - 20041108
```

Assume there is a directory, Ratios, that just contains one file, *ratios.rb*. You could run RDoc without any options or file specifications:

```
$ rdoc
```

or run rdoc on *ratios.rb*:

```
rdoc ratios.rb
```

Either way, as long at there is only one file in the directory, you will see output from the command like the following:

```
                    ratios.rb: c....
Generating HTML...

Files:   1
Classes: 1
Modules: 0
Methods: 4
Elapsed: 0.363s
```

As RDoc generated XHTML, it also created the doc subdirectory, which contains a variety of files:

```
$ ls doc
classes            fr_class_index.html    index.html
created.rid        fr_file_index.html     rdoc-style.css
files              fr_method_index.html
```

I won't drill down to what each of the files is for, but here are the brass tacks: *index. html* in Example 10-12 contains frames that link to all the files prefixed by fr_; the *rdoc-style.css* file is a Cascading Style Sheet (CSS); the file *created.rid* contains text, a timestamp of when everything was created; the directories classes and files contains files to make everything work together (that's all you really need to know about them at this point).

Example 10-12. RDoc-generated index.html

```
<html xmlns="http://www.w3.org/1999/xhtml" xml:lang="en" lang="en">
<head>
  <title>Ratios</title>
  <meta http-equiv="Content-Type" content="text/html; charset=iso-8859-1" />
</head>
<frameset rows="20%, 80%">
    <frameset cols="25%,35%,45%">
        <frame src="fr_file_index.html"   title="Files" name="Files" />
        <frame src="fr_class_index.html"  name="Classes" />
        <frame src="fr_method_index.html" name="Methods" />
    </frameset>
    <frame src="files/ratios_rb.html" name="docwin" />
</frameset>
```

To generate *ri* (command-line) documentation, use the option --ri (or -r).

```
$rdoc --ri
```

No XHTML documentation will be generated if you use this option. This command places an .rdoc directory in your home directory ~/.rdoc, where ~/ is an abbreviation for the full path of the home directory, which contains all the *ri* files (these files are actually in YAML format, by the way).

To place the files in a system-wide directory, use the --ri-system (or -Y) option with sudo, which requires a root or superuser password.

```
$ sudo rdoc --ri-system
Password:


                         ratios.rb: c....
Generating RI...

Files:   1
Classes: 1
Modules: 0
Methods: 4
Elapsed: 0.342s
```

Once you have the *ri* files generated, you can look at them with the ri command:

```
$ ri Ratios#der
------------------------------------------------------------ Ratios#der
     der( debt=@debt, equity=@equity )
------------------------------------------------------------------------
     The +der+ method returns a debt-equity ratio.

     Formula
         long-term debt
     ------------------- = debt-equity ratio
             equity

     Parameters
```

```
The parameters are:

*    _debt_ = long-term debt

*    _equity_ = equity

Example
 ratios = Ratios.new( 2456, 9876 )
 ratios.der # => The debt-equity ratio is 0.25.
 ratios.der( 1301, 7690 ) # => The debt-equity ratio is 0.17.
```

 If you have *ri* files in both ~/.rdoc and in a system directory, *ri* may get tripped up. An easy though hacky solution to this collision is to simply delete the ~/.rdoc directory and then regenerate the files. You won't delete the source files by deleting ~/.rdoc, just the generated files. Don't delete the source files!

If you have extra files in the directory that you do not want to process with RDoc, use the --exclude (or -x) option.

```
$ ls
ratios.rb       test.rb
$ rdoc --exclude test.rb

                            ratios.rb: c....
Generating HTML...

Files:   1
Classes: 1
Modules: 0
Methods: 4
Elapsed: 0.387s
```

You can put everything in one XHTML file if you want (I do not recommended this for beginners).

```
rdoc --one-file >> my_rdoc.html
```

Embedded Ruby

Embedded Ruby (ERB or eRuby) allows you to embed arbitrary Ruby code in text files. The code is executed when the file is processed. If you have ever used JavaServer Pages (JSP), ERB syntax will seem familiar to you. Like JSP, ERB uses template tags to embed code.

ERB comes with the Ruby distribution. However, there are other, faster embedded Ruby engines, such as Makoto Kuwata's Erubis (*http://rubyforge.org/projects/erubis*). I'll focus on the syntax of an ERB page, not on implementations.

It's very common to embed code in HTML or XHTML, or to generate web pages on the fly with ERB. However, that's not the only place you'll see ERB. Example 10-13 shows you how ERB works in very simple terms.

Example 10-13. simple_erb.rb

```
#!/usr/bin/env ruby

require 'erb'

person = "Matz!"

temp = ERB.new( "Hello, <%= person %>" )

puts temp.result( binding ) # => Hello, Matz!
```

To get ERB to work, you must require the erb library. The class method new creates an instance of ERB (temp), with a string as an argument. Embedded in the string are a pair of template tags, <%= and %>. These tags contain a reference to the local variable person. When the program runs, the tags and the expression in the tags are replaced with the result of the expression. This means that <%= person %> will be replaced with the value of person, Matz!, when the program is run.

When the instance method result is called, temp is the receiver, and binding is the argument. This produces the result Hello, Matz!.

The tags <%= and %> are just one possible pair of tags. All the ERB template tags are shown in Table 10-4.

Table 10-4. ERB template tags

Tag	Description
<% ... %>	Ruby code; inline with output.
<%= ... %>	Ruby expression; replace with result.
<%# ... %>	Comment; ignored; useful in testing.
%	A line of Ruby code; treated as <% .. %>; set with trim_mode argument in ERB.new.
%%	Replace with % if it is the first thing on a line and % processing is used.
<%% ... %%>	Replace with <% or %> , respectively.

Example 10-14 uses an XHTML template to create individual records for horses. These templates are often stored in *.rhtml* files by convention. This program is a simplified version of a program in the ERB documentation (*http://ruby-doc.org/core/classes/ERB.html*).

Example 10-14. erb.rb

```
#!/usr/bin/env ruby

require 'erb'
```

Example 10-14. erb.rb (continued)

```
document = %[
<html xmlns="http://www.w3.org/1999/xhtml" xml:lang="en" lang="en">
<head>
<title><%= @name %></title>
</head>
<body>
<h1><%= @name %></h1>

<p><b>Breed:</b> <%= @breed %></p>
<p><b>Sex:</b> <%= @sex %></p>

<h2>Foals</h2>
<ul><% @foals.each do |foals| %>
 <li><%= foals %></li> <% end %>
</ul>

</body>
</html>
]

class Horse

  def initialize( name, breed, sex )
   @name = name
   @breed = breed
   @sex = sex
   @foals = []
  end

  def foal( name )
    @foals << name
  end

  def context
    binding
  end

end

output = ERB.new( document )

horse = Horse.new( "Monarch's Sunrise", "Quarter Horse", "Mare" )
horse.foal( "Dash" )
horse.foal( "Pepper" )

output.run( horse.context )
```

The XHTML template document is formed inside a general delimited string (%[...]). It uses instance variables from the Horse class to produce output. The array @foals accumulates names via the foal method. The context method returns the binding.

A new ERB instance output is created, and a new instance of Horse is also created with appropriate arguments. The foal method is called several times to append names to the @foals array. These names are retrieved via the each method and a block. Notice the tags <% and %>. These hold Ruby code, whereas the <%= and %> tags return a result from an expression.

```
<h2>Foals</h2>
<ul><% @foals.each do |foals| %>
 <li><%= foals %></li> <% end %>
</ul>
```

When this program runs, it yields the output shown in Example 10-15.

Example 10-15. Output from erb.rb

```
<html xmlns="http://www.w3.org/1999/xhtml" xml:lang="en" lang="en">
<head>
<title>Monarch's Sunrise</title>
</head>
<body>
<h1>Monarch's Sunrise</h1>

<p><b>Breed:</b> Quarter Horse</p>
<p><b>Sex:</b> Mare</p>

<h2>Foals</h2>
<ul>
 <li>Dash</li>
 <li>Pepper</li>
</ul>

</body>
</html>
```

One place you're likely to encounter these tags is in the *.rhml* files produced by Ruby on Rails, the subject of Chapter 11.

Review Questions

1. What is the b format field used for in `sprintf` (`printf`)?
2. What method would you use to pretty-print with Builder?
3. What does the `superclass` method do?
4. How can you test whether a given class will respond to a method?
5. How do you require a RubyGems package in a Ruby program?
6. What is the name of a key method for metaprogramming in Ruby?
7. What RubyGems command would you use to install a package?
8. What Tk class is used for creating labels?
9. The Ruby keywords rescue and ensure are synonyms for what keywords in Java?
10. How do you format headings for consumption by RDoc?

## CHAPTER 11

A Short Guide to Ruby on Rails

Ruby on Rails (*http://www.rubyonrails.org*) is an open source web development framework for creating database-enabled web applications without all the usual agony. It is written in Ruby, and, as I mentioned in Chapter 1, Matz calls it Ruby's "killer app."

Rails lets you build complex web sites quickly and easily, because you can let Rails do a truckload of work for you. On the other hand, all the work Rails does is relatively transparent, so it is easy to take as much control as you want. After some introductory remarks, you'll find a Rails tutorial at the end of the chapter.

Where Did Rails Come From?

The private, Chicago-based company 37signals (*http://www.37signals.com*) was founded by Jason Fried in 1999. The company makes web-based applications, such as Basecamp for project management (*http://www.basecamphq.com*) and Backpack, a nifty organizational tool (*http://www.backpackit.com*). 37signals asked David Heinemeier Hansson (or *DHH*) to write Basecamp in PHP. He had met Matz at a conference when he was a student and really liked what Ruby had to offer. He preferred to write Basecamp in Ruby over PHP, and the 37signals folks let him do it his way. The rest, as they say, is history.

After he finished writing the code, DHH started extracting base code out of Basecamp to use with another project, Ta-da Lists (*http://www.tadalist.com*). He later turned that code into an open source project (MIT license) and called it Ruby on Rails.

Rails version 0.5 was first released by DHH to the public on RubyForge on July 24, 2004 (*http://rubyforge.org/frs/?group_id=307*). Version 1.0 was released on December 13, 2005. The current version at the time of this writing is version 1.2.3, released in early 2007.

Why Rails?

Does the world really need another web app framework? Don't we already have things like Apache Struts (*http://struts.apache.org*), Apache Cocoon (*http://cocoon.apache.org*), Horde (*http://www.horde.org*), Maypole (*http://maypole.perl.org*), Tapestry (*http://jakarta.apache.org/tapestry*), WebSphere (*http://www.ibm.com/websphere*), and a whole bunch of others?

Yes, we do have all those, but Rails is different. It just *works*. It is intelligently designed, and the deeper you dig, the more you'll like. Not that you won't find some flaws. Problems exist, just as they do in Ruby, but they are not the glaring, odious kinds of horrors that send you flailing from your cubicle. They are minor annoyances compared to the overall strength of Rails. So I don't worry about them much, and neither should you.

Another good thing is that people you can trust—people like Dave Thomas (*http://blogs.pragprog.com/cgi-bin/pragdave.cgi*), Mike Clark (*http://clarkware.com/cgi/blosxom*), Andy Hunt (*http://toolshed.com/blog/*), Chad Fowler (*http://www.chadfowler.com*), and James Duncan Davidson (*http://www.duncandavidson.com*), among many others— have given Rails everything from a thorough thrashing to glowing, hard-won reviews. None of these folks just rolled off the turnip truck. Davidson, the creator of Apache Java apps Tomcat and Ant, has said, "Rails is the most well thought-out web development framework I've ever used…. Nobody has done it like this before." Tim O'Reilly has called it "a breakthrough in lowering the barriers of entry to programming." I find it hard to ignore statements like these (*http://www.rubyonrails.com/quotes*).

Rails has some critics. You can easily find their blogs, but I'm too busy to focus much energy on who is railing against Rails, though DHH himself doesn't often shrink from a fight (*http://weblog.rubyonrails.org*). There is a lot of fear out there, because we are approaching a bit of a paradigm shift. I say hang onto your current languages and frameworks and improve on them, but it would be wise to read up on Ruby and Rails. It won't be too taxing and you'll be better prepared for the future.

I think we have more than a few web frameworks around because people really don't worry too much about "the competition," whatever that is. They worry about making life and work easier for themselves and others, so they can't help creating something that fits a need. They worry about making the environment they work in more productive and comfortable and even more enjoyable. This was likely the case with DHH and others who ventured into creative space to produce Basecamp, Rails' direct ancestor. The difference is that Rails makes people remarkably productive, even if they knew little about Ruby. If they don't know Ruby, they learn in a hurry, and with grace and ease.

Now allow me to elaborate on Rails' coolness.

A Full-Stack Framework

Rails has been described as a full-stack framework. What does that mean? Basically, that means that Rails supplies the pieces of code necessary to build robust web applications in one neatly tied package. In other words, you won't need to bolt on code for writing XML, or scramble to find a database adapter, or fumble around after dark for a package to run your unit tests. All the parts are already there. A synonym for "full stack," at least in my book, is "well thought out."

Don't Repeat Yourself

Rails abides by the philosophy of "don't repeat yourself," or DRY. DRY espouses the precept that, in computer programming, you shouldn't have to, and don't want to, repeat code or data in software. Ruby helps with that concept.

Under DRY, data, information, or code exists in one place and therefore requires that any changes be made in one place only. This, of course, reduces errors, menial work, and worry, and makes for happier, ulcer-free programmers.

Convention over Configuration

Rails is XML-free. Not that XML is a bad thing in and of itself (in my view), but the way it is used is sometimes unfortunate—in bloated configuration files, for example. Rails does it better: instead of verbose config files, it uses "convention over configuration."

Here is an example of what that means. Rails uses a simple convention for URL routing: the names of a controller (a class name), action (a method name), and primary key (ID) are used in a consistent manner in the URL, so they don't need to be supplied through some other mechanism. By the way, this convention can be overridden.

Rails doesn't completely eschew configuration. You'll find a YAML file (*http://www.yaml.org*) for configuring a database (in *database.yml*), but that's about it.

I Want My MVC

The Model-View-Controller or MVC software architecture cooks up data, presentation, and control logic in three separate pots instead of one kettle, which makes it a lot easier to keep track of what you are doing and where things are going. Instead of having the three mixed together, MVC enables you to manipulate, control, and track each. Under Rails, the MVC scheme is divided up this way:

Model
> The model architecture is managed by ActiveRecord (*http://api.rubyonrails.org/files/vendor/rails/activerecord/README.html*), the layer of Rails code that provides the object-relational mapping (ORM) between Rails and a database such as MySQL (*http://www.mysql.com*), PostgreSQL (*http://www.postgresql.org*), SQLite (*http://www.sqlite.org*), or some other database. You can use Rails without a database, but that isn't common.

View

The view part of the architecture handles the presentation of the data, such as in a web browser. Files with the `.rhtml` suffix under Rails can handle HTML in an implicit or explicit way, spit out XML, or use Embedded Ruby (ERB)—similar to JSP, ASP, or PHP—to display data from the model or whatever is in your `.rhtml` pages. This code comes from ActionPack (*http://api.rubyonrails.org/files/vendor/ rails/actionpack/README.html*), the Rails code that handles view and controller actions.

Controller

This controller code, which, like View, is also part of ActionPack, takes user input and responds by operating on the model, and then prepares the result for display. The view code displays the result.

Scripts

Rails' scripts make it very easy to do many tasks, such as:

- Starting a web server like Ruby's own WEBrick
- Generating scaffolding to help put instant web views of a database in place
- Creating controllers and models for a Rails application
- Migrating to a new database table schema and then backing it out to any previous version
- Bringing up a console to investigate a model and launching actions in a controller

Many more scripts are available—this is only a sample of what Rails can do to reduce your workload.

Validation

Rails has methods that validate all kinds of things—the creation of things, the presence of things, the size or length of things, and so forth (see *http://api.rubyonrails. org/classes/ActiveRecord/Validations/ClassMethods.html*). For example, the `validate_ presence_of` method validates that specified attributes (symbols) are not blank. The following code says that the `title` attribute must be in the object and it cannot be blank. Such validation is done for you upon saving an object.

```
class Novel < ActiveRecord::Base
  validates_presence_of :title
end
```

Ajax

Rails supports Ajax, or Asynchronous JavaScript and XML. The term was coined by Jesse James Garrett of Adaptive Path early in 2005 (*http://www.adaptivepath.com/ publications/essays/archives/000385.php*). It describes the ability of a browser to update or change a portion of a web page by means of the XMLHttpRequest object, which makes it possible for such updates to be done in the background (see *http:// www.xml.com/pub/a/2005/02/09/xml-http-request.html*). That's only a brief description of an important topic on the web landscape. Rails supports Ajax by using the Prototype JavaScript framework (*http://prototype.conio.net*) and Thomas Fuch's script.aculo.us JavaScript library of effects (*http://script.aculo.us*).

Migrations

As I mentioned in the previous section, Rails has the ability to easily migrate from one database schema to another. These migrations are done with pure Ruby code rather than with SQL Data Definition Language (DDL) or with an application. Even if you can have multiple versions of a table, you can switch between versions, and even to the original, with a single command.

Console

Rails allows you to test your Rails application using Interactive Ruby (*irb*) in a console, as I discussed earlier. This allows you to examine and test code that exists in your models and to touch off actions in controllers. *irb* lets you walk through your code step by step to watch what happens along the way. In other words, you can work close to the bone, and if you specify that the console is in "sandbox" mode, any changes you make are thrown away when you close the console.

Environments and Testing

One of the best features of Rails is its built-in environments and testing. By default, Rails provides three parallel environments: development, test, and production. This allows you to create freely in one environment (development), to hammer out bugs in another (test), and to mind your p's and q's in another that is designed for public consumption (production).

The test environment helps you easily design and perform functional and unit tests. Fixtures containing sample data in YAML are also provided in the mix, and mocks (mock HTTP requests and responses) are readily available. Because much of the testing environment is set up for you automatically while you are working on your app, many of the common worries and fears are allayed as you get ready to deploy the app to the world. For unit testing, just run rake test_units. For more information on testing with Rails, see "A Guide to Testing with Rails" at *http://manuals.rubyonrails.com/ read/book/5*.

Capistrano

While you can do much more with it, Capistrano (formerly SwitchTower) is mostly used as a highly configurable Ruby utility for securely deploying applications to one or more remote servers with a single command. This headache reliever was written by Jamis Buck (*http://jamis.jamisbuck.org*), who now works for 37signals. While Capistrano is not a part of Rails, it is a close relative. To learn more about Capistrano, see "Capistrano: Automating Application Deployment" at *http://manuals.rubyonrails.com/read/book/17*.

Rake

A build tool helps you build, compile, or otherwise process files, sometimes large numbers of them. Rake is a build tool like make (*http://www.gnu.org/software/make*) and Apache Ant (*http://ant.apache.org*), but it is written in Ruby. It is used by many applications, not just Rails. Rails operations use Rake frequently, so it is worth mentioning here.

Rake uses a Rakefile to figure out what to do. A Rakefile contains named tasks. When you create a Rails project, a Rakefile is automatically created to help you deal with a variety of jobs, such as running tests and looking at project statistics. (After creating a Rails project with one of the tutorials below, run rake --tasks or rake stats while in the main Rails project directory to get a flavor of what Rake does.)

Rake was written by Jim Weirich (*http://onestepback.org*). You'll find documentation on Rake at *http://rake.rubyforge.org*. A good introduction to Rake by Martin Fowler may be found at *http://www.martinfowler.com/articles/rake.html*. For Rake's command-line options, type rake --help or see Appendix A.

What Have Other Folks Done with Rails?

Is Rails for real? With all this hype, don't you wonder if it's too good to be true? If you do, I don't blame you. So, let's consider the real thing. We'll have a look at just three sites.

The original Rails app is Basecamp, the on-line, collaborative project-management tool from 37signals. With over 100,000 users, it's clear that Rails can handle traffic and can scale enough to handle the real-world toe-to-toe. Figure 11-1 shows what it looks like.

43things (*http://www.43things.com*) is the ultimate global to-do list, an example of social software done right created by Robot Co-op (see Figure 11-2). It is also written in Rails, and has over 700,000 users and counting (and probably way more by the time you read this.) Watch 43places as well (*http://www.43places.com*).

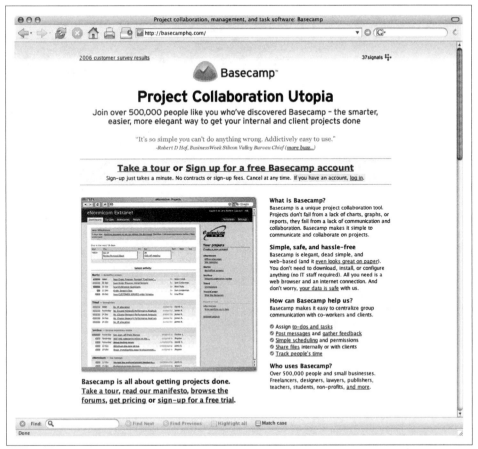

Figure 11-1. Basecamp

Rails app Blinksale from Firewheel Design, shown in Figure 11-3, provides a simple way to send invoices over the Internet and keep track of them, too. You can also send reminders and thank you notes.

Basecamp, 43things, and Blinksale are examples of what Web 2.0 looks like: user focused, collaborative, decentralized. They demonstrate well what is possible for true web-based applications. In the next few years, watch more and more desktop applications move to the web, and new, unheard of apps show up there as well. Deployment and revenue models are changing. I'd like to get caught up in the change, not caught by it, wouldn't you?

If you'd like to look at a long and growing list of real-world Rails applications, go to *http://wiki.rubyonrails.org/rails/pages/RealWorldUsage* or *http://happycodr.com* and follow links to your heart's content. There is a lot of promise out there.

Figure 11-2. 43things

Hosting Rails

A host of options are available for hosting Rails applications. For a growing list, go to *http://wiki.rubyonrails.com/rails/pages/RailsWebHosts*. TextDrive (*http://textdrive.com*) is the official Ruby on Rails host. DreamHost (*http://dreamhost.com*) has been highly recommended to me. With low monthly costs, you'll profit from trying several sites to see which one you like the best.

Installing Rails

Before installing Rails, you should also have version 1.8.6 or higher of Ruby installed (1.8.4 or 1.8.5 are acceptable, but 1.8.6 is best). At this point, you probably already have Ruby installed. If not, well, I'm crushed. It's time to head back to Chapter 1. Please don't tell me you need to do that!

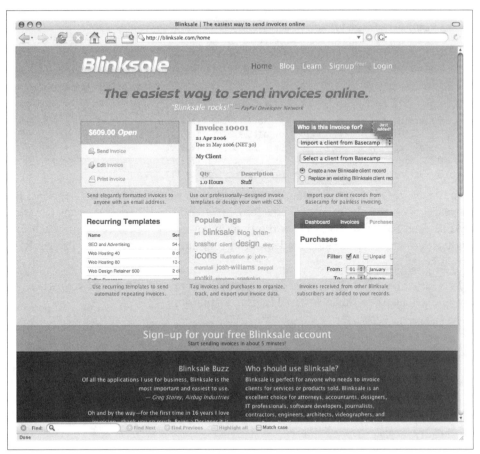

Figure 11-3. Blinksale

Using RubyGems to install Rails

RubyGems is the best way to install Rails or any Ruby package. In the previous chapter, you learned about RubyGems. Here is how you install Rails with gem on Mac OS X 1.4. You need sudo so you can issue the command as a *superuser*—that is, someone who has the proper administrative privileges to install software, among other things. You will be prompted for the root or superuser password. Just type in:

```
$ sudo gem install rails --include-dependencies
Password:
```

At this point, gem will talk back at you like this:

```
$ sudo gem install rails --include-dependencies
Password:
Bulk updating Gem source index for: http://gems.rubyforge.org
Successfully installed rails-1.2.3
Successfully installed activesupport-1.4.2
Successfully installed activerecord-1.15.3
```

```
Successfully installed actionpack-1.13.3
Successfully installed actionmailer-1.3.3
Successfully installed actionwebservice-1.2.3
Installing ri documentation for activesupport-1.4.2...
Installing ri documentation for activerecord-1.15.3...
Installing ri documentation for actionpack-1.13.3...
Installing ri documentation for actionmailer-1.3.3...
Installing ri documentation for actionwebservice-1.2.3...
Installing RDoc documentation for activesupport-1.4.2...
Installing RDoc documentation for activerecord-1.15.3...
Installing RDoc documentation for actionpack-1.13.3...
Installing RDoc documentation for actionmailer-1.3.3...
Installing RDoc documentation for actionwebservice-1.2.3...
```

It's that easy. Gems knows what directories to put things in for you. The --include-dependencies switch installs ActiveRecord, ActionPack, ActiveSupport, Action-Mailer, and ActionWebService, without stopping to ask you if you want each individual package (they are independent packages bundled in Rails). You also get RDoc documentation.

On Tiger (Mac OS X 1.4), if you go to a shell prompt and type the following, you should get a path to the location of Rails in response:

```
$ which rails
/usr/local/bin/rails
```

Now find out what version Rails is at:

```
$ rails --version
Rails 1.2.1
```

Then get a little help from your new friend:

```
$ rails --help
Usage: /usr/local/bin/rails /path/to/your/app [options]

Options:
    -r, --ruby=path                  Path to the Ruby binary of your choice
(otherwise scripts use env, dispatchers current path).
                                     Default: /usr/local/bin/ruby
    -d, --database=name              Preconfigure for selected database (options:
mysql/oracle/postgresql/sqlite2/sqlite3).
                                     Default: mysql
    -f, --freeze                     Freeze Rails in vendor/rails from the gems
generating the skeleton
                                     Default: false

General Options:
    -p, --pretend                    Run but do not make any changes.
        --force                      Overwrite files that already exist.
    -s, --skip                       Skip files that already exist.
    -q, --quiet                      Suppress normal output.
    -t, --backtrace                  Debugging: show backtrace on errors.
```

```
    -h, --help                        Show this help message.
    -c, --svn                         Modify files with subversion. (Note: svn must be
in path)

Description:
    The 'rails' command creates a new Rails application with a default
    directory structure and configuration at the path you specify.

Example:
    rails ~/Code/Ruby/weblog

    This generates a skeletal Rails installation in ~/Code/Ruby/weblog.
    See the README in the newly created application to get going.

WARNING:
    Only specify --without-gems if you did not use gems to install Rails.
    Your application will expect to find activerecord, actionpack, and
    actionmailer directories in the vendor directory.  A popular way to track
    the bleeding edge of Rails development is to checkout from source control
    directly to the vendor directory.  See http://dev.rubyonrails.com
```

Other Installation Information

Using gem is best, but there are other options. For Mac OS X, you can also turn to Dan Benjamin's HiveLogic site mentioned in Chapter 1 (*http://hivelogic.com/articles/2005/12/01/ruby_rails_lighttpd_mysql_tiger*). Beyond Ruby and Rails, Dan's instructions also get you MySQL and the lighttpd server. Another option for Mac OS X is Ryan Rauum's Locomotive (*http://locomotive.raaum.org/home/show/HomePage*), which offers lighttpd and SQLite. For Windows, there is also Instant Rails (*http://instantrails.rubyforge.org/wiki/wiki.pl*), which gives you Ruby, Rails, the Apache server, and MySQL. For Linux, there is Brian Ketelsen's Rails Live CD at *http://www.railslivecd.org*.

Once you get Ruby and Rails installed, it's time to start having some fun.

Learning Rails

By now, I am sure you are itching to start learning Rails. I'll show you where you can learn more.

The first thing to do is to watch the screencasts at *http://www.rubyonrails.org/screencasts*. You could start with DHH's colloquia presentation at Roskilde University (*http://www.ruc.dk/ruc_en/*) in 2004 (*http://media.rubyonrails.org/video/rubyonrails.mov*). It is actually under the "Presentations" heading on the screencast page; it is good foundational material.

Then watch "Creating a weblog in 15 minutes" (*http://media.rubyonrails.org/video/rails_take2_with_sound.mov*). Here you'll learn how to create a complete weblog from scratch with only 58 lines of code, with time left over for unit testing.

Next, watch "Putting Flickr on Rails" (*http://media.rubyonrails.org/video/flickr-rails-ajax.mov*). In five minutes, you'll see Rails and the Flickr API (*http://www.flickr.com/services/api/*) used to create a search engine for Flickr, the popular photo sharing web site.

 All the screencasts are in Apple's QuickTime movie (*.mov*) format.

This site has one other screencast on migrations, and a half-dozen presentations, all worth viewing.

Ruby Tutorials and Books

If you watched those screencasts, you have already been through tutorials in the form of video. They got you to second base. Here are a few hands-on, learn-by-doing tutorials that will get you across home plate.

Bill Walton and Curt Hibbs wrote an excellent tutorial called "Rolling with Ruby on Rails Revisited." Part 1 is at *http://www.onlamp.com/pub/a/onlamp/2006/12/14/revisiting-ruby-on-rails-revisited.html,* and Part 2 is at *http://www.onlamp.com/pub/a/onlamp/2007/01/05/revisiting-ruby-on-rails-revisited-2.html.* These appeared in late 2006 and early 2007. (The originals, written by Curt Hibbs alone, came out in late 2005. You'll find Part 1 at *http://www.onlamp.com/pub/a/onlamp/2005/01/20/rails.html* and Part 2 at (*http://www.onlamp.com/pub/a/onlamp/2005/03/03/rails.html*).

These tutorials will take you step-by-step through the process of setting up and configuring a Rails app and a MySQL server, and then playing with the interface. The tutorials are based on the Windows platform, so you might have to do some real-time translation along the way to use them on other platforms. Curt has also written a book with Bruce Tate called *Ruby on Rails: Up and Running* (O'Reilly). You can get a PDF version as well as a print version from *http://www.oreilly.com/catalog/rubyrails/index.html.*

If you are on the Mac, Apple's Developer Connection also has a tutorial, "Using Ruby on Rails for Web Development on Mac OS X," at *http://developer.apple.com/tools/rubyonrails.html.*

A sure bet is *Agile Web Development with Rails,* by Dave Thomas et al. (Pragmatic). This is a must-have for Rails programmers.

A Brief Tutorial

There are other sources for Rails tutorials, but I can't resist the temptation to provide one here for you. It will be brief and very gentle on you—just enough to get your feet wet. Don't think too hard; just follow the step-by-step instructions and let the process sink in. I'll provide some tips along the way.

I'll use Rails to create a simple address book on Mac OS X; Unix/Linux will be very similar, but you will have to translate the steps a little if you are on Windows. These instructions assume that Rails and MySQL are already installed. If you used the HiveLogic or Instant Rails instructions under "Other installation information," you should be set to go.

In a shell window, move to your home directory, and just for sanity, test the existence of Rails and MySQL. Then create a directory where you will generate the Rails project (address), and change directories to that new location.

```
$ cd ~/
$ rails --version
Rails 1.2.3
$ mysql --version
mysql  Ver 14.12 Distrib 5.0.27, for apple-darwin8.6.0 (powerpc) using readline 5.0
$ mkdir address
$ cd address
```

So far so good? Now run the `rails` command with the name addressbook, and Rails creates a number of directories and files.

```
$ rails addressbook
      create
      create  app/controllers
      create  app/helpers
      create  app/models
      create  app/views/layouts
      create  config/environments
      create  components
      create  db
      create  doc
      create  lib
      ...
```

At this point you have a Rails application in skeletal form. In a matter of seconds, Rails has done an unbelievable amount of work for you. This should become a little more clear in the next few minutes.

Change directories to the directory created by Rails:

```
$ cd addressbook
```

We'll use the WEBrick server to host Ruby, as it won't require any other installation on your part (it's bundled with Ruby, so you got it when you installed Ruby). You could run some other server, but we'll stick with WEBrick for simplicity.

 Pay attention to Mongrel—if you do much with Rails, you'll probably want to be using it soon. Mongrel is a speedy, up-and-coming little HTTP server written mostly in Ruby. It can host web frameworks such as Rails directly with HTTP rather than having to use FastCGI or SCGI. See the Mongrel project page at *http://rubyforge.org/projects/mongrel* on RubyForge for more information.

Run WEBrick with this command:

```
$ ./script/server webrick &
=> Booting WEBrick...
=> Rails application started on http://0.0.0.0:3000
=> Ctrl-C to shutdown server; call with --help for options
[2007-01-30 11:43:09] INFO  WEBrick 1.3.1
[2007-01-30 11:43:09] INFO  ruby 1.8.6 (2006-08-25) [powerpc-darwin8.8.0]
[2007-01-30 11:43:09] INFO  WEBrick::HTTPServer#start: pid=863 port=3000
```

 The & at the end of the command places the process in the background, so I can still use the shell prompt. It's just my preference. You don't have to do this. It doesn't work on Windows, by the way, unless you have something like Cygwin installed (see *http://www.cygwin.com*). To close WEBrick, type fg then Control-C.

Normally, you can just type ./script/server, without specifying webrick, but I have another server installed, so I have to be specific about what server I want. On Windows, issue this command as ruby script/server webrick or ruby script\server webrick.

Highlight the URL *http://0.0.0.0:3000* (*http://127.0.0.1:3000* or *http://localhost:3000* on Windows), copy it, and then paste it into the address or location bar of your browser. I am using Firefox 2 (*http://www.mozilla.com/en-US/firefox*). Figure 11-4 shows what I see when Firefox loads this URL. When you get this far, it means that you are in good shape—ready to start making things happen.

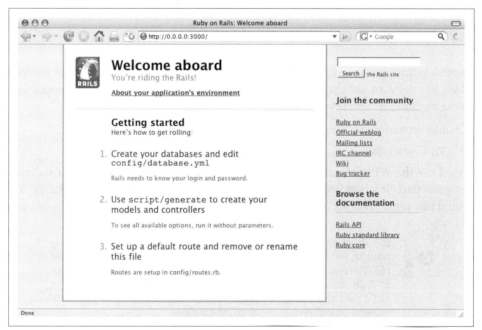

Figure 11-4. Rails welcome in Firefox 2

Let's get MySQL working. I assume you'll have it installed; if not, see "Other Installation Information," earlier in this chapter. Usually, the MySQL server runs when you start your computer, so you should have a service instance running. (If not, on Mac OS X, run System Preferences on the Apple menu, and click on the MySQL preference pane, then click the Start MySQL Server button.)

We are going to set up the MySQL database by hand using SQL command, without using a GUI tool. It is simpler that way, because you don't have to download yet another tool or try to figure out how to get your tool to work when it looks so much different from mine. It won't be hard to do—just follow along and connect the dots.

Create a database by logging in as root and entering a `create database addressbook_development` command, followed by a semicolon:

```
$ mysql -u root -p
Enter password:
Welcome to the MySQL monitor.  Commands end with ; or \g.
Your MySQL connection id is 236 to server version: 5.0.27-standard

Type 'help;' or '\h' for help. Type '\c' to clear the buffer.

mysql> create database addressbook_development;
Query OK, 1 row affected (0.00 sec)
```

It is important that you use the name `addressbook_development`, as Rails is automatically configured to use a database of that name.

Use the SQL command `show databases`, select our new database with the use `addressbook` command, and then use `show tables` to see that no tables exist yet in the current database `addressbook`.

```
mysql> show databases;
+------------------------+
| Database               |
+------------------------+
| information_schema      |
| addressbook_development |
| mysql                   |
| test                    |
+------------------------+
4 rows in set (0.00 sec)

mysql> use addressbook_development;
Database changed
mysql> show tables;
Empty set (0.06 sec)
```

Create a table in `addressbook` with the `create table` command, followed by field specifications for the address book—`name`, `address`, `citystate`, and so forth:

```
mysql> create table addresses (
    -> id           int            not null auto_increment,
    -> name         varchar(100)   not null,
```

```
      -> address           varchar(255)      not null,
      -> citystate         varchar(100)      not null,
      -> postcode          varchar(20)       not null,
      -> country           varchar(100)      not null,
      -> primary key(id) );
   Query OK, 0 rows affected (0.18 sec)
```

Verify your work with the show tables and describe addresses command, then quit MySQL:

```
mysql> show tables;
+-----------------------------------+
| Tables_in_addressbook_development |
+-----------------------------------+
| addresses                         |
+-----------------------------------+
1 row in set (0.00 sec)

mysql> describe addresses;
+-----------+--------------+------+-----+---------+----------------+
| Field     | Type         | Null | Key | Default | Extra          |
+-----------+--------------+------+-----+---------+----------------+
| id        | int(11)      | NO   | PRI | NULL    | auto_increment |
| name      | varchar(100) | NO   |     |         |                |
| address   | varchar(255) | NO   |     |         |                |
| citystate | varchar(100) | NO   |     |         |                |
| postcode  | varchar(20)  | NO   |     |         |                |
| country   | varchar(100) | NO   |     |         |                |
+-----------+--------------+------+-----+---------+----------------+
6 rows in set (0.01 sec)

mysql> quit
Bye
```

In earlier versions of Rails, it was necessary to change a configuration file *config/ database.yml* to use a given database. Now Rails does this for you automatically by assuming that the name of the Rails application addressbook will hook up to a database called addressbook_development. This means you don't have to change a configuration file or restart the web server.

With the database and table in place, you are ready to generate the scaffolding for a model and controller with a simple script command. This is where the rubber hits the road: the scaffolding magically makes everything work. Enter the following script to make it happen:

```
$ ./script/generate scaffold address address
      exists  app/controllers/
      exists  app/helpers/
      create  app/views/address
      exists  app/views/layouts/
      exists  test/functional/
```

```
dependency  model
    exists      app/models/
    exists      test/unit/
    exists      test/fixtures/
    create      app/models/address.rb
    create      test/unit/address_test.rb
    create      test/fixtures/addresses.yml
    create  app/views/address/_form.rhtml
    create  app/views/address/list.rhtml
    create  app/views/address/show.rhtml
    create  app/views/address/new.rhtml
    create  app/views/address/edit.rhtml
    create  app/controllers/address_controller.rb
    create  test/functional/address_controller_test.rb
    create  app/helpers/address_helper.rb
    create  app/views/layouts/address.rhtml
    create  public/stylesheets/scaffold.css
```

The generate scaffold script has the arguments address and address. The first is the name for the model, which is the object-relational mapping (ORM) layer for the database (ActiveRecord), and the second is the name for the controller, which takes user input and responds by operating on the model, then prepares the result for display (part of ActionPack). With the scaffolding in place, add address to the URL, as in *http://0.0.0.0:3000/address*, and you will witness the magic (see Figure 11-5).

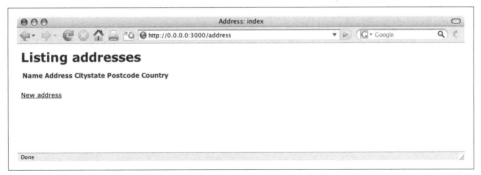

Figure 11-5. Rails-generated list

Using the embedded Ruby code (ERB) in *list.rhtml* (which you learned about in Chapter 10), Rails has translated the names of table fields into the column headings of an XHTML table! This is an example of what scaffolding does for you. It produces files like *list.rhtml*, *new.rhtml*, *edit.rhtml*, and so forth, to enable you to load data into the database table and manipulate it using a web interface.

It is amazing how much work you don't have to do with Rails! Now you are left with the pleasant job of playing with the application until it becomes the web application you want it to be.

Time to take the next step. Click the "New address" link to bring up the "New address" (*new.rhtml*) page. Enter a new address—something similar to what's shown in Figure 11-6—then click the Create button; the list page reappears (Figure 11-7), with the new address on it.

Figure 11-6. Creating a new address

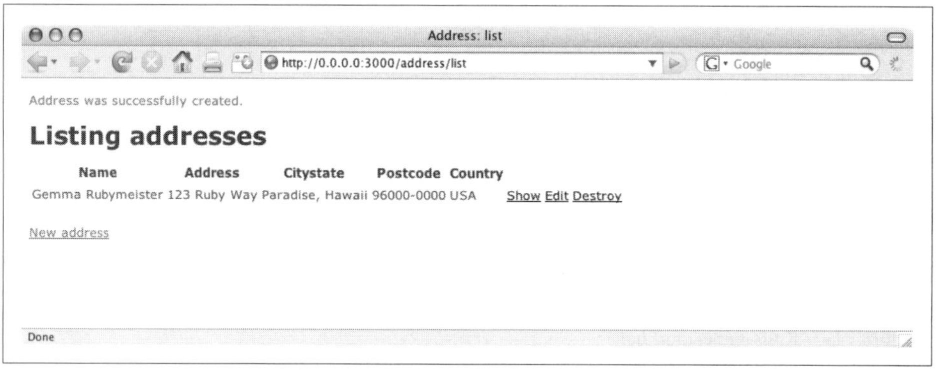

Figure 11-7. Rails listing of new address

There you are. That's as far as we'll go with this little tutorial. Click the Show, Edit, and Destroy links, and give yourself a full tour of the landscape.

Use the resources described in the earlier section "Learning Rails" to take your Rails development to the next level. The exciting thing for me is to watch how far someone can go with Ruby and Rails in a relatively short period. Have a great time!

Review Questions

1. From what program was the Rails framework extracted?
2. What does *MVC* stand for?
3. What part of Rails handles databases?
4. What do migrations do?
5. What are some applications that use Rails?
6. What is the Rake tool?
7. What is the purpose of Capistrano?
8. What is a preferred method for installing Rails?
9. Where is Rails' database configuration stored?
10. What is the role of scaffolding in Rails?

Ruby Reference

Reference material on Ruby is gathered in this appendix for your convenience. You will find information about the following: interpreter options, reserved words (keywords), operators, escape characters, predefined variables, global constants, regular expressions, String unpack directives, Array pack directives, flags and fields for sprintf, file tests from Kernel#test, time formatting directives, RDoc options, and Rake options.

Ruby Interpreter

Here is the syntax for the Ruby interpreter:

    ruby [switches] [--] [program filename] [arguments]

Switches (or command-line options) include:

-0[octal]
    Specify record separator (\0 if no argument)

-a
    Set autosplit mode with -n or -p (splits $_ into $F)

-c
    Check syntax only

-Cdirectory
    cd to directory before executing your script

-d
    Set debugging flags (set $DEBUG to true)

-e 'command'
    Execute one line of script; several -e's allowed; omit [program filename]

-Fpattern
    split( ) pattern for autosplit (-a)

-i[extension]
    Edit ARGV files in place (make backup if extension is supplied)

-Idirectory
    Specify $LOAD_PATH directory (may be used more than once)
-Kkcode
    Specify KANJI (Japanese) code-set
-l

    Enable line-ending processing
-n

    Assume 'while gets( ); ... end' loop around your script
-p

    Assume loop similar to -n but print line similar to sed
-rlibrary
    Require the library, before executing your script
-s

    Enable some switch parsing for switches after script name
-S

    Look for the script using a PATH environment variable
-T[level]
    Turn on tainting checks
-v

    Print version number, then turn on verbose mode
-w

    Turn on warnings for your script
-W[level]
    Set warning level: 0 for silence, 1 for medium, 2 for verbose (default)
-x[directory]
    Strip off text before #!ruby line and perhaps cd to directory
--copyright
    Print the copyright
--version
    Print the version (compare with -v)

Ruby's Reserved Words

Table A-1 lists all of Ruby's reserved words.

Table A-1. Ruby's reserved words

Reserved word	Description
BEGIN	Code, enclosed in { and }, to run before the program runs.
END	Code, enclosed in { and }, to run when the program ends.
alias	Creates an alias for an existing method, operator, or global variable.

Table A-1. Ruby's reserved words (continued)

Reserved word	Description
and	Logical operator; same as && except and has lower precedence. Compare with or.
begin	Begins a code block or group of statements; closes with end.
break	Terminates a while or until loop or a method inside a block.
case	Compares an expression with a matching when clause; closes with end. See when.
class	Defines a class; closes with end.
def	Defines a method; closes with end.
defined?	A special operator that determines if a variable, method, super method, or block exists.
do	Begins a block and executes code in that block; closes with end.
else	Executes following code if previous conditional, in if, elsif, unless, or when, is not true.
elsif	Executes following code if previous conditional, in if or elsif, is not true.
end	Ends a code block (group of statements) started with begin, def, do, if, etc.
ensure	Always executes at block termination; use after last rescue.
false	Logical or Boolean false; instance of FalseClass. See true.
for	Begins a for loop; used with in.
if	Executes code block if conditional statement is true; closes with end. Compare with unless, until.
in	Used with for loop. See for.
module	Defines a module; closes with end.
next	Jumps before a loop's conditional. Compare with redo.
nil	Empty, uninitialized, or invalid, but not the same as zero; object of NilClass.
not	Logical operator; same as !.
or	Logical operator; same as || except or has lower precedence. Compare with and.
redo	Jumps after a loop's conditional. Compare with next.
rescue	Evaluates an expression after an exception is raised; used before ensure.
retry	Repeats a method call outside of rescue; jumps to top of block (begin) if inside rescue.
return	Returns a value from a method or block; may be omitted.
self	Current object (invoked by a method).
super	Calls method of the same name in the superclass. The superclass is the parent of this class.
then	A continuation for if, unless, and when; may be omitted.
true	Logical or Boolean true; instance of TrueClass. See false.
undef	Makes a method in current class undefined.
unless	Executes code block if conditional statement is false. Compare with if, until.
until	Executes code block while conditional statement is false. Compare with if, unless.
when	Starts a clause (one or more) under case.
while	Executes code while the conditional statement is true.
yield	Executes the block passed to the method.
__FILE__	Name of current source file.
__LINE__	Number of current line in the current source file.

Operators

Table A-2 lists all of Ruby's operators in the order of precedence. If the operator is defined as a method, it is indicated in the Method column, and may be overridden.

Table A-2. Ruby operators

Operator	Description	Method
::	Scope resolution	
[] []=	Reference, set	✓
**	Raise to power (exponentiation)	✓
+ - ! ~	Positive (unary), negative (unary), logical negation, complement	✓ (but not !)
* / %	Multiplication, division, modulo (remainder)	✓
+ -	Addition, subtraction	✓
<< >>	Shift left, shift right	✓
&	Bitwise *and*	✓
| ^	Bitwise *or*, bitwise exclusive *or*	✓
> >= < <=	Greater than, greater than or equal to, less than, less than or equal to	✓
<=> == === != =~ !~	Equality comparison (spaceship), equality, equality, not equal to, match, not match	✓ (but not != !~)
&&	Logical *and*	
||	Logical *or*	
.. ...	Range inclusive, range exclusive	✓ (but not ...)
? :	Ternary	
= += -= *= /= %= **= <<= >>= &= |= ^= &&= ||=	Assignment, abbreviated assignment	
not	Logical negation	
and or	Logical composition	
defined?	Special operator (no precedence)	

Escape Characters

Table A-3 lists all of Ruby's escape characters.

Table A-3. Escape (nonprintable) characters

Backslash notation	Hexadecimal character	Description
\a	0x07	Bell or alert
\b	0x08	Backspace
\cx		Control-*x*

Table A-3. Escape (nonprintable) characters (continued)

Backslash notation	Hexadecimal character	Description
\C-x		Control-x
\e	0x1b	Escape
\f	0x0c	Formfeed
\M-\C-x		Meta-Control-x
\n	0x0a	Newline
\nnn		Octal notation, where n is in the range 0–7
\r	0x0d	Carriage return
\s	0x20	Space
\t	0x09	Tab
\v	0x0b	Vertical tab
\x		Character x
\xnn		Hexadecimal notation, where n is in the range 0–9, a–f, or A–F

Predefined Variables

Table A-4 lists all of Ruby's predefined variables.

Table A-4. Predefined variables

Predefined variable	Description
$!	Exception-information message containing the last exception raised. raise sets this variable. Access with => in a rescue clause.
$@	Stack backtrace of the last exception, retrievable via Exception#backtrace.
$&	String matched by the last successful pattern match in this scope, or nil if the last pattern match failed. Same as m[0] where m is a MatchData object. Read only. Local.
$`	String preceding whatever was matched by the last successful pattern match in the current scope, or nil if the last pattern match failed. Same as m.pre_match where m is a MatchData object. Read only. Local.
$'	String following whatever was matched by the last successful pattern match in the current scope, or nil if the last pattern match failed. Same as m.post_match where m is a MatchData object. Read only. Local.
$+	Last bracket matched by the last successful search pattern, or nil if the last pattern match failed. Useful if you don't know which of a set of alternative patterns matched. Read only. Local.
$1, $2...	Subpattern from the corresponding set of parentheses in the last successful pattern matched, not counting patterns matched in nested blocks that have been exited already, or nil if the last pattern match failed. Same as m[n] where m is a MatchData object. Read only. Local.
$~	Information about the last match in the current scope. Regex#match returns the last match information. Setting this variable affects match variables like $&, $+, $1, $2, etc. The nth subexpression can be retrieved by $~[nth]. Local.
$=	Case-insensitive flag; nil by default.

Predefined variable	Description
$/	Input record separator; newline by default. Works like awk's RS variable. If it is set to nil, a whole file will be read at once. gets, readline, etc., take the input record separator as an optional argument.
$\	Output record separator for print and IO#write; nil by default.
$,	Output field separator between arguments; also the default separator for Array#join, which allows you to indicate a separator explicitly.
$;	Default separator for String#split; nil by default.
$.	Current input line number of the last file that was read. Same as ARGF.lineno.
$<	Virtual concatenation file of the files given by command-line arguments, or standard input (in case no argument file is supplied). $<.*filename* returns the current filename. Synonym for ARGF.
$>	Default output for print, printf, and $stdout by default. Synonym for $defout.
$_	Last input line of string by gets or readline in the current scope; set to nil if gets or readline meets EOF. Local.
$0	Name of the current Ruby program being executed.
$*	Command-line arguments given for the script. The options for the Ruby interpreter are already removed.
$$	Process number (process.pid) of the Ruby program being executed.
$?	Exit status of the last executed process.
$:	Synonym for $LOAD_PATH.
$"	Array containing the module names loaded by require. Used to prevent require from loading modules twice.
$DEBUG	True if -d or --debug switch is set.
$defout	Default output for print, printf, and $stdout by default. Synonym for $>.
$F	Receives output from split when -a is specified. Set if -a is set along with -p and -n.
$FILENAME	Name of the file currently being read from ARGF. Same as ARGF.*filename* or $<.*filename*.
$LOAD_PATH	Synonym for $:.

$SAFE	Security level:
	0
	    No checks on externally supplied (tainted) data are allowed (default).
	1
	    Potentially dangerous operations using tainted data are forbidden.
	2
	    Potentially dangerous operations performed on processes and files are forbidden.
	3
	    All newly created objects are considered tainted.
	4
	    Modification of global data is forbidden.

$stdin	Current standard input; STDIN by default.
$stdout	Current standard output; STDOUT by default.
$stderr	Current standard error output; STDERR by default.

Table A-4. Predefined variables (continued)

Predefined variable	Description
$VERBOSE	True if verbose flag is set by the -v, -w, or --verbose switch of the Ruby interpreter.
$-0	Alias of $/.
$-a	True if option -a is set. Read only.
$-d	Alias of $DEBUG.
$-F	Alias of $;.
$-i	In in-place-edit mode, holds the extension; otherwise nil. Can enable or disable in-place-edit mode.
$-I	Alias of $:.
$-l	True if option -lis is set. Read only.
$-p	True if option -pis is set. Read only.

Global Constants

Table A-5 lists all of Ruby's global constants.

Table A-5. Global constants

Constant	Description
ARGF	I/O-like stream that allows access to a virtual concatenation of all files provided on the command line, or standard input if no files are provided. Synonym for $<.
ARGV	Array that contains all the command-line arguments passed to a program. Synonym for $*.
DATA	Input stream for reading the lines of code following the __END__ directive. Not defined if __END__ is not present in code.
ENV	Hash-like object containing the program's environment variables; can be treated as a hash.
FALSE	Synonym for false; false is preferred.
NIL	Synonym for nil; nil is preferred.
PLATFORM	Synonym for RUBY_PLATFORM. Deprecated.
RELEASE_DATE	Synonym for RUBY_RELEASE_DATE. Deprecated.
RUBY_PLATFORM	String indicating the platform of the Ruby interpreter; e.g., "powerpc-darwin8.8.0".
RUBY_RELEASE_DATE	String indicating the release date of the Ruby interpreter; e.g., "2006-08-25".
RUBY_VERSION	The Ruby version; e.g., "1.8.5".
STDERR	Standard error output stream with default value of $stderr.
STDIN	Standard input stream with default value of $stdin.
STDOUT	Standard output stream with default value of $stdout.
TOPLEVEL_BINDING	Binding object at Ruby's top level.
TRUE	Synonym for true; true is preferred.
VERSION	Synonym for RUBY_VERSION. Deprecated.

Regular Expressions

Table A-6 lists regular expressions in Ruby.

Table A-6. Regular expressions in Ruby

Pattern	Description
`/pattern/options`	Pattern `pattern` in slashes, followed by optional options, one or more of: i for case-insensitive; o for substitute once; x for ignore whitespace, allow comments; m for match multiple lines and newlines as normal characters.
`%r!pattern!`	General delimited string for a regular expression, where ! can be an arbitrary character.
`^`	Matches beginning of line.
`$`	Matches end of line.
`.`	Matches any character.
`\1...\9`	Matches *n*th grouped subexpression.
`\10`	Matches *n*th grouped subexpression if already matched; otherwise, refers to octal representation of a character code.
`\n, \r, \t, etc.`	Matches character in backslash notation.
`\w`	Matches word character; same as `[0-9A-Za-z_]`.
`\W`	Matches nonword character; same as `[^0-9A-Za-z_]`.
`\s`	Matches whitespace character; same as `[\t\n\r\f]`.
`\S`	Matches nonwhitespace character; same as `[^\t\n\r\f]`.
`\d`	Matches digit; same as `[0-9]`.
`\D`	Matches nondigit; same as `[^0-9]`.
`\A`	Matches beginning of a string.
`\Z`	Matches end of a string, or before newline at the end.
`\z`	Matches end of a string.
`\b`	Matches word boundary outside [ ] or backspace (0x08) inside [ ].
`\B`	Matches nonword boundary.
`\G`	Matches point where last match finished.
`[..]`	Matches any single character in brackets, such as `[ch]`.
`[^..]`	Matches any single character *not* in brackets.
`*`	Matches zero or more of previous regular expressions.
`*?`	Matches zero or more of previous regular expressions (nongreedy).
`+`	Matches one or more of previous regular expressions.
`+?`	Matches one or more of previous regular expressions (nongreedy).
`{m}`	Matches exactly *m* number of previous regular expressions.
`{m,}`	Matches at least *m* number of previous regular expressions.
`{m,n}`	Matches at least *m* but at most *n* number of previous regular expressions.
`{m,n}?`	Matches at least *m* but at most *n* number of previous regular expressions (nongreedy).

Table A-6. Regular expressions in Ruby (continued)

Pattern	Description
?	Matches zero or one of previous regular expression.
|	Alternation, such as `color|colour`.
( )	Groups regular expressions or subexpression, such as `col(o|ou)r`.
(?#..)	Comment.
(?:..)	Groups without back-references (without remembering matched text).
(?=..)	Specifies position with pattern.
(?!..)	Specifies position with pattern negation.
(?>..)	Matches independent pattern without backtracking.
(?imx)	Toggles i, m, or x options on.
(?-imx)	Toggles i, m, or x options off.
(?imx:..)	Toggles i, m, or x options on within parentheses.
(?-imx:..)	Toggles i, m, or x options off within parentheses.
(?ix-ix:)	Turns on (or off) i and x options within this noncapturing group.
[:alnum:]	POSIX character class for alphanumeric.
[:alpha:]	POSIX character class for uppercase and lowercase letters.
[:blank:]	POSIX character class for blank and tab.
[:cntrl:]	POSIX character class for Control characters.
[:digit:]	POSIX character class for digits.
[:graph:]	POSIX character class for printable characters (but not space).
[:lower:]	POSIX character class for lowercase letter.
[:print:]	POSIX character class for printable characters (space included).
[:punct:]	POSIX character class for printable characters (but not space and alphanumeric).
[:space:]	POSIX character class for whitespace.
[:upper:]	POSIX character class for uppercase letters.
[:xdigit:]	POSIX character class for hex digits: A–F, a–f, and 0–9.

String Unpack Directives

Table A-7 lists unpack directives for `String#unpack`.

Table A-7. String unpack directives

Directive	Returns	Description
A	String	Removes trailing nulls and spaces
a	String	String
B	String	Extracts bits from each character (most significant bit first)
b	String	Extracts bits from each character (least significant bit first)

Directive	Returns	Description
C	Fixnum	Extracts a character as an unsigned integer
c	Fixnum	Extracts a character as an integer
d, D	Float	Treats `sizeof(double)` characters as a native double
E	Float	Treats `sizeof(double)` characters as a double in little-endian byte order
e	Float	Treats `sizeof(float)` characters as a float in little-endian byte order
f, F	Float	Treats `sizeof(float)` characters as a native float
G	Float	Treats `sizeof(double)` characters as a double in network byte order
g	Float	Treats `sizeof(float)` characters as a float in network byte order
H	String	Extracts hex nibbles from each character (most significant bit first)
h	String	Extracts hex nibbles from each character (least significant bit first)
I	Integer	Treats `sizeof(int)` (modified by _) successive characters as an unsigned native integer
i	Integer	Treats `sizeof(int)` (modified by _) successive characters as a signed native integer
L	Integer	Treats four (modified by _) successive characters as an unsigned native long integer
l	Integer	Treats four (modified by _) successive characters as a signed native long integer
M	String	Quoted-printable
m	String	Base64-encoded
N	Integer	Treats four characters as an unsigned long in network byte order
n	Fixnum	Treats two characters as an unsigned short in network byte order
P	String	Treats `sizeof(char *)` characters as a pointer and return \emph{len} characters from the referenced location
p	String	Treats `sizeof(char *)` characters as a pointer to a null-terminated string
Q	Integer	Treats eight characters as an unsigned quad word (64 bits)
q	Integer	Treats eight characters as a signed quad word (64 bits)
S	Fixnum	Treats two (different if _ is used) successive characters as an unsigned short in native byte order
s	Fixnum	Treats two (different if _ is used) successive characters as a signed short in native byte order
U	Integer	UTF-8 characters as unsigned integers
u	String	UU-encoded
V	Fixnum	Treats four characters as an unsigned long in little-endian byte order
v	Fixnum	Treats two characters as an unsigned short in little-endian byte order
w	Integer	BER-compressed integer (see `Array#pack`)
X		Skips backward one character
x		Skips forward one character
Z	String	With trailing nulls removed up to first null with *
@		Skips to the offset given by the length argument

Array Pack Directives

Table A-8 lists pack directives for use with `Array#pack`.

Table A-8. Array pack directives

Directive	Description
@	Moves to absolute position
A	ASCII string (space padded; count is width)
a	ASCII string (null padded; count is width)
B	Bit string (descending bit order)
b	Bit string (ascending bit order)
C	Unsigned char
c	Char
D, d	Double-precision float, native format
E	Double-precision float, little-endian byte order
e	Single-precision float, little-endian byte order
F, f	Single-precision float, native format
G	Double-precision float, network (big-endian) byte order
g	Single-precision float, network (big-endian) byte order
H	Hex string (high nibble first)
h	Hex string (low nibble first)
I	Unsigned integer
i	Integer
L	Unsigned long
l	Long
M	Quoted-printable, MIME encoding (see RFC 2045)
m	Base64-encoded string
N	Long, network (big-endian) byte order
n	Short, network (big-endian) byte order
P	Pointer to a structure (fixed-length string)
p	Pointer to a null-terminated string
Q, q	64-bit number
S	Unsigned short
s	Short
U	UTF-8
u	UU-encoded string

Table A-8. Array pack directives (continued)

Directive	Description
V	Long, little-endian byte order
v	Short, little-endian byte order
w	BER-compressed integer\fnm
X	Backs up a byte
x	Null byte
Z	Same as a, except that null is added with *

Sprintf Flags and Field Types

Tables A-9 and A-10 list flags and field types for Kernel#sprintf (or its synonym Kernel#format), respectively.

Table A-9. Flag characters for sprintf

Flag	For field types	Description
[*space*]	bdeEfgGiouxX	Places a space at the start of a positive number.
[1–9]$	All field types	Absolute number of an argument for this field.
#	beEfgGoxX	For the field b, prefixes the result with 0b; for o, with 0; for x, with 0x; for X, with 0X. For e, E, f, g, and G, adds decimal point. For g and G, does not remove trailing spaces.
+	bdeEfgGiouxX	Adds a leading plus sign (+) to positive numbers.
-	All field types	Left-justifies the result.
0	bdeEfgGiouxX	Pads the result with zeros (0) instead of spaces.
*	All field types	Uses the next argument as the field width. If negative, left-justifies the result. If asterisk (*) is followed by a number and a dollar sign ($), uses argument as width.

Table A-10. Field types for sprintf

Field	Description
b	Converts a numeric argument to binary.
c	Converts a numeric argument (character code) to a character.
d	Converts a numeric argument to a decimal number. Same as i.
e	Converts a floating-point argument into exponential notation using one digit before the decimal point. Defaults to six fractional digits. Compare with g.
E	Same as e, but uses E in result.
f	Converts a numeric argument to a floating-point number. Defaults to six fractional digits. Precision determines the number of fractional digits.
g	Converts a numeric argument to a floating point number using the exponential form if the exponent is less than -4 or greater than or equal to precision, otherwise using the form d.dddd. Compare with e.
G	Same as g, but uses E in result.
i	Converts a numeric argument to a decimal number. Same as d.

Field	Description
o	Converts a numeric argument to octal.
p	Same as `argument.inspect` where `inspect` gives you a printable version of the argument, with special characters escaped.
s	Substitutes an argument as a string. If the format string contains precision, at most that many characters are copied in the substitution.
u	Treats argument as an unsigned decimal. Negative integers are displayed as a 32-bit two's complement plus one for the underlying architecture (for example, 2**32+n). Because Ruby has no inherent limit on the number of bits used to represent an integer, negative values are preceded by two leading periods, indicating an infinite number of leading sign bits.
x	Converts a numeric argument to hexadecimal with lowercase letters a through f. Negative numbers are displayed with two leading periods, indicating an infinite string of leading ffs.
X	Same as x, but uses uppercase letters A through F in the result. Negative numbers are displayed with two leading periods, indicating an infinite string of leading FFs.

File Tests

Tables A-11 and A-12 list file tests for one and two files from Kernel#test, respectively.

Table A-11. File tests

Test	Returns	Meaning
?A	Time	Last access time for file1
?b	Boolean	True if file1 is a block device
?c	Boolean	True if file1 is a character device
?C	Time	Last change time for file1
?d	Boolean	True if file1 exists and is a directory
?e	Boolean	True if file1 exists
?f	Boolean	True if file1 exists and is a regular file
?g	Boolean	True if file1 has the \CF{setgid} bit set (false under NT)
?G	Boolean	True if file1 exists and has a group ownership equal to the caller's group
?k	Boolean	True if file1 exists and has the sticky bit set
?l	Boolean	True if file1 exists and is a symbolic link
?M	Time	Last modification time for file1
?o	Boolean	True if file1 exists and is owned by the caller's effective uid
?O	Boolean	True if file1 exists and is owned by the caller's real uid
?p	Boolean	True if file1 exists and is a FIFO
?r	Boolean	True if file1 is readable by the effective uid/gid of the caller
?R	Boolean	True if file1 is readable by the real uid/gid of the caller
?s	Int/nil	If file1 has nonzero size, return the size; otherwise return `nil`

Table A-11. File tests (continued)

Test	Returns	Meaning
?S	Boolean	True if file1 exists and is a socket
?u	Boolean	True if file1 has the setuid bit set
?w	Boolean	True if file1 exists and is writable by the effective uid/gid
?W	Boolean	True if file1 exists and is writable by the real uid/gid
?x	Boolean	True if file1 exists and is executable by the effective uid/gid
?X	Boolean	True if file1 exists and is executable by the real uid/gid
?z	Boolean	True if file1 exists and has a zero length

Table A-12. File tests for two files

Test	Returns	Description
?-	Boolean	True if file1 and file2 are identical
?=	Boolean	True if the modification times of file1 and file2 are equal
?<	Boolean	True if the modification time of file1 is prior to that of file2
?>	Boolean	True if the modification time of file1 is after that of file2

Time Formatting Directives

The directives listed in Table A-13 are used with the method `Time#strftime`.

Table A-13. Directives for formatting time

Directive	Description
%a	Abbreviated weekday name (Sun)
%A	Full weekday name (Sunday)
%b	Abbreviated month name (Jan)
%B	Full month name (January)
%c	Preferred local date and time representation
%d	Day of the month (01 to 31)
%H	Hour of the day, 24-hour clock (00 to 23)
%I	Hour of the day, 12-hour clock (01 to 12)
%j	Day of the year (001 to 366)
%m	Month of the year (01 to 12)
%M	Minute of the hour (00 to 59)
%p	Meridian indicator (AM or PM)
%S	Second of the minute (00 to 60)
%U	Week number of the current year, starting with the first Sunday as the first day of the first week (00 to 53)

Directive	Description
%W	Week number of the current year, starting with the first Monday as the first day of the first week (00 to 53)
%w	Day of the week (0 to 6; Sunday is 0)
%x	Preferred representation for the date alone, no time
%X	Preferred representation for the time alone, no date
%y	Year without a century (00 to 99)
%Y	Year with a century
%Z	Time zone name
%%	Literal % character

RDoc Options

RDoc options are used like this:

```
rdoc [options] [names...]
```

Files are parsed, and the information they contain collected, before any output is produced. This allows cross-references between all files to be resolved. If a name on the command line is a directory, it is traversed. If no names are specified on the command line, all Ruby files in the current directory (and subdirectories) are processed.

Options include:

`--accessor, -A accessorname[,..]`
Comma-separated list of additional class methods that should be treated like attr_reader and friends. Option may be repeated. Each accessorname may have =text appended, in which case that text appears where the r/w/rw appears for normal accessors.

`--all, -a`
Include all methods (not just public) in the output.

`--charset, -c charset`
Specify HTML character-set.

`--debug, -D`
Display lots on internal stuff.

`--diagram, -d`
Generate diagrams showing modules and classes. You need *dot* v1.8.6 or later to use the --diagram option correctly. *Dot* is available from *http://www.research.att.com/sw/tools/graphviz*.

--exclude, -x *pattern*

> Do not process files or directories matching pattern. Files given explicitly on the command line will never be excluded.

--extension, -E *new=old*

> Treat files ending with *.new* as if they ended with *.old*. Using '-E cgi=rb' will cause *xxx.cgi* to be parsed as a Ruby file.

--fileboxes, -F

> Classes are put in boxes, which represents files, where these classes reside. Classes shared among more than one file are shown with a list of files that are sharing them. Silently discarded if --diagram is not given Experimental.

--fmt, -f *chm/html/ri/xml*

> Set the output formatter. Available output formatters are chm, html, ri, and xml.

--help, -h

> You're looking at it.

--help-output, -O

> Explain the various output options.

--image-format, -I *gif/png/jpg/jpeg*

> Sets output image format for diagrams. Can be png, gif, jpeg, jpg. If this option is omitted, png is used. Requires --diagram.

--include, -i *dir[,dir...]*

> Set (or add to) the list of directories to be searched when satisfying :include: requests. Can be used more than once.

--inline-source, -S

> Show method source code inline rather than via a pop-up link.

--line-numbers, -N

> Include line numbers in the source code.

--main, -m *name*

> name will be the initial page displayed.

--merge, -M

> When creating *ri* output, merge processed classes into previously documented classes of the name name.

--one-file, -1

> Put all the output into a single file.

--op, -o *dir*

> Set the output directory.

--opname, -n *name*

> Set the name of the output. Has no effect for HTML.

--promiscuous, -p

When documenting a file that contains a module or class also defined in other files, show all stuff for that module/class in each files page. By default, only show stuff defined in that particular file.

--quiet, -q

Don't show progress as we parse.

--ri, -r

Generate output for use by *ri*. The files are stored in the *.rdoc* directory under your home directory unless overridden by a subsequent --op parameter, so no special privileges are needed.

--ri-site, -R

Generate output for use by *ri*. The files are stored in a site-wide directory, making them accessible to others, so special privileges are needed.

--ri-system, -Y

Generate output for use by *ri*. The files are stored in a system-level directory, making them accessible to others, so special privileges are needed. This option is intended to be used during Ruby installations.

--show-hash, -H

A name of the form #name in a comment is a possible hyperlink to an instance method name. When displayed, the # is removed unless this option is specified.

--style, -s *stylesheet* url

Specifies the URL of a separate stylesheet.

--tab-width, -w *n*

Set the width of tab characters (default is 8).

--template, -T *template name*

Set the template used when generating output.

--title, -t *text*

Set txt as the title for the output.

--version, -v

Display RDoc's version.

--webcvs, -W *url*

Specify a URL for linking to a web frontend to CVS. If the URL contains a "%s," the name of the current file will be substituted; if the URL doesn't contain a "%s," the filename will be appended to it.

For information on where the output goes, use:

```
rdoc --help-output
```

How RDoc generates output depends on the output formatter being used and on the options you give.

- HTML output is normally produced into a number of separate files (one per class, module, and file, along with various indices). These files will appear in the directory given by the --op option (*doc/* by default).

- XML output by default is written to standard output. If a --opname option is given, the output will instead be written to a file with that name in the output directory.

- *.chm* files (Windows help files) are written in the --op directory. If an --opname parameter is present, that name is used; otherwise, the file will be called *rdoc.chm*.

Rake

A build tool helps you build, compile, or otherwise process files, sometimes large numbers of them. Rake is a build tool like make (*http://www.gnu.org/software/make*) and Apache Ant (*http://ant.apache.org*), but it is written in Ruby. It is used by many Ruby applications, not just Rails. Rails operations use Rake frequently, so it is worth mentioning here.

Rake uses a Rakefile to figure out what to do. A Rakefile contains names tasks. When you create a Rails project, a Rakefile is automatically created to help you deal with a variety of jobs, such as running tests and looking at project statistics. (After creating a Rails project with one of the tutorials below, while in the main Rails project directory, run rake --tasks or rails stats to get a flavor of what Rake does.)

Rake was written by Jim Weirich (*http://onestepback.org*). You'll find documentation on Rake at *http://rake.rubyforge.org*. A good introduction to Rake by Martin Fowler may be found at *http://www.martinfowler.com/articles/rake.html*.

To run Rake help, type:

```
$ rake --help
```

Here's how Rake is used:

```
rake [-f rakefile] {options} targets...
```

Options include:

--classic-namespace (-C)
: Put Task and FileTask in the top-level namespace.

--dry-run (-n)
: Do a dry run without executing actions.

--help (-H)
: Display this help message.

`--libdir=libdir (-I)`

    Include *libdir* in the search path for required modules.

`--nosearch (-N)`

    Do not search parent directories for the Rakefile.

`--prereqs (-P)`

    Display the tasks and dependencies, then exit.

`--quiet (-q)`

    Do not log messages to standard output.

`--rakefile (-f)`

    Use FILE as the Rakefile.

`--rakelibdir=rakelibdir (-R)`

    Auto-import any *.rake* files in *rakelibdir* (default is `rakelib`).

`--require=module (-r)`

    Require *module* before executing the Rakefile.

`--silent (-s)`

    Like `--quiet`, but also suppresses the "in directory" announcement.

`--tasks (-T)`

    Display the tasks (matching optional PATTERN) with descriptions, then exit.

`--trace (-t)`

    Turn on invoke/execute tracing. Enable full backtrace.

`--usage (-h)`

    Display usage.

`--verbose (-v)`

    Log message to standard output (default).

`--version (-V)`

    Display the program version.

Answers to Review Questions

Chapter 1 Review Questions

1. What is the nickname of the inventor of Ruby? *Matz*

2. Ruby came out in 1995. What other programming language was released to the public that year? *Java*

3. Is everyone who writes a programming book morally or otherwise obligated to write a "Hello, World!" program? *No!*

4. What does the abbreviation *irb* stand for? *Interactive Ruby, the line-oriented Ruby sandbox*

5. What is Ruby's killer app? *Ruby on Rails*

6. What is the name of the funny book on Ruby? *why's (poignant) guide to Ruby*

7. Who wrote the pickaxe book? *Dave Thomas*

8. What's one of the author's favorite programming environments on the Mac? *TextMate*

Chapter 2 Review Questions

1. What is one of the main differences between a class and a module? *You can instantiate a class, but not a module*

2. What module does the Object class include? *Kernel*

3. What syntax do you use to form block comments? *=begin/=end*

4. What special character begins an instance variable? A class variable? A global variable? *@, @@, $*

5. What is the main feature that distinguishes a constant? *A constant must begin with an uppercase letter*

6. When a method ends with a ?, what does that signify by convention? *Returns true or false*

7. A block is a sort of nameless _____ . *Method or function*

8. What is a proc? *A stored procedure, with context*

9. What is the most important characteristic of a symbol? *It occupies a single memory location*

10. What is RDoc? *The Ruby documentation tool*

Chapter 3 Review Questions

1. Why is case/when somewhat more convenient than if/elsif/else? *It is more succinct because == is assumed*

2. What is the ternary operator? *expr ? expr : expr*

3. What is a statement modifier? *A conditional, such as* if, *at the end of a statement*

4. Why is upto or downto more convenient than a regular for loop? *They are more concise and use blocks*

5. An unless statement is the negated form of what other control structure? if

6. What are the synonyms for && and ||? and/or *but have lower precedence*

7. What is probably the most common control structure used in Ruby and other languages? if

8. What is the benefit of using begin/end with a while statement? *Statements in the loop are evaluated once before the condition is checked*

Chapter 4 Review Questions

1. How do chop and chomp differ? *chop removes the last character; chomp, the last record separator*

2. Name two ways to concatenate strings. *With* <<, concat, *or* +

3. What happens when you reverse a palindrome? *Nothing*

4. How do you iterate over a string? *With the method* each *or* each_line

5. Name two or more case conversion methods. capitalize, capitalize!, casecmp, downcase, downcase!, swapcase, swapcase!, upcase, upcase!

6. What methods would you use to adjust space in a string? center, ljust, lstrip, lstrip!, rjust, rstrip, rstrip!, strip, strip!

7. Describe alteration in a regular expression pattern? *The* | *character (use one or the other)*

8. What does /\d{3}/ match? *Three digits*

9. How do you convert a string to an array? *The* to_a *method*

10. What do you think is the easiest way to create a string? *Reader's choice, but I think the easiest way is to just enclose the string in quotes*

Chapter 5 Review Questions

1. In Ruby, are numbers primitives or objects? *Objects*

2. What method can you use to discover what modules a Ruby class includes? `included_modules`

3. What is the possible range of numbers represented by the `Fixnum` class? *What the computer can hold in its machine word (32 or 64 bits, minus 1)*

4. How can you avoid truncating the result of division? *Use at least one floating-point number as an operator*

5. Rational numbers are another name for _____. *Fractions*

6. If a unary operator is absent, what is the sign of the number that follows? *Positive*

7. What are the two constants in the `Math` module? `Math::PI` *and* `Math::E`

8. What method can you use to convert an integer into a character representation? *The* `chr` *method*

Chapter 6 Review Questions

1. Name the class methods for `Array`. Come on, there's only two of them. `new` *and* `[]`

2. Show three ways to create an array. `Array( )`, `[]`, `%w{}`, *and so forth*

3. Use two methods to access the last element in an array. `ary.last` *and* `ary[-1]`

4. True or false: `shift` and `unshift` perform reverse stack operations. *True*

5. What is the difference between `delete` and `delete_at`? `delete` *deletes a matching object;* `delete_at` *deletes a matching index*

6. Multiple choice: You need to add an object to every element in an array. Where do you turn? `map`

   a. `value_at`

   b. `length`

   c. **`map`**

   d. `[]=`

7. What are two methods for comparing arrays for equality? `==` *or* `<=>` *or* `eql?`

8. What method can you use to remove `nil`s from an array? `compact`

Chapter 7 Review Questions

1. What is the difference between a hash and an array? *A hash is an unordered collection, with keys and values; an array is an ordered collection, with an index starting with 0, and whose values are called elements*

2. Why would you choose a hash over an array? *When order is not important and when the association of a key with a value is*

---

3. How would you check to see if a hash has a given key, or a given value? `has_key?`, `key?`, `has_value?`, `value?`

4. The Hash class is based on what other class? *Array*

5. What is the benefit of converting a hash to a hash? *Both will have the same object ID*

6. What is the difference between has_key? and key?? *Nothing, they are synonyms, as are* `member?` *and* `include?`

7. Show how to create a hash with Hash[]. `Hash[ key => value ]` *or* `Hash[ key, value ]`

8. What is the result of sorting a hash? *An array of two-element arrays*

Chapter 8 Review Questions

1. How is `ARGV` useful? *It represents the names of all the files on the command line*

2. How would you obtain a file type from a file on disk with Ruby? `ftype`

3. What does the mask `0700` do to a file's permissions? *Creates rwx mask for the owner*

4. How would you access the date and time a file was created? `ctime`, `mtime`, `atime`

5. What kind of object does the `entries` method from `Dir` return? *An array*

Chapter 9 Review Questions

1. True or false: You cannot add methods or variables to built-in classes. *False*

2. An instance variable is prefixed by a _____ character. *At sign (@)*

3. What is one distinguishing characteristic of a class method? *It is prefixed with the class name*

4. True or false: In Ruby, even a class is an object. *True*

5. What is a singleton method, and how do you create one? *A method tied to a singleton class; using an instance method of an instance of a singleton class*

6. Can you instantiate a module? *No, but you can include one*

7. What is the main difference between single and multiple inheritance? *With single, you can inherit from only one class; with multiple, you can inherit from multiple classes*

8. What is Ruby's base class? *Object*

9. What is the default visibility for members of a class? *Public*

Chapter 10 Review Questions

1. What is the b format field used for in `sprintf` (`printf`)? *Binary*

2. What method would you use to pretty-print with Builder? `to_xs`

3. What does the `superclass` method do? *Returns the name of the parent class*

4. How can you test whether a given class will respond to a method? `respond_to?`

5. How do you require a RubyGems package in a Ruby program? `require 'rubygems'` *and* `require_gem`

6. What is the name of a key method for metaprogramming in Ruby? `define_method`

7. What RubyGems command would you use to install a package? `[sudo] gem install` *pkg_name*

8. What Tk class is used for creating labels? `TkLabel`

9. The Ruby keywords `rescue` and `ensure` are synonyms for what keywords in Java? `catch` *and* `finally`

10. How do you format headings for consumption by RDoc? *Using equals signs*

Chapter 11 Review Questions

1. From what program was the Rails framework extracted? *Basecamp, from 37signals*

2. What does *MVC* stand for? *Model-View-Controller*

3. What part of Rails handles databases? *ActiveRecord or the model*

4. What do migrations do? *Allow you to migrate from one database schema to another*

5. What are some applications that use Rails? *Basecamp, Blinksale, 43things, to name a few*

6. What is the Rake tool? *It is a build tool written in Ruby*

7. What is the purpose of Capistrano? *Deploying applications*

8. What is a preferred method for installing Rails? *RubyGems*

9. Where is Rails' database configuration stored? *config/database.yml*

10. What is the role of scaffolding in Rails? *To create instant web views of your Rails application*

Glossary

accessor

A method for accessing data in a class that is usually inaccessible otherwise. Also called getter and setter.

Ajax

Originally an abbreviation for *Asynchronous JavaScript and XML*. A web design technique that uses `XMLHttpRequest` to load data (often small bits of data) onto a web page without requiring the entire page to be refreshed from the server.

aliasing

Using the Ruby keyword `alias`, you can alias a method, operator, or global constant by specifying an old and a new name.

ARGF

An I/O-like stream that allows access to a virtual concatenation of all files provided on the command line, or standard input if no files are provided.

ARGV

An array that contains all of the command-line arguments passed to a program.

argument

Variables passed to a method. In the method call `hello( name )`, the variable `name` is an argument. See method.

array

A data structure containing an ordered list of elements—any Ruby object—starting with an index of `0`. Compare hash.

ASCII

Abbreviation for *American Standard Code for Information Interchange*. ASCII is a character set representing 128 letters, numbers, symbols, and special codes, in the range 0–127. Each character can be represented by an 8-bit byte (octet). Compare with UTF-8. Ruby default. Set with `$KCODE = 'a'`.

block

A nameless function, always associated with a method call, contained in a pair of braces ({}) or do/end.

block comment

See comment.

C extensions

Ruby is written in the C programming language. You can extend Ruby with C code, perhaps for performance gains or to do some heavy lifting. For instructions on how to do this, see Peter Cooper's article "How to create a Ruby Extension in C in under 5 minutes" at *http://www.rubyinside.com/how-to-create-a-ruby-extension-in-c-in-under-5-minutes-100.html*.

carriage return

See newline.

child class

A class that is derived from a parent or superclass. Compare with superclass.

class

A collection of code, including methods and variables called members. The code in a class sets the rules for objects of the given class. See instance, module, object.

class variable

A variable that can be shared between objects of a given class. In Ruby, prefixed with two at signs, as in @@count. See global variable, instance variable, local variable.

closure

A nameless function or method. It is like a method within a method, that refers to or shares variables with the enclosing or outer method. In Ruby, the closure or block is wrapped by braces ({}) or do/end, and depends on the associated method to work.

comment

Program text that is ignored by the Ruby interpreter. If it is preceded by a #, and not buried in double quotes, it is ignored by the Ruby interpreter. Block comments, enclosed by =begin/=code, can contain comments that cover more than one line. These are also called *embedded documents*.

composability

The degree to which you can express logic by combining and recombining parts of a language (see "The Design of RELAX NG," by James Clark, at *http://www.thaiopensource.com/relaxng/ design.html#section:5*).

concatenation

Joining or chaining two character strings performed in Ruby with the +, <<, and concat methods.

conditional expression

See ternary operator.

conditional statement

Tests whether a given statement is true or false, executing code (or not) based on the outcome. Conditional statements are formed with keywords such as if, while, and unless.

constant

In Ruby, a constant name is capitalized or all uppercase. It is not fixed as in other languages, though when you change the value of a constant, the Ruby interpreter

warns you that the constant is already initialized. Compare with variable.

data structure

Data stored in a computer in a way that (usually) allows efficient retrieval of the data. Arrays and hashes are examples of data structures.

database

A systematic collection of information, stored on a computer. Ruby on Rails is a database-enabled web application framework.

default

A value that is assigned automatically when interacting with code or a program.

each

In Ruby, a method named each (or similarly, like each_line) iterates over a given block, processing the data piece by piece—by bytes, characters, lines, elements, and so forth, depending on the structure of the data. See block.

embedded document

See comment.

embedded Ruby

See ERB.

enumerable

In Ruby, collection classes that have traversal and searching methods and sort capability.

error

A problem or defect in code that usually causes a program to halt. Common errors in Ruby programs are identified with classes such as ArgumentError, EOFError, and ZeroDivisionError. Compare with exception.

ERB

An abbreviation for *Embedded Ruby*. A technique, similar to JavaServer Pages, for embedding Ruby code in tags—such as <%= and %>—in text files, including HTML and XHTML, that is executed when the files are processed. Ruby on Rails makes extensive use of embedded Ruby. ERB is actually a built-in implementation of embedded Ruby, but other, faster implementations also exist, such as Erubis (*http://rubyforge.org/projects/erubis*).

eRuby

See ERB.

exception

Allows you to catch and manage runtime and other errors while programming. Managed with rescue, ensure, and raise. Compare with error.

expression

A programming statement that includes keywords, operators, variables, and so forth, and returns a value.

expression substitution

In Ruby, a syntax that allows you to embed expressions in strings and other contexts. The substitution is enclosed in #{ and }, and the result of the expression replaces the substitution in place when the code runs through the interpreting.

extension, file

The part of the filename (if present) that follows the period. The conventional file extension for Ruby is *.rb*.

extension, C

See C extensions.

file mode

Depending on how it is set, determines the ability to read, write, and execute a file. One way you can set a file's mode is with File.new at the time the file is created.

float

In Ruby, objects that represent real numbers, such as 1.0.

gem

See RubyGems.

general delimited strings

A technique for creating strings using %! and !, where ! can be an arbitrary nonalphanumeric character. Alternative syntax: %Q!*string*! for double-quoted strings, %q!*string*! for single-quoted strings, and %x!*string*! for back-quoted strings.

getter method

See accessor.

global variable

A variable whose scope includes the entire program. Compare with class variable, instance variable, local variable.

graphical user interface

See GUI.

GUI

An abbreviation for *graphical user interface*. A user interface that focuses on graphics rather than text. Mac OS X is an example. Tcl/Tk is Ruby's built-in GUI library.

hash

An unordered collection of data where keys and values are mapped. Compare with array.

hash code

An integer calculated from an object. Identical objects have the same hash code. Generated by a hash method.

here document

A technique that allows you to build strings from multiple lines, using <<*name*/*name* where *name* is an arbitrary name. Alternative syntax: <<"*string*"/*string* for double-quoted strings, <<'*string*'/*string* for single-quoted strings, <<`*string*`/*string* for back-quoted strings, and <<-*string*/*string* for indented strings.

hexadecimal

A base-16 number, represented by the digits 0–9 and the letters A–F or a–f. Often prefixed with 0x. For example, the base-10 number 26 is represented as 0x1A in hexadecimal.

index

An integer, beginning with 0, that numbers or identifies the elements in an array. See array.

inheritance

The ability of a class to inherit features from another class via the < operator. See multiple inheritance, single inheritance.

instance

An object that is created when a class is instantiated, often with the new class method—for example, str = String.new creates an instance of the String class.

instance variable

A variable associated with an instance of a class. In Ruby, instance variables are prefixed with a single at sign—for example,

@name. See class variable, local variable, global variable.

I/O

An abbreviation for *input/output*. Refers to the flow of data to and from the computer, such as reading data to and from a file. The IO class is the basis for all of Ruby's I/O, and the File class is a subclass of IO.

key

A key is associated with a value in a hash. You can use keys to access hash values. See hash.

keyword

See reserved word.

lambda

A method that creates a Proc object that is bound to the current context and does parameter checking (checks the number) when called. See proc.

library

See standard library.

line-end character

See newline.

linefeed

See newline.

local variable

A variable with local scope, such as inside a method. You cannot access a local variable from outside of its scope. In Ruby, local variables begin with a lowercase letter or an underscore (_). num and _outer are examples of local variables. See class variable, global variable, instance variable.

loop

A repeatable iteration of one or more statements. Ruby uses for loops, and even has a loop method for such a task. A loop may be stopped (break). Control then passes to the next statement in the program, or a special location, or may even exit the program.

match

When a method finds a specified regular expression, it is said to match. See regular expression.

member

Variables and methods are considered members of a class or object. See class, method, object, variable.

metaprogramming

Programming that creates and/or manipulates other programs. Ruby's define_method method is one tool that can be used in metaprogramming. Reflection is another capability that plays a role in metaprogramming. See reflection.

method

A named collection of statements, with or without arguments, and a return value. A member of a class. See class.

mixin

When a module is included in a class, it is mixed into the class, hence the name mixin. Using mixins helps overcome the problems that stem from multiple inheritance.

mode, file

See file mode.

module

A module is like a class, but it cannot be instantiated like a class. A class can include a module so that when the class is instantiated, it gets the included module's methods and so forth. The methods from an included module become instance methods in the class that includes the module. This is called mixing in, and a module is referred to as a mixin. See class, mixin.

modulo

A division operation that returns the remainder of the operation. The percent sign (%) is used as the modulo operator.

multiple inheritance

When a class can inherit more than one class. C++, for example, supports multiple inheritance, which has disadvantages that, in the opinion of many, outweigh the advantages. See single inheritance.

namespace

In Ruby, a module acts as a namespace. A namespace is a set of names—such as method names—that have a scope or context. A Ruby module associates a single name with a set of method and constant names. The module name can be used in classes in other modules. Generally, the scope or context of such a namespace is the class or module where the namespace (module name) is included. A Ruby class can also be considered a namespace.

newline

A character that ends a line, such as a linefeed (Mac OS X and Unix/Linux) or a combination of characters such as character return and linefeed (Windows).

nil

Empty, uninitialized, or invalid. nil is always false, but is not the same as zero. It is an object of NilClass.

object

An instance of a class, a thing, an entity, or a concept that is represented in contiguous memory in a computer. See instance, class.

object-oriented programming

Refers to a programming practice that is based on organizing data with methods that can manipulate that data. The methods and data (members) are organized into classes that can be instantiated as objects. See class.

octal

A base-8 number, represented by the digits 0–7. Often prefixed with 0 (zero). For example, the base-10 number 26 is represented as 32 in octal.

OOP

See object-oriented programming.

operators

Perform operations such as addition and subtraction. Ruby operators include, like other languages, + for addition, - for subtraction, * for multiplication, / for division, % for modulo, and so forth. Many Ruby operators are methods.

overloading

Method or function overloading is a practice in object-oriented programming that allows methods with the same name to operate on different kinds of data (methods or functions with the same name but different signatures). You can't really overload methods in Ruby without branching the logic *inside* the method. See overriding.

overriding

Redefining a method. The latest definition is the one recognized by the Ruby interpreter. Compare with overloading.

package

See RubyGems.

parent class

See superclass.

path

The location of a file on a filesystem. Used to help locate files for opening, executing, and so forth. Contained in the PATH environment variable.

pattern

A sequence of ordinary and special characters that enables a regular expression engine to locate a string. See regular expression.

pop

A term related to a stack—a last-in, first-out (LIFO) data structure. When you pop an element off a stack, you are removing the last element first. You can pop elements off (out of) an array in Ruby. Compare with push.

push

A term related to a stack—a last-in, first-out (LIFO) data structure. When you push an element onto a stack, you are adding an element onto the end of the array. You can pop elements off (out of) an array in Ruby. Compare with pop.

precision

Refers to the preciseness with which a numerical quantity is expressed. The Precision module in Ruby enables you to convert numbers (float to integer, integer to float).

private

A method that is marked private can only be accessed, or is only visible, within its own class. Compare with protected, public.

proc

In Ruby, a procedure that is stored as an object, complete with context; an object of the Proc class. See lambda.

protected

A method that is marked protected can only be accessed or visible within its own class, or child classes. Compare with private, public.

pseudovariable

An object that looks like a variable and acts like a constant but can't be assigned a value.

public

A method that is marked public (which is the default) is accessible or visible in its own class and from other classes. Compare with private, protected.

RAA

See Ruby Application Archive.

RDoc

A tool for generating documentation embedded in comments in Ruby source code. See *http://rdoc.sourceforge.net*.

Rails

See Ruby on Rails.

Rake

A build tool written in Ruby with capabilities like make, a predecessor. See *http://rake.rubyforge.org*.

random number

With the Kernel#rand or Kernel#srand methods, Ruby can generate an arbitrary, pseudo-random number.

range

In Ruby, a way of representing inclusive (..) and exclusive (...) ranges of objects, usually numbers. For example, 1..10 is a range of numbers from 1 to 10, inclusive; using ... instead of .. excludes the last value from the range.

rational number

A fraction. In Ruby, rational numbers are handled via the Rational class.

RoR

Abbreviation for Ruby on Rails. See Ruby on Rails.

receiver

An object that receives or is the context for the action that a method performs. In the method call str.length, str is the receiver of the length method.

reflection

The ability of a language such as Ruby to examine and manipulate itself.

regular expression

A concise sequence or pattern of special characters used to search for strings. See match.

reserved word

Another name for *keyword*. Reserved words such as begin, end, if, else, and so forth are set aside and have special meaning to the Ruby interpreter.

Ruby Application Archive

A web-based archive for Ruby applications. Not the same as RubyForge.

RubyForge

A web-based archive for Ruby applications. Not the same as Ruby Application Archive.

RubyGems

The premier packing system for Ruby applications. A RubyGems package is called a gem. It comes with Ruby (though you must choose to install it with certain installation procedures).

Ruby on Rails

A productive, popular web application framework written in Ruby. Matz, the inventor of Ruby, has called it Ruby's killer app.

setter method

See accessor.

single inheritance

When a class can inherit only one class, as opposed to multiple inheritance, which allows a class to inherit from multiple classes. See multiple inheritance.

singleton

A singleton class is tied to a particular object, can be instantiated only once, and is not distinguished by a prefixed name. A singleton method is tied to the singleton class.

standard library

A library or collection of Ruby code containing packages that perform specialized tasks. Some example packages are REXML for XML processing, and Iconv for character set conversion. Online documentation is available at *http://ruby-doc.org/stdlib*.

statement

An instruction for a program to carry out.

string

A sequence of objects, usually characters.

substitution

See expression substitution.

superclass

The parent class. A child class is derived from the parent or superclass. Compare with child class.

Tcl/Tk

The Tcl scripting language with the Tk user interface toolkit, Ruby's built-in GUI library or system.

ternary operator

An operator that takes three arguments separated by ? and :, a concise form of if/then/else. For example, label = length == 1 ? " argument" : " arguments".

thread

Ruby supports threading. Threading allows programs to execute multiple tasks simultaneously (or almost simultaneously) by slicing the time on the clock that runs the computer processor. The threads in Ruby are operating-system independent, so threading is available on all platforms that run Ruby, even if the OS doesn't support them.

Unicode

An international character coding system that allows approximately 65,000 characters. See *http://www.unicode.org*.

UTF-8

A character set, based on one to four bytes, that can describe most characters in human writing systems. Set with $KCODE = 'n'. Compare with ASCII.

variable

A name that may be assigned a quantity or a value. See class variable, global variable, instance variable, local variable.

XML

An abbreviation for *Extensible Markup Language*. A language specified by the W3C that enables you to create vocabularies using tags and other markup. Ruby uses REXML, Builder, and libxml to process XML.

Index

Symbols

& (array intersection), 99, 100
& (background), 10, 155
&& (and operator), 48
<< method, 4, 62, 99
< operator, 133
* method, 5, 66
@ (instance variable), 29
@@ (class variable), 29
` (backtick or grave), 5
=begin/=end (block comment), 27
{ } (braces), 42, 59
   use in Builder, 146
[] (brackets) method, 31
[ ] class method, 108
: (colon), 43
:title directive, 165
- (difference) array operation, 99
$ (dollar sign), 29
$stdin, $stderr, $stdout, 123
.rb file extension, 3
=~ method, 76
=> (in comments), 5
= (equals sign), 37
== method, 101
== (equals operator), 47, 65
=== (range) method, 86
=== (range operator), 52
! (exclamation point), 37, 93
(hash mark), 27
% (percent) as format specifier, 140
% method, 6
%o field type, 141

+ method, 4, 63
# (pound character), 3
? (question mark), 37, 93
?: (ternary operator), 51
; (semicolon), 2
#! (shebang), 3
// (forward slashes), 32
<=> (spaceship operator), 65, 83, 101, 148
[ ] (square brackets), 95
[ ]= method, 66, 110
[ ] method, 63
[] method, 97
_ (underscore), 29
_ _FILE_ _, 27, 197
_ _LINE_ _, 27, 197
| (union array operation), 99

Numerals

37signals, 175
43things and 43places, 180

A

abbreviated assignment operators, 83
abs method, 88
abstract classes and methods, Java, 125
accessor methods, 128–130, 219
acos and acos! methods, 89
acosh and acosh! methods, 89
ActionPack, 178
ActiveRecord, 177, 178
add_element method, 144
Ajax (Asynchronous JavaScript and
       XML), 178, 219

We'd like to hear your suggestions for improving our indexes. Send email to *index@oreilly.com*.

ajd method, 151
alias, 26, 196, 219
aliasing methods, 39, 219
alternation syntax (regular expression), 75
ancestors method, 80, 153
anchors syntax (regular expression), 75
and, 26, 197
and (&&) operator, 48
appending to a string, 4
ARGF, 115, 119, 200, 201, 219
argf.rb, 119
ArgumentError, 140
arguments, 219
   default arguments (method), 38
   variable arguments (method), 38
ARGV (command-line arguments
      variable), 6, 115, 118, 201, 219
argv.rb, 118
arrays, 8, 34, 93–106, 219
   Array class, 93
   array methods, 95, 105
   Array pack directives, 205
   blocks and, 103
   clear, 95
   comparing, 101
   concatenation, 99
   creating, 94–97
   elements, 93
      accessing, 97–98
      changing, 101–103
      deleting, 103
      referencing of, 93
      unique elements, 100
   indexes, 93
   later Ruby versions and, 105
   multidimensional arrays, 104
   new, 95
   set operations, 99
   sorting, 104
   stacks, 100
   string conversion to via split method, 69
ASCII, 70, 219
asctime, 148
asin and asin! methods, 89
assoc command (Windows), 21
asterisk (*) method, 66
at method, 97
atan and atan! methods, 89
atime method, 121
attr method, 129, 157
attr_accessor method, 129, 157
attr_reader method, 129, 157

attr_writer method, 129, 157
Austen, Jane, 158
autoexec.bat, 22

B

backslash (escape) characters, 198
backticks (`), 5
base class, 125
Basecamp, 175, 180
base-three operator, 51
BEGIN, 26, 59, 196
begin, 26, 53, 55, 162, 197
Benjamin, Dan, 16, 185
Bignum class, 79
bitwise operators, 84
Blinksale, 181
block_given? method, 41
blocks, 8, 40–43, 219
   arrays and, 103
   procs, 42
      converting to, 9
   yield statement, 40
braces ({ }), 42
brackets ([]) method, 31
break, 26, 54, 197
Buck, Jamis, 180
bucket analogy, 25
Builder, 145–146
   RubyGems require_gem method, 145

C

C extensions, 219
calendar forms, 150
call method, 9, 43
canonical standards, 147
Capistrano, 180
capitalize method, 64, 70
carriage return, 12, 199
Cascading Style Sheet (CSS), 169
case, 26, 197
case conversion on strings, 70–71
case statement, 51
casecmp method, 66
catch method, 162, 164
ceil method, 88
center method, 72
chdir method, 115
child class, 125, 219
chmod masks, 122
chmod method, 121
chomp and chomp! methods, 67

S

scaffolding, 190
    generate scaffold script, 190, 191
scan method, 120
scope, 135, 137
scrape.rb, 119
screen scraping, 119
screencasts, 185
scRubyt toolkit, 119
seconds method, 147
select method, 109
self, 27, 197
semicolon (;), 2
setter methods, 224
shebang (#!), 3
shell commands, inserting output from, 5
shift method, 103
shortcut syntax (regular expressions), 75
sin and sin! methods, 89
single inheritance, 125, 133, 224
singleton classes, 132, 225
singleton methods, 132
singleton_methods method, 154
sinh and sinh! methods, 89
size method, 60, 94, 107
size? method, 121
sleep method, 58
slice and slice! methods, 98
slice method, 63
sonnet_119.txt, 118
sonnet_129, 117
sort method, 104, 111
spaceship operator (<=>), 65, 83, 101, 148
split method, 69, 92
sprintf, 139–142
    field types, 139, 142, 206
    flag characters, 141
    flags, 206
    format specifiers (%), 140
    precision indicators, 141
sprintf method, 6
SQLite, 177, 185
sqrt and sqrt! methods, 89, 131
square brackets ([ ]), 63
stacks, 100
standard error, standard output, and
    standard input, 123
standard input, 7, 123
standard library, 224
standard streams, 123

statements, 2, 26, 40
    conditional statements, 34, 41, 47, 220
    statement modifiers, 48, 53
static methods, 131
STDERR, 123, 201
STDIN, 123, 201
STDOUT, 123, 201
store method, 110
strftime method, 58
strings, 30, 60–78, 224
    appending to, 4
    case conversion, 70–71
    comparing, 65
        case-insensitive comparisons, 66
    concatenating, 63
    converting, 74
    creating, 60
    general delimited strings, 221
    here documents, 62
    incrementing, 73
    iterating over, 70
    manipulating, 66–69
        arrays, conversion to via split
            method, 69
        changing all or part, 66
        chop, chop!, chomp and chomp!, 67
        delete method, 68
        gsub method, 68
        inserting a string in a string, 66
        reverse method, 69
        substring substitution, 68
    regular expressions and, 74–77
    String methods, accessing via, 31, 63–65
    string methods, information resources
        for, 60
    string unpack (String#unpack)
        directives, 203
    substrings, substitution, 68
    unpack directives, 203
    whitespace, managing, 71
strings, appending, 4
strip and strip! methods, 72
subscripts, 93
substrings, substitution, 68
succ method, 73, 88, 91, 149
succ! method, 73
sudo, 16, 161, 183
Sunrise (Quarter Horse), 155
super, 27, 197
superclass method, 152
superclasses, 125, 133, 225

About the Author

Michael Fitzgerald has more than 20 years of experience as a writer and programmer and describes Ruby as his "favorite language so far." Michael is also the author of *Learning XSLT*, *XML Hacks*, and *Ruby Pocket Reference*, and coauthor of *XML Pocket Reference*, all published by O'Reilly.

Colophon

The animals on the cover of *Learning Ruby* are giraffes (*Giraffa camelopardalis*), the tallest of all land animals. A giraffe can reach 16 to 18 feet in height and weigh up to 3,000 pounds. Its species name, *camelopardalis*, is derived from an early Roman name, which described the giraffe as resembling both a camel and a leopard. The spots that cover its body act as camouflage in the African savanna. Its long neck and tough, prehensile tongue allow it to feed in treetops, consuming about 140 pounds of leaves and twigs daily. And its complex cardiovascular system and 24-pound heart regulate circulation throughout its tremendous body: in the upper neck, a pressure-regulation system prevents excess blood flow to the brain when the giraffe lowers its head to drink, while thick sheaths of skin on the lower legs maintain high extravascular pressure to compensate for the weight of the fluid pressing down on them.

Giraffes travel in herds comprised of about a dozen females, one or two males, and their young. Other males may travel alone, in pairs, or in bachelor herds. Male giraffes determine female fertility by tasting the female's urine to detect estrus. Yet sexual relations in male giraffes are most frequently homosexual: the proportion of same-sex courtships varies between 30 and 75 percent. Among females, homosexual mounting appears to comprise only 1 percent of all incidents. Gestation lasts between 14 and 15 months, after which a single calf is born. Only 25 to 50 percent of calves reach adulthood, as the giraffe's predators—including lions, leopards, hyenas, and African wild dogs—mainly prey on young.

Giraffes use their long necks and keen sense of smell, hearing, and eyesight to guard against attacks. They can reach speeds of up to 30 miles per hour and fight off predators using their muscular hind legs. A single kick from an adult giraffe can shatter a lion's skull. Giraffes were once hunted for their skin and tail but are currently a protected species.

The cover image is from *Wood's Animate Creation*. The cover font is Adobe ITC Garamond. The text font is Linotype Birka; the heading font is Adobe Myriad Condensed; and the code font is LucasFont's TheSans Mono Condensed.

Better than e-books

Buy *Learning Ruby* and access the digital
edition FREE on Safari for 45 days.

Go to www.oreilly.com/go/safarienabled
and type in coupon code FSIVJGA

Search
thousands of
top tech books

Download
whole chapters

Cut and Paste
code examples

Find
answers fast

Search Safari! The premier electronic reference
library for programmers and IT professionals.